The Church in the Nineteenth Century

THE I.B.TAURIS HISTORY OF THE CHRISTIAN CHURCH

The Church in the Nineteenth Century

Frances Knight

I.B. TAURIS

LONDON · NEW YORK

Published in 2008 by I.B.Tauris & Co. Ltd
6 Salem Road, London W2 4BU
175 Fifth Avenue, New York, NY 10010
www.ibtauris.com

In the United States of America and Canada distributed by
Palgrave Macmillan, a division of St Martin's Press
175 Fifth Avenue, New York, NY 10010

Vol 1: *The Early Church*   978 1 84511 366 7
Vol 2: *The Church in the Early Middle Ages*   978 1 84511 150 2
Vol 3: *The Church in the Later Middle Ages*   978 1 84511 438 1
Vol 4: *Early Modern Christianity*   978 1 84511 439 8
Vol 5: *The Church in the Long Eighteenth Century*   978 1 84511 440 4
Vol 6: *The Church in the Nineteenth Century*   978 1 85043 899 1
Vol 7: *The Church in the Modern Age*   978 1 84511 317 9

A full CIP record for this book is available from the British Library
A full CIP record for this book is available from the Library of Congress
Library of Congress catalog card: available

Typeset in Adobe Caslon Pro by A. & D. Worthington, Newmarket, Suffolk
Printed and bound in the Czech Republic by FINIDR, s. r. o.

THE I.B.TAURIS HISTORY OF THE CHRISTIAN CHURCH

Since the first disciples were sent out by Jesus, Christianity has been of its essence a missionary religion. That religion has proved to be an ideology and a subversive one. Profoundly though it became 'inculturated' in the societies it converted, it was never syncretistic. It had, by the twentieth century, brought its own view of things to the ends of the earth. The Christian Church, first defined as a religion of love, has interacted with Judaism, Islam and other world religions in ways in which there has been as much warfare as charity. Some of the results are seen in the tensions of the modern world, tensions which are proving very hard to resolve – not least because of a lack of awareness of the history behind the thinking which has brought the Church to where it is now.

In the light of that lack, a new history of the Christian Church is badly needed. There is much to be said for restoring to the general reader a familiarity with the network of ideas about what the Church 'is' and what it should be 'doing' as a vessel of Christian life and thought. This series aims to be both fresh and traditional. It will be organized so that the boundary-dates between volumes fall in some unexpected places. It will attempt to look at its conventional subject matter from the critical perspective of the early twenty-first century, where the Church has a confusing myriad of faces. Behind all these manifestations is a rich history of thinking, effort and struggle. And within it, at the heart of matters, is the Church. *The I.B.Tauris History of the Christian Church* seeks to discover that innermost self through the layers of its multiple manifestations over twenty centuries.

SERIES EDITOR'S PREFACE

Against the background of global conflict involving interfaith resentments and misunderstandings, threatening 'religious wars' on a scale possibly unprecedented in history, Christians and the Christian Church are locked in internal disputes. On 2 November 2003, a practising homosexual was made a bishop in the Episcopal Church in the United States, America's 'province' of the Anglican Communion. This was done in defiance of the strong opinion in other parts of the 'Communion' that if it happened Anglicanism would fall apart into schism. A few years earlier there had been similar rumblings over the ordination of women to ministry in the same Church. A century before that period, the Roman Catholic Church had pronounced all Anglican ordination to the priestly or episcopal ministry to be utterly null and void because of an alleged breach of communion and continuity in the sixteenth century. And the Orthodox Churches watched all this in the secure conviction that Roman Catholic, Anglican and all other Christian communities were not communions at all because they had departed from the truth as it had been defined in the ecumenical Councils of the first few centuries. Orthodoxy alone was orthodox. Even the baptism of other Christians was of dubious validity.

Those heated by the consecration of a 'gay' bishop spoke on the one side of faithfulness to the teaching of the Bible and on the other of the leading of the Holy Spirit into a new world which knew no discrimination. Yet both the notion of faithfulness to Scripture and the idea that Jesus particularly wanted to draw the outcasts and disadvantaged to himself have a long and complex history which makes it impossible to make either statement in simple black-and-white terms.

One of the most significant factors in the frightening failures of communication and goodwill which make daily headlines is a loss of contact with the past on the part of those taking a stand on one side or another of such disagreements. The study of 'history' is fashionable as this series is launched, but the colourful narrative of past lives and episodes does not necessarily make familiar the patterns of thought and assumption in the minds of those involved. A modern history of the Church must embody that awareness in every sinew. Those embattled in disputes within the Church and disputes involving Christian and other-faith communities have tended to take their stand on principles they claim to be of eternal validity, and to represent the will of God. But as they appear in front of television cameras or speak to journalists the accounts they give – on either side – frequently reflect a lack of knowledge of the tradition they seek to protect or to challenge.

The creation of a new history of the Church at the beginning of the third millennium is an ambitious project, but it is needed. The cultural, social and political dominance of Christendom in what we now call 'the West' during the first two millennia made the Christian Church a shaper of the modern world in respects which go far beyond its strictly religious influence. Since the first disciples were sent out to preach the Gospel by Jesus, Christianity has been of its essence a missionary religion. It took the faith across the world in a style which has rightly been criticized as 'imperialist'. Christianity has proved to be an ideology and a subversive one. Profoundly though it became 'inculturated' in the societies converted, it was never syncretistic. It had, by the twentieth century, brought its own view of things to the ends of the earth. The Christian Church, first defined as a religion of love, has interacted with Judaism, Islam and the other world religions in ways in which there has been as much warfare as charity. We see some of the results in tensions in the modern world which are now proving very hard to resolve, not least because of the sheer failure of awareness of the history of the thinking which has brought the Church to where it is now.

Such a history has of course purposes more fundamental, more positive, more universal, but no less timely. There may not be a danger of the loss of the full picture while the libraries of the world and its historic buildings and pictures and music preserve the evidence. But the connecting thread in living minds is easily broken. There is much to be said for restoring as familiar to the general reader, whether Christian or not, a command of the sequence and network of ideas about what the Church *is* and what it should be *doing* as a vessel of Christian thought and life.

This new series aims, then, to be both new and traditional. It is organized so that the boundary-dates between volumes come in some unexpected places. It attempts to look at the conventional subject matter of histories of the Church from the vantage-point of the early twenty-first century, where the Church has confusingly many faces: from Vatican strictures on the use of birth-control and the indissolubility of marriage, and the condemnation of outspoken German academic theologians who challenge the Churches' authority to tell them what to think and write, to the enthusiasm of Black Baptist congregations in the USA joyously affirming a faith with few defining parameters. Behind all these variations is a history of thought and effort and struggle. And within, at the heart of matters, is the Church. It is to be discovered in its innermost self through the layers of its multiple manifestations over twenty centuries. That is the subject of this series.

Contents

In memory of

Annette Ros Knight, 1925–1998

and

Edmund Alan Knight, 1919–2006

Abbreviations

ABCFM	American Board of Commissioners for Foreign Missions
CIM	China Inland Mission
CMS	Church Missionary Society
LMS	London Missionary Society
SPCK	Society for Promoting Christian Knowledge
SPG	Society for the Propagation of the Gospel
UMCA	Universities' Mission to Central Africa
WCTU	Women's Christian Temperance Union

In keeping with current conventions, I have only adopted a capital letter for 'Evangelical' and cognate words when referring to those who were Anglicans or members of the established Church of Scotland. In all other cases, the lower case is preferred. I have adopted a capital letter for 'Church' when referring to the idea of the universal Church or to a specific denomination. Lower-case usage means that I am referring to a church building, or using the word as an adjective.

Acknowledgements

A book of this nature relies to a large degree on its author making judicious use of the research of others. I am therefore hugely indebted to the scholars whose works are cited in the endnotes, and to others whose works are not cited, but who I have read, listened to or conversed with in the past. I have tried to simplify complex arguments and lengthy debates without doing violence to the integrity of their work, but if I have not succeeded in this, I offer sincere apologies.

This book would never have been written without the practical support and kindness of many people. Being the head of a large university department leaves very little time for scholarly activity, so I am particularly grateful to three of the professors, D.P. Davies, Tom O'Loughlin and Nigel Yates, who decided that if this book was ever going to appear I would have to take study leave, and to make that possible they would all have to assume significant extra duties. This they did during the summer of 2006 with great willingness and efficiency. Tom O'Loughlin provided moral and intellectual support at key moments and was a great source of ideas. Nigel Yates read the whole manuscript in its final draft and made a number of extremely helpful observations, as did Ruth Russell-Jones. Andrea Garner, the queen of personal assistants, did a magnificent job in holding the fort while I was away and easing the burdens when I returned. Laura Jarvis acted as research assistant by producing relevant journal articles and she also read several chapters as they were being written. Other colleagues in the Department of Theology and Religious Studies at Lampeter, and friends elsewhere, offered encouragement and helpful suggestions. I am particularly indebted to Nancy Christie and Michael Gauvreau, who, on the strength of a brief meeting in Atlanta, kindly emailed me the draft chapters of their forthcoming study on the churches in Canada. I would like to thank Alex Wright at I.B.Tauris for suggesting the book in the first place, and then for being patient. Clive Bright, once again, generously put up with me in writing mode, as I spent what seemed to be every spare moment at home for months on end staring at my computer screen. I am hugely grateful to you all.

My father was looking forward to seeing this book, but he died when I was about two-thirds of the way through writing. This book is dedicated to his memory and to that of my mother. Both of them enjoyed history and always encouraged me with my writing. I hope that they would have found it a good read.

Lampeter, September 2007

INTRODUCTION

Interpreting the Church in the Nineteenth Century

This is a book intended for readers who are studying the nineteenth-century Church for the first time, as well as for those who already have some familiarity with the subject. Writing it has been enjoyable, but also rather daunting, and people have sometimes marvelled at my willingness (or stupidity?) in taking it on. The current pressures for specialization mean that it is relatively unusual for historians, particularly those of us working within the United Kingdom, to tackle global histories, and any who do so normally limit themselves to a much more narrowly defined theme than the gargantuan topic that is Western Christianity. The pictures I paint in this book inevitably contain plenty of broad brush strokes, and a certain lack of subtlety. Nevertheless, having previously concentrated my historical attention largely on one particular Christian tradition (Anglicanism) in two particular geographical locations (England and Wales), I have found it eye-opening to stand back and survey the vista of Christian history much more widely. I hope that you too will find that this book enables you to make fresh connections and that reading it will be rather like making a train journey through a varied and interesting landscape. The book introduces concisely and quickly the large panorama of the nineteenth-century Church, but I hope it will also provide you with some ideas for further expeditions into particular areas.

This book is about the Western Christian tradition, that is to say Roman Catholicism and the many varieties of Protestantism, in the nineteenth century. It is arranged in two parts: the first, longer section deals with 'Places', and the second with 'Themes'. The places are England and Wales, Protestant Europe (which includes Scotland), Catholic Europe (which includes Ireland), the United States and Canada, and finally Africa, India, China and Australasia and Oceania, all of which were regions extensively visited by nineteenth-century Christians as a result of missionary activity, and some of which were extensively populated by European migration. In selecting the themes for the second part of the book, my aim is to highlight some of the big subjects which had transnational significance in nineteenth-century Christianity, and which are also regarded as being particularly relevant by historians writing today. In this way I hope that the book will provide an introduction to some of the major current scholarly perspectives.

Over the last two or three decades, the study of nineteenth-century Christianity has been shaped by two perspectives in particular, both of which have now become so influential that each may be seen as offering a 'master narrative', or a framework for explaining the shape of religious history as a whole. The first master narrative is that of religious revival, which is predominantly, although not exclusively, understood as evangelical awakening. This account places in the foreground movements which began in Britain, parts of Europe and America from the 1720s, and which spread and replicated themselves throughout the world in the decades that followed, with varying levels of ease and speed. Evangelical revival massively extended the overall size of Christianity's global footprint, reshaped its institutions and patterns of thought and involved a far greater cross-section of women and men, of all social groups and cultural and ethnic backgrounds, in its regular activities. The interpretation which focuses on the primacy of revival can also encompass non-evangelical forms of Christianity, such as Roman Catholicism and some of the Protestant state Churches, as they too experienced their own forms of renewal during the nineteenth century. Devotees of the revival narrative are usually accommodating towards these very distinctive phenomena as sub-sections within their overall framework, although scholars whose primary interest is the history of Roman Catholicism, or Anglo-Catholicism or indeed the revival of the Church as an institution, are sometimes less willing to place their work within the larger framework of revival studies, and will (quite rightly) want to emphasize the differences between, for example, Catholicism in its various forms, and evangelicalism. Roman Catholicism and evangelicalism, the two ecclesiastical pillars upon which this book rests, are indeed very different, and were more different in the nineteenth century than they are today. I shall return to this point shortly. Chapter 6, 'Revival and Renewal', attempts to do justice to the revival narrative. It explores evangelical revivalism in America and Europe, Anglo-Catholic revivalism in England and overseas, and Roman Catholic developments associated with missions and Ultramontanism (the belief, which became prevalent in the nineteenth century, that Catholicism should focus more on Rome, and less on the national or diocesan level).

The second master narrative is that of secularization. The idea of secularization, traditionally understood as the withering away of religion and its replacement with a humanistic philosophy based on a liberal view of progress and personal freedom in which the spiritual gives way to (or has already given way to) the material, has long had a powerful hold over the European imagination. The intellectual roots of the theory of secularization are found in the works of Auguste Comte, Karl Marx, Max Weber and Emile Durkheim, all highly significant thinkers whose work did much to encourage subsequent generations to develop the study of sociology. From the 1960s, sociologists, and then historians, began to put forward versions of the secularization thesis in order to explain when and why Europeans had weakened (or abandoned) their long-standing allegiance to Christianity. In recent times, theories of secularization have undergone significant modifications, with debates centring in particular on the moment when secularization occurred, which some scholars now see as being a mid-twentieth century, rather than a nineteenth-century phenomenon.[1] There have also been lively discussions about the extent and the causes of secularization, and any scholarly consensus that might have been detected a few decades ago has now evaporated.[2] Yet the approach itself continues to offer a very powerful master narrative, with secularization being seen by many historians as the central theme, at least in the history of Europe. As Jeffrey Cox puts it, 'If we set aside celebratory stories of religious triumphalism, the secularisation story is the *only* master narrative of religion in modern history.'[3] Current debates focus on the nature of secularization, not on its reality. Chapter 7, 'Dislocation and Decline', investigates the various manifestations of the secularization thesis, together with some of the major events associated with it, because they sparked the traumas that brought about de-Christianization. These include the impact of the writings of Darwin, the inter-communal crisis that was the American Civil War, changing views on biblical authority, the decline in belief in hell and the rise in the importance of leisure.

To what extent can highlighting the two narratives sketched out above provide an adequate interpretative framework for understanding the history of the Church in the nineteenth century worldwide? It would be over-simplistic to suggest that all who study the topic fall into one of the two camps, seeing it either in terms of growth and revival or dislocation and de-Christianization. Nevertheless, both paradigms have had a very profound influence on the way in which the subject has been understood. What are we to make of the obvious paradox, which is that the first model indicates religious growth as the key factor and the second indicates decline? Is the glass half full or half empty? Are we more compelled by a positive, up-beat interpretation of the role of Christianity in society, or by a more negative view which sees it as an ideology that had become oppressive and outdated?

What are we to make of confusing evidence, such as that from Scandinavia, which indicates that the Awakening was actually a key factor in bringing about secularization?[4]

Whether it is a model based on revival or decline which attracts us more, we need to remember that the nineteenth-century world indisputably contained a large and growing number of Christians. It also contained significant numbers of people who had little to do with the Churches, who show up for the first time statistically in documents such as Britain's 1851 religious census. Their statistical appearance (or non-appearance in church terms) caused shock to contemporaries, who had been largely lacking in awareness of the extent of what Horace Mann, the author of the census report, termed 'unconscious secularists'. In the New World – but also in working-class districts in Paris and other major French cities – people frequently became secularized because of circumstances beyond their control, such as having nowhere to worship or no contact with clergy who could offer support or pass on knowledge about Christianity. Yet elsewhere in France, despite the violent de-Christianization which had been experienced in the aftermath of the revolution (1789), levels of churchgoing recovered in some places, for example Brittany and Lorraine, dramatically.[5] Here we see a demonstration of both paradigms, but in the unexpected order – secularization, and then revival. At the same time, elsewhere in Europe, some people who had previously readily identified themselves as Christians began to struggle with faith as a result of evolutionary biology, moral difficulties in believing in hell or substitutionary atonement, or seemingly threatening approaches to reading the Bible. Historians need to attend to the bearers of both labels, 'Christians' and 'secularists', and also to that quite significant body of people who combined elements of both perspectives. We need to remember that religion also grows by intrinsic means, quite apart from revival. Partly because this book is a history of the Church, I tend to give more weight to Christianization, rather than to secularization, although that does not mean that I consider the latter unimportant. It is, however, the case that secularization in the nineteenth century is a more exclusively European rather than a global phenomenon. In its classical form (Christianity withering away to be replaced by a doctrine of human progress) it had almost no impact in those many parts of the world where Christianity was newly introduced. Arguably, it also had far less impact in Canada and the United States of America, which at an early point in its post-independence history more or less departed from Thomas Jefferson's 'secular' ideal to become a nation that was profoundly affected by repeated pulses of evangelical revival and Catholic immigration, and which remains one of the most overtly Christian countries on earth.

Although I have tried to take account of the very significant body of scholarly opinion encompassed in what I have termed the master narratives of revival and secularization, this book has inevitably been shaped by my own historical priorities. Readers will discover that my central interest is in what Christianity meant to ordinary people, as a supernatural belief-system and as an institution that impinged on their daily lives. This approach asserts itself throughout the text, and I return to it again in Chapter 8. This puts me closer to the 'revivalism' than to the 'secularism' paradigm, although my approach does not fit easily there, as I tend to emphasize Christianity's non-emotional side and the fact that Christianity simply continues for intrinsic reasons, most notably the tendency of Christians in the past to have children who continued in the faith. Another important factor was the usually newly acquired capacity of nineteenth-century Christians for exercising choice in matters of religion. 'Pluralism', a term reflecting the increasing opportunities for choice in religion, is perhaps the best one-word summary for the paradigm I seek to explore. It is, however, worth noting that 'pluralism' is a concept harnessed both by advocates of the revivalism paradigm, as in 'revival produced many new ways of being a Christian', as well as by devotees of the secularization thesis, as in 'secularization produced many new choices, which were often non-religious'.[6] But to develop this point a little further, undoubtedly the excessive zeal and energy which some Christians demonstrated, coupled with the particular circumstances of post-revolutionary Europe and America, did indeed lead to a wide array of different ways of being a Christian. Variety led naturally to the necessity for choice, and the ways in which choice was exercised at the individual and local level, through the decision to attend one type of chapel rather than another, or to switch from Protestantism to Catholicism, or from Catholicism to unbelief, is a matter of interest.

The opportunity for exercising individual choice existed in many places by the end of the century, but was greatest for the residents of Britain, the USA and Canada. In Britain, the 1851 religious census identified 28 major and 11 minor denominations, of which all but one (the Jews) were Christian. A similar number of major denominations and a larger number of minor ones could be found in the USA at the same period. Recent work on Canada has revealed that people took full advantage of the religious free market, and that the model of flexible or double denominational allegiance, which I identified in the nineteenth-century Church of England over a decade ago, where a double allegiance with Wesleyan Methodism was not uncommon, was particularly prevalent there.[7] However, this focus on denominational identity, whether fixed or flexible, begs an important question raised by Hugh McLeod, which it is worth posing again here: 'To what extent was religion a fundamental social category shaping the self-image and behaviour of the majority of the population, or was it only important for the identity of those who were highly devout?'[8] In other words, how many times in a week did a Roman Catholic remember that she was a Roman Catholic? What other terms would she have used to define herself? This book does not pretend to be able to answer this question, but it is an important one for the reader to keep in mind.

Within the exotic denominational flowering which had created a garden of religious choice, there were, naturally, certain family resemblances between Churches which had either grown from the same root stock or been pollinated from the same sources. In particular, as already noted, many of the British and American denominations had either been created or reinvigorated by the evangelical revival. The evangelical denominations were counterweighted by the apparent monolith of Roman Catholicism, which was also undergoing major transitions as it adjusted to the rapidly changing political and social circumstances of the nineteenth century. Before we embark upon our world tour of nineteenth-century Christianity, it may be helpful to say a little more about the two 'ecclesiastical pillars' of evangelicalism and Catholicism. Both groups were well organized, rapidly growing and internally competitive. But in almost every other way, they were very different from each other. Catholicism was conceptually a single entity, tightly regulated and with clear boundaries. Evangelicalism was a much more diffuse and diverse movement, a broad federation of denominations and parts of denominations. Both were, and have remained, the major players on Christianity's world stage, of much greater significance than the non-evangelical Protestant state Churches.

An immediate sense of these differences can be obtained by comparing a recent observation from a Roman Catholic historian, Terence Fay, with David Bebbington's famous and now standard definition of evangelicalism. Writing about the development of the Catholic Church in Canada, Fay describes it (perhaps rather too simplistically) in military terms: 'These units [metropolitan provinces, dioceses and parishes] like the ships and fleets of the Royal Navy, were run by well-educated and carefully selected bishops and clergy. At their head the bishop of Rome gave leadership in matters of faith and morals and enjoyed primacy of jurisdiction over fledgling Canadian dioceses.'[9] He goes on to explain how Catholics were bound by the ecumenical councils of the Catholic Church and by canon law, and how bishops and clergy in Canada functioned within the guidelines laid down by Rome. Protestant evangelicalism, by contrast, operated with a completely different model. There was no hierarchical pyramid of leadership (although certain leaders could exert great influence), relatively little interest in the

creation of formal structures and (with the exception of Lutherans, Presbyterians and Anglicans) much less emphasis on education as a qualification
for ministry. The creeds which had been formulated by the councils of the
early Church were assented to, but there was no equivalent to Roman canon
law. Supreme authority notionally rested in the Bible, or more accurately in
the human interpretation of the Bible. The defining tenets of evangelicalism were a strong belief in the Bible as governing everything relating to
Christian life, the belief in the saving power of Jesus's death on the cross,
the necessity for conversion, and the belief that conversion would lead to the
active desire to seek the conversion of others. Writing about evangelicalism
in the whole of the English-speaking world, David Bebbington restates
the four-point definition which he first articulated in the 1980s and which
has been widely adopted since: 'A stress on the Scriptures as the source
of faith, on conversion as its beginning, on redemption as its object, and
activity as its consequence were hallmarks of the evangelicals.'[10] In this
way, all converted Christians became active foot soldiers for Christ in the
war against sin and the loss of souls, but that was a rather different military
metaphor from the one applied by Fay to the structures of Rome.

Both Roman Catholicism and Protestant evangelicalism possessed a
phenomenal ability to spread themselves and to replicate their structures
all over the globe. The state Churches were less able to do this, although
Anglicans, Presbyterians and Lutherans all made major advances outside
Europe. Although this book focuses to some extent on some of the areas
of similarity between Catholicism and evangelicalism, it is in fact difficult to exaggerate the extent of the cultural and theological separation that
existed between them. Although there was an increasing level of cooperation between Protestants, particularly in the second half of the century, this
was the age before ecumenism. Readers who think that today the differences between the mainstream denominations are of little significance, or
who understand the differences but regard their brothers and sisters in other
denominations with kindly feelings, or who have witnessed the transpo-
sition of theological boundaries which have produced sacramental Methodists on the one hand and charismatic Catholics on the other, need to
remember that these perspectives are the result of huge changes in Christian thought and practice that occurred in the twentieth century. In the
nineteenth century, Catholics and Protestants normally viewed each other
with suspicion and fear, avoided contact if possible, but clashed when they
felt under threat. In those Protestant nations where Catholicism was relatively weak, it was the state Church that was likely to replace Catholicism as
evangelicalism's bitter rival and sworn enemy. This can be seen in England,
where Protestant evangelicals made a particular attack upon what they

saw as the popish tendencies of the Anglo-Catholic wing of the Church of England, in Scotland, where the established Church split in two as a result of a struggle between Evangelical and non-Evangelical elements within it, and in Scandinavia and some of the Lutheran parts of Germany, where Pietists sometimes denounced Lutheranism's intensely close links with the state.

In another respect too, nineteenth-century Christians differed very much from their twenty-first century counterparts. Encouraged by the massive expansion of Christianity that they had witnessed in their life-time, many of them believed that the whole world was on the point of turning Christian. This produced a great sense of optimism and enormous energy. Almost all of them, however, failed to consider the challenge which a growth in other world religions would pose to the global dominance of Christianity. Despite the fact that in the twentieth century this expansion in other faiths occurred, and was coupled with Christianity's European decline, the footprints left by nineteenth-century Church growth are still clearly visible in today's religious landscape. For example, Christianity today is experiencing its fastest growth on the continent of Africa, and this is due in part to the missionary efforts that were made a century and a half ago. To take another example, in 1990 Catholicism had the largest market share among the Churches in 31 out of the 51 states in the USA.[11] This would have astonished the Protestant evangelicals who dominated early nineteenth-century America, but it is in part the result of the massive influx of Catholics from Europe, who have arrived steadily ever since. A third example is that although Catholicism remains the biggest denomination globally, by the middle of the twenty-first century Pentecostalism is predicted to become the dominant form of world Christianity. Pentecostalism developed directly out of the nineteenth-century holiness movement, which in turn developed out of evangelicalism. If we look carefully, we will find that almost everything that happens in our time has an antecedent in the nineteenth century. It should be obvious that we cannot understand the role of Christianity in the world today unless we know something about how it shaped that world in the recent past.

PART I
PLACES

CHAPTER I

England and Wales

The 1851 religious census in the city of Nottingham

The 30th of March 1851 was an unsettled day. As dawn broke across the fens and wolds of central England, rain was already in the air, yet there was a mildness which hinted that a storm might be on the way. The wind was rising. It was the lambing season, and the insistent, high-pitched cry of the newly born carried across gently undulating fields, mixing with the deeper notes of early morning cockerels and cattle. There was evidence of fields being prepared for seed drilling, but on this morning the only signs of agricultural activity related to the welfare of livestock, for this was a Sunday, in a country where Sunday churchgoing and Sabbath rest were generally regarded as being of paramount importance.

In a town in the English Midlands, in the newly built vicarage of St Mary's Nottingham, the Reverend Joshua Brooks was feeling anxious. Since moving from Retford to be vicar of Nottingham, his health had deteriorated, and his adoption of the 'water system' – going to bed with towels steeped in cold water around his neck – had not provided him with much relief. Today was a particularly anxious day. It was the day appointed for the first national census of religious attendance. He had been sent forms to fill in, which required him to give details of the numbers attending at each of the services that would take place that day, the numbers attending the Sunday schools, the average attendance over the last 12 months and the number of sittings available in each of the places of worship for which he was responsible. He was worried about how he was supposed to manage all this counting, and how the information would be used once he had collected it. Was he supposed to stand in the pulpit and count every individual, jabbing his finger at every worshipper and muttering under his breath? Or stand at the door like a footman and count the congregation in and out? Or would round numbers do? Brooks decided that the London bureaucrats who were due to receive his census return would have to put up with round numbers. In any case, Brooks knew that attendance would not be as good as usual because of the measles epidemic which had hit the town, and because it was Mid-Lent Sunday, when younger people living away from home would make a special effort to go back to their villages to visit their mothers. How foolish of the authorities to commission this survey for Mothering Sunday, and at such a wet time of year! Then there was the problem of what to do with the forms once he had filled them in. He knew that he was supposed to return them to one of the local census enumerators, and that they would dispatch them to London. But he did not trust them. None of them were Church of England; in fact he considered that they were all Dissenters of the worst sort, the type who would try to make political capital out of any weakness that they could detect in the returns for St Mary's, or for the cemetery chapel or the school room for which Brooks was also responsible.

To entrust his census returns to Dissenters was an appalling prospect. They might tamper with figures, and they were bound to exaggerate the numbers at their own places of worship! Brooks remembered the time when, a decade previously, dissenting radicals had seized control of St Mary's by getting themselves elected as the churchwardens. They had refused to set a church rate or to spend any money on the upkeep of the building. Eventually the church had been declared unsafe and was closed for months on end, with a massive £4,600 needed for repairs. The incident had resulted in uproar in the town, and the resignation of his predecessor. Numbers had never recovered, and many couples who would once have come to St Mary's for marriage or to have their babies baptized had resorted instead to the office of the Superintendent Registrar. Brooks had been under more or less constant stress since his arrival in the parish in 1843. As the vicar of the most prominent Church of England church in the heart of the city of Nottingham, he regarded himself as the senior ecclesiastic in the town. But now that there was such a free market in religion, it was such a hard position to defend. It seemed to Joshua Brooks that Protestant Dissenters of all types – and now Catholics – were everywhere in Nottingham. There were several Baptist and Independent congregations, and a bewildering variety of Methodists. There were Presbyterians who were on the way to Unitarianism, and there were Quakers and Mormons. Only the previous October, the Swedenborgians had opened a branch of the New Jerusalem Church in Trinity Street. Meanwhile the Roman Catholics had a new church on the Derby Road designed by the leading Gothic revival architect A.W.N. Pugin, which was reputed to accommodate well over 1,000. Their old chapel, in George Street, was being converted into a ragged school, to be run by the Sisters of Mercy. Thus, all within easy walking distance of St Mary's parish church, there was a host of vibrant and often newly established Christian communities, all developing their own infrastructure and distinctive ways of believing.

Brooks knew that every minister from Francis Cheadle, the senior Roman Catholic priest in the town, to Cuthbert Orlebar, who styled himself the Angel or Bishop of the Catholic and Apostolic Church in Nottingham, would be filling in their census forms on that Sunday or on the following Monday, if ministerial commitments or sabbatarian principles prevented him from doing it on the day. All denominations, whether sectarian or papist, treated as equal by the London bureaucrats! This was a painful thought for a Church of England clergyman who had been brought up to believe not only that his religion gave him particular privileges, such as entry into the universities of Cambridge and Oxford, but also the right to expect that the government would support him in the promotion of the Anglican form of Christianity. Brooks believed in the importance of maintaining the special privileges of the Church – an Anglican establishment in England and Wales. Yet he knew that in Nottingham at least, the Church of England was unlikely to emerge from the census as the majority denomination, and that the case for a state-supported establishment rested to a large extent on its continuing to have the support of the majority of the population. He also knew that nothing would make him entrust his census forms to men whom he regarded as dissenting infidels. He would send them direct to George Graham, the Registrar General, with a covering letter.[1] It must have been a stressful day all told – and no doubt the water system did not help him get a good night's rest, as the world moved on to Monday 31 March 1851.

When the results of the religious census of 1851 were published in January 1854, they revealed that 31 per cent of the churchgoing citizens of Nottingham had attended Anglican worship, as against 62 per cent who attended Nonconformist chapels.[2] In the Nottingham registration district, the central city area which covered 1,870 acres, there were 38 places of worship. Nine of these were Anglican, seven were Baptist, seven were some variety of Methodist, five were Independent, five belonged to the smaller sects, two were Roman Catholic, one was Presbyterian/Unitarian, one was Quaker and one was Jewish.[3] It was a bewildering array of different types of religion to have in such close proximity in a single English town, all of them making claims about the veracity of their own doctrine and order, in most cases directly against the claims of their rivals. As one Protestant pamphlet that circulated in Nottingham in the 1840s put it, 'If the Protestant is right, then a Roman Catholic cannot be saved; but if the Roman Catholic be right, then a Protestant cannot be saved.'[4] This was the stark dilemma that faced the ordinary Sunday churchgoer, as she made her way past perhaps half a dozen different places of worship until she reached the church or chapel which appeared to her to have the greatest claim on religious truth, as well as providing the most congenial environment for worship, among those with whom she could feel a sense of kinship.

Denominations in competition at mid-century

This sectarian model of religious life, in which competing and mutually hostile religious groups operated cheek by jowl as they attempted to attract and retain the support of the local population, was repeated all over England and Wales. It was, however, subject to considerable regional variation, which has been mapped for England by Hugh McLeod, and in greater detail for England and Wales by K.D.M. Snell and Paul S. Ell.[5] The Church of England had not been everywhere as eclipsed by Nonconformity as it was in Nottingham, and it retained strongholds in the southern rural counties of east Hampshire, west Sussex, much of Surrey, and also in east Devon, central and west Somerset and most of Dorset. It was strong in east Kent, much of Herefordshire, parts of Worcestershire and south Shropshire, in some districts immediately east of Leicester, and in some areas of central East Anglia.[6] It had ceased to be the majority denomination in much of north east and central England. In Cornwall, and a vast swathe of the north east stretching from central Northumberland to the south of Lincolnshire, Wesleyan Methodists were the strongest denomination.[7] Primitive Methodists were strongest in north Lincolnshire, much of Norfolk and in parts of Yorkshire, Northumberland and county Durham.[8] Independents and Baptists thrived across central and eastern England, and were also strong in Wales. The Church of England and Nonconformist denominations were fairly evenly weighted in much of East Anglia and the east Midlands, and in parts of the north Midlands, north Somerset, north Wiltshire and south Gloucestershire.[9] Although the Catholic population in England had risen steeply since the beginning of the nineteenth century, the only places in which Roman Catholics were the largest non-established denomination in 1851 were Liverpool, Preston, the Strand district of central London and St George's Southwark, immediately south of the Thames.[10]

It has been estimated that at the time of the 1851 census, some 60 per cent of the English population regarded themselves as Anglicans, and perhaps 30 per would have defined themselves as Nonconformist. Four per cent were Roman Catholics. Because less than the total Anglican population attended worship on census Sunday, and many of the Nonconformists attended more than one service, the census results, which counted attendances at all services, rather than the number of individual worshippers, gave the impression of almost equal numbers of Anglicans and Nonconformists.[11] The other 6 per cent of the population in 1851 comprised Jews, very small numbers of adherents of other world faiths and new religious movements, such as Theosophists and Spiritualists, and a small but vocal group of freethinkers, atheists and secularists.[12]

In Wales differences in language and religious culture resulted in different patterns of denominational allegiance.[13] The Church of England operated as an established Church in Wales until 1920, and was known, rather oddly, as the Church of England in Wales, with the four Welsh dioceses regarded as part of the province of Canterbury, in the same way that the southern English dioceses were. The Welsh dioceses were, however, very much less strongly supported than the English dioceses, in what was an intensely religious country in 1851. Wales offered an enormously high level of religious provision for its population, with 4,006 separate places of worship. These places contained a total of 1,005,410 sittings for a population of 1,188,914; thus overall 84.5 per cent of the population could have been seated at worship. Horace Mann, the author of the census report, described Wales as 'fortunately basking in an excess of spiritual privileges'.[14] Indeed, the counties of Merioneth and Breconshire had more seats available than population to fill them.[15] Wales also recorded much higher levels of attendance than England – equivalent to 83.4 per cent of the population in South Wales and 86.6 per cent in North Wales.[16]

Thus the concept of secularization, which became widely discussed in British society after the census findings were published, is something which was much less meaningful in mid-nineteenth-century Wales than it was in England, where worship was attended by 59.1 per cent of the population. Equally, it challenges the assertion that was made by Horace Mann, and widely picked up by others, both at the time and since, that it was the working classes, the 'unconscious secularists', who stayed away from religion. Working-class Welsh people had, at this date, clearly not abandoned the practice of religion. The sheer size of Welsh Protestant Dissent is another obvious and important finding: the Welsh were far more likely than the English to be Nonconformists, and Anglicans were a minority throughout the principality. In the south, the main source of rivalry for the Anglicans came from the Independents; in the north, Calvinistic Methodists were in the majority.[17] There is also evidence of an east–west split within Nonconformity, with Calvinistic Methodist and Independent congregations noticeably strongest in the Welsh-speaking west, and Wesleyan Methodism more densely clustered in the east of Wales. The strength of Nonconformity is revealed by the sheer number of their sittings, particularly in the south. The percentage share of Anglican sittings was lowest in Wales, with a dramatic decline being visible along the southern part of the English–Welsh border, between the dioceses of Hereford and St Davids. The place with the lowest share of Anglican sittings anywhere in England or Wales was Merthyr

Tydfil. In about half of Wales, the Anglican share was less than 30 per cent. This differentiated Wales very significantly from most of England, where large parts of the south and Midlands registered a share in excess of 60 per cent, with five registration districts in Sussex all recording well over 80 per cent. Merthyr also registered the lowest share of Anglican attendances – 6.2 per cent. Indeed, the 14 districts with the lowest Anglican attendance were all in Wales. In parts of Hampshire, meanwhile, Anglican attendance ran at 90 per cent.[18]

Despite the very significant importance of regional diversity, the predominant religious paradigm in nineteenth-century England and Wales was therefore two very large and finely balanced Anglican and Nonconformist blocs, eyeing each other with mutual jealousy whilst simultaneously aware of the splits and divisions within their own ranks. This is the national variation on the global picture which was sketched out in the Introduction, in which the two large groupings dominating Christianity were identified as Protestant evangelicalism and Roman Catholicism. It reflects the power of the state Church in England and Wales, and the relative weakness at this date of Roman Catholicism within a largely Protestant society. The more global Protestant–Catholic hostility had been transferred into a Nonconformist–Anglican one. As Anglicans and Nonconformists exchanged hostile glances, they were also acutely aware of the presence of two other alien entities. On the one hand there were Roman Catholics, threatening because they were growing, who were perceived as owing their primary allegiance to a foreign power, and who were newly organized into diocesan structures. On the other there were secularists, freethinkers and atheists, threatening because they were seen as having no vested interest in the maintenance of the status quo, or indeed of traditional Christian morality, which was believed to be the bedrock of Victorian society.

In reality, both Catholics and secularists were still tiny in number. The power which they wielded over the English and Welsh Protestant majority was more psychological than actual. It was markedly different from the pattern in Catholic countries, such as France, Spain, Italy and Portugal, where the fault-lines between Catholics and anti-clerical socialists were deep, and where non-Catholic varieties of Christianity made little impact. It was different again from the predominant patterns in parts of North America and Africa, where particular denominations grew because of the work of individual mission agencies, but where there was little internal competition between different denominations. In these places, a traveller could move quite unconsciously from the stronghold of one denomination to the stronghold of another, or pass into an unevangelized 'no man's land' for no other reason than that he had passed over the invisible boundary that marked the outer reaches of the missionary agency's evangelistic endeavours.

Nonconformist consolidation

By the mid-nineteenth century, there was, as we have seen, a flourishing free market for Christianity in England and Wales. This was not something which had been intended, but it turned out to be one of the longer-term consequences of the nation's official adoption of Protestantism from 1559. In 1662, the passing of the Act of Uniformity had meant that, in theory at least, England had declared itself as having just one officially sanctioned form of religion, and that was the *Ecclesia Anglicana* (the term 'Anglican' did not come into use until the middle of the nineteenth century). The Act of Uniformity worked on the basis of imposing a single liturgical framework on the people of England and Wales. All ministers were required to use only those forms of worship that were in the Book of Common Prayer, the service book that had been compiled mainly by Thomas Cranmer in the 1540s and 1550s. Those ministers who by 24 August 1662 had refused to conform to the Book of Common Prayer, or to seek episcopal ordination, were ejected from the Church of England. It was from the ranks of these 2,000 men that the first generation of Nonconformist (in the strict sense) ministers emerged – men who espoused Presbyterian theology and church government. They joined already existing Baptists, Quakers and Independents (also known as Congregationalists) to provide distinctive, Protestant alternatives to the established Church.

These emerging denominations had some shared emphases, but also certain distinctive features which set them apart from each other. They shared in common a belief in preaching the pure word of God, in simplicity in worship and life, in Christ's sole headship of the Church, in the priesthood of all believers and in the locus of the Church as in the locally gathered congregation. They were all strongly anti-episcopal; whatever constituted the true Church, they were sure that bishops were not part of it. The Quakers were the most radical in theology and had a history of passive resistance to those actions of the state of which they disapproved. Thus they refused to pay church rate, or, being pacifist, taxes in support of the army. By the nineteenth century, some Quakers had come under the influence of the evangelical revival, whilst others retained the simple, quietist piety of waiting on God in silence, and the characteristic plain dress and forms of speech that set them apart from other denominations.

The Presbyterians, Independents and Baptists were, in contrast, broadly Calvinist in theology, as befitted their Reformation origins. Since the 1630s, the Baptists had, however, been divided into two groups. On the one hand, the General Baptists were Arminian in outlook, which meant that they believed that the possibility of redemption was 'general'; meanwhile the more numerous Particular Baptists were orthodox Calvinists, believing that the possibility of redemption was 'particular', in other words confined to the elect. Both Independents and Baptists believed that the essential form of the Church was the local congregation of believers, which was independent and autonomous. The two groups differed sharply over baptism, with the Baptists baptizing by immersion only adult believers. In the late eighteenth century, under the influence of the evangelical revival, the Baptists softened their Calvinist theology considerably, although there was no official abandonment of the Calvinist position. The changed approach was symbolized by the foundation in 1792 of the Baptist Missionary Society, an action indicative of the belief that man could influence his brothers and sisters towards Christ, and that the number of the elect had not already been predetermined by God. In contrast to the Congregationalists and the Baptists, it was the Presbyterians who attempted to realize most fully the Calvinist model of church government. Rather than emphasizing the autonomy of the local congregation, they focused on church government as a hierarchy of church courts, from the local congregation at the bottom to a national assembly at the top. This worked in Scotland, but south of the border congregations were often too scattered to implement Presbyterian government effectively, and from the eighteenth century onwards many formerly Presbyterian congregations began to move in the direction of Congregationalism or Unitarianism. The decisive move towards Unitarianism was what was occurring to the High Pavement congregation in Nottingham at the time of the 1851 census. Unitarians were distinctive in rejecting the doctrines of the Trinity and the divinity of Christ. This made them heretical in the eyes of most Christians.

All these Dissenting denominations had been severely penalized until the passing of the Toleration Act in 1689, and in the case of the Unitarians, up until 1813. The Toleration Act was designed to give Dissenters some freedom of worship in exchange for their support (signified by assent to the Oaths of Allegiance and Supremacy, and in the case of ministers, to the Thirty-Nine Articles of the Church of England) against the deposed Catholic monarch, James II. In time, they would be known as the Old Dissent, in acknowledgement of their seventeenth-century roots, and in contrast to the mainly Methodist groups that would arise from the eighteenth-century evangelical revival, which became known as the New Dissent. Historians who write about the nineteenth century sometimes use the terms 'Dissenter' and 'Nonconformist' interchangeably. In fact, 'Dissenter' is a more correct term to use when describing the earlier part of the century.

The term 'Nonconformist' did not come into vogue until the second half of the century, having been popularized by the title of Edward Miall's newspaper, *The Nonconformist*, which began publication in 1841.[19] By the end of the century, the nomenclature of 'Free Churchman' was becoming fashionable, following the formation of the National Free Church Council in 1892. This terminology was intended to express the positive nature of religious freedom rather than to dwell on the negativity of opposition to the established Church.

Although, as we have seen, Old Dissent was much influenced by the evangelical revival, New Dissent was entirely the product of it. In England, greatest among New Dissent in terms of numbers and influence was Wesleyan Methodism. In Wales it was Calvinistic Methodism. For decades both were part of the established Church and both had begun more or less simultaneously in the 1730s. In England the leaders were John Wesley and George Whitefield; in Wales, they were Daniel Rowland and Howell Harris. By 1800 the Wesleyans had caught up and overtaken all the old Dissenting denominations put together in some English counties, but they were not without their difficulties. After the death of John Wesley in 1791, they were divided between those who wished to remain a supplementary society of the Church of England and those who wished to recognize that they were now in effect a separate denomination and should have their own sacraments. The Plan of Pacification of 1795 allowed societies to have their own sacraments if the majority of trustees, stewards and leaders agreed, but it was followed by a further dispute over ministers and laity. Some Wesleyans objected to the fact that the Conference consisted only of travelling preachers, and in 1797 a small group broke away to form the Methodist New Connexion, in which ministers and laymen had equal representation in the Conference.

In the early years of the nineteenth century, other groups grew up in the Methodist tradition, but splintered away from Wesleyanism, largely because they felt that the Wesleyan parent organization had lost the evangelistic immediacy of its founder. These new denominations included the Independent Methodists, who broke away in 1806, the Primitive Methodists (1811) and the Bible Christians (1815). Within a few decades, however, Methodists of almost all hues were deciding that there was more that united than divided them. By the final quarter of the nineteenth century, the mood had changed decisively, and the Methodist denominations began on a programme of cooperation and reunion which resulted in all the major English Methodist bodies being reunited by 1932. In Wales, the hugely influential Calvinistic Methodist movement remained part of the established Church until 1811. It was able to remain within the Church because it was attuned to the evangelical tone of much Welsh Anglicanism; Methodism, whether Wesleyan or Calvinist, was seen as something which could be accommodated quite happily within the Anglican mainstream. In Haverfordwest, a 'Wesley room' was opened next door to St Mary's church in 1772, and at Newport (Pembs), a 'church chapel' was built next to the parish church in 1799. There were, inevitably, individual clergy and bishops who remained hostile to Methodism, seeing it as 'a cloak to hide every vice which can disgrace the Christian character'.[20] In the end the split occurred because there were too few Anglican clergy willing to celebrate communion services for the burgeoning number of Calvinistic Methodist denominations, and this led the movement's leader, Thomas Charles, to realize that some lay preachers would have to be ordained to fill the breach. The newly independent denomination adopted a presbyterian form of church government, and in 1933 it took the name the Presbyterian Church of Wales, by which it had been unofficially known for some time.

Among the new denominations that began to make an impact in the second half of the nineteenth century, the Salvation Army was undoubtedly the most significant. This too was an offshoot of Methodism, in so far as its founder, William Booth, was a former minister in the Methodist New Connexion, breaking away in 1861 when the Connexion refused to sanction him as a travelling evangelist. Booth with his wife Catherine founded the Christian Mission in the East End of London in 1865. By 1878 the Mission had developed into the Salvation Army. Far removed from the genteel world of much of Victorian Nonconformity, the Army sought to present itself in self-consciously proletarian terms, dispensing with all 'churchy' language and associations. Rather than organs and surpliced choirs, it had brass bands and songster brigades. It had no chapels, but citadels or barracks, designed to look like music halls. It used the flags, uniforms and language reminiscent of contemporary popular imperialism. It was an autocratic organization, with Booth himself as the first General. In one important respect, however, it departed from militaristic codes and metaphors. From the beginning the Army gave equal status to women, who were eligible not simply to become soldiers but to be officers (ministers) on equal terms with men. This was revolutionary for its time, and it suggests that in this respect, the Salvation Army was returning to the patterns of early Methodist revivalism, in which eighteenth-century women had also played a large part. Catherine Booth played a central role in the Salvation Army and was in many ways the brains behind the organization. The Booths' daughter and grand-daughters were also active in what became a dynastic form of leadership that lasted well into the twentieth century.

It would have been easy for late Victorian society to pour scorn on the bogus General, in his military tunic and top hat, but in fact he became a national institution. People were impressed by the Army's social-work activities, which were firmly in place by the 1890s. They ran soup kitchens and hostels for the homeless, and Booth experimented with some quite radical ideas for getting the poor out of poverty. The Salvation Army's theology was firmly Arminian: God's love embraced everyone, and all could be saved. In other respects, it was distinctly less orthodox. The emphasis on evangelistic preaching meant that the Lord's Supper was totally abandoned, perhaps because of Booth's fear that even with the use of unfermented grape juice it might prove an obstacle for alcoholics. Nor was baptism celebrated. Instead infants were given a military-style dedication ceremony. Growth was phenomenal. In 1900, about 25 years after its foundation, it had a total membership approaching 100,000, with 4,000 full-time officers and workers and over 1,300 buildings and centres. Booth remained at the helm until his death in 1912, when his son, Bramwell Booth, became the second General. In the twentieth century, the Salvation Army became a worldwide denomination, with members in almost every country.

Just as the Salvation Army saw itself, initially at least, as having a specific mission to the very poor, so other Nonconformist bodies had a clear sense of identity with particular social groups. Nonconformity lacked aristocrats and had very few of the very poor, and in this respect it differed from both Anglicans and Roman Catholics, who were represented in both categories. The range of Nonconformity ran from the respectable worker to the wealthy business and professional classes.[21] The Unitarians and Quakers were probably the wealthiest denominations, the so-called aristocracy of Dissent. They were well represented among merchants and manufacturers. The Quakers were known as successful bankers, and for their chocolate products: Lloyds and Barclays, Cadbury, Fry and Rowntree are all names which remain familiar in the twenty-first-century British high street. The Congregationalists, Baptists and Wesleyans tended to be the main middle-class denominations, but there were interesting and subtle differences. The Congregationalists tended to include the wealthiest manufacturers – for example, the Colmans of Norwich, Titus Salt, Leverhulme, Unwin, Remington, Crossley and Wills.[22] The Baptists were stronger among the small business classes; the Wesleyans were particularly strong among shopkeepers. The smaller Methodist bodies, the General Baptists of the New Connexion and the Primitive Methodists, flourished best among those of more humble status, appealing particularly to artisans, small craftsmen and other manual workers. In rural areas, Congregationalists and Baptists tended to be strong among the farmers and independent craftsmen, while Wesleyans and Primitive Methodists attracted agricultural labourers. In South Wales, some wealthy industrialists embraced Nonconformity, such as the Cory family, who were prominent ship and colliery owners. The majority of Welsh Nonconformists were artisans, and in the first half of the century at least it was more usual for Dissenting ministers to be supported by secular employment than was the case in England. Many Baptist ministers were shopkeepers.[23] Although the exercise of individual choice was clearly a crucial factor in defining the religious identity of nineteenth-century England and Wales, in rural areas the social composition of chapels depended very much on what else was available; social differentiations proliferated with the number of chapels in the vicinity. If there was only one chapel available, religious identity tended to be defined in terms of dissent from the Church of England, and was not the prerogative of any particular social group.

Anglican high-church revival

Of the many developments that occurred within the nineteenth-century Church of England, we shall concentrate here on one that contributed to a change in its internal religious culture, bringing about a Catholic revival within the national Church. The Church of England had always had its 'high' and its 'low' ends. The 'high' emphasized continuity with early Christianity, the theology of the seventeenth-century Caroline divines, the sacraments and the importance of the Church keeping its distance from Nonconformity. The 'low' emphasized the importance of biblical faith, atonement theology, vital religion and the importance of cooperating with other evangelicals where possible. At the beginning of the century, only about 500 clergy identified themselves with Evangelicalism, but the number had grown to no fewer than 6,500, or one-third of the whole, by the middle of the century. By this date, an even greater number had grown up in a world favourable to Evangelical religion.[24] It contributed a major part of the culture of Victorian Britain.

The catalyst for growth of the Catholic wing was both political and religious. At the political level, the immediate trigger was the Irish Church Temporalities Act of 1833, a political measure that was mainly designed to reduce the resentment felt by Irish Catholics. In 1833, there were 22 Anglican bishops in Ireland, with a combined episcopal income of £150,000, which at an average of £6,800 per bishop was significantly higher than the average received by most English bishops. They served an Anglican population of about 850,000, a figure which represented about 12 per cent of the total Irish population at that time. The Irish Church Temporalities Act reduced the number of Anglican bishops in Ireland from 22 to 12. For Anglican loyalists, the measure might have been slightly less controversial if it had been the legislative enactment of the pre-reform parliament, fulfilling its traditional role as an Anglican lay synod, by managing the Church's affairs. But a trio of measures passed between 1828 and 1832 had provided the final nails in the coffin of the notion that parliament's major function in relation to religion was to protect the best interests of the established Church.[25] In July 1833, John Keble, Professor of Poetry at the University of Oxford, who was to become one of the leaders of what would be known as the Oxford Movement, thundered that:

> The Legislature of England and Ireland, (*the members of which are not even bound to profess belief in the Atonement,*) ... has virtually usurped the commission of those whom our Saviour entrusted with at *least one voice* in making ecclesiastical laws, on matters wholly or partly spiritual. The same Legislature has also ratified, to its full extent, this principle; – that the Apostolic Church in this realm is henceforth to stand in the eye of the State, as *one sect among many.*[26]

Against the essentially utilitarian model of Church government that parliament was adopting, the leaders of the Oxford Movement proposed a transcendental model. In addition to John Keble, the most famous were John Henry Newman, Edward Bouverie Pusey and Richard Hurrell Froude. For them, the Church was a supernatural institution, with a spiritual mandate that could not be interfered with by political processes. The bishops were the successors of the Apostles, not primarily peers of the realm with seats in the House of Lords. The clergy were priests with a divinely validated vocation which resulted from the 'honourable badge' of their episcopal ordination; they were not primarily English gentlemen with a mission to behave like characters in a Jane Austen novel. The Oxford Movement was one factor, although not the main factor, in the drastic revision which took place in the relationship between church and state in England and Wales in the nineteenth century.

The Anglican high church revival developed a number of distinct strands. One phase, from 1833 to 1841, was marked by the publication of tracts, which led to the Oxford Movement gaining its alternative name, 'Tractarianism'. The Tracts started off as short, pithy little publications of only a few pages, designed to be read by the clergy over the breakfast table, or at some other brief but convenient moment. Principally the early Tracts were designed to make the clergy stop and think about the nature of their vocation. Later they became much longer, more verbose and therefore less easily readable. In order to demonstrate the continuity in thought between themselves and the much older high-church tradition within the Church of England, a number of the later Tracts became heavily dependent on reproducing large chunks from the writings of the Caroline divines.

Some of the later Tracts aroused controversy on account of the seeming novelty of their teaching. This was true of Tract 80, 'On Reserve in Communicating Religious Knowledge', written by Isaac Williams in 1838. This Tract, which revealed a key aspect of Tractarian thought, was based on the idea that the apprehension of religious truth requires moral maturity. If this were the case, then it made sense for religious truth to be revealed gradually to those who wished to be fully initiated Christians; once they had been weaned on milk they could be introduced to stronger food. The Tractarians thought that there were good early Church precedents for adopting this particular approach. The Evangelicals thought that they were up to something sinister. What was this religious truth which could not be spoken of openly? It seemed to run counter to the imperative to preach the Gospel to all people. It also led to anxieties about the Tractarians not being all that they seemed. If they could not be open about what they believed in, could they be relied upon to be what they said they were? Were those who appeared to be Anglicans in fact secret converts to Rome, infiltrating the Church from within and attempting to subvert the principles of the Reformation? As some of the Oxford Movement's associates began to convert to Rome from 1843, the Evangelicals felt that their fears had been vindicated.

Although in most respects the leaders of the Oxford Movement were keen to emphasize the continuity of their ideas with both the early Church and with the older high-church tradition within Anglicanism, on the subject of the Reformation they were distinctly different, and spoke with a voice which jarred with the traditional high Anglican understanding, which saw the English Reformation as having been both desirable and necessary. Hurrell Froude, who had leanings towards disestablishment, particularly hated the Reformation for having, as he saw it, enslaved the Church to the state. After Froude's early death in 1836, a particular flashpoint was the refusal of the remaining Tractarian leaders to make a donation to the Oxford martyrs' memorial, which was planned in memory of those divines of the English Reformation, Cranmer, Latimer and Ridley, who had been burnt under Mary. Once again, it seemed incomprehensible that Anglican clergy should repudiate the principles of the Reformation, and their loyalty to the Church and its principles was called severely into question.

It was to be Newman's entanglement with one of the foundations of the English Reformation, the Thirty-Nine Articles, which led to the Tracts coming to an end in 1841. The episode was also part of the process which led to Newman's eventual conversion to Roman Catholicism in 1845. In Tract 90, Newman tried to show that the Thirty-Nine Articles, to which every Anglican clergyman (and indeed Oxford student) had to subscribe, could be interpreted in a Catholic sense, fully consonant with the faith of the early Church. If this task could be accomplished successfully, it would have the effect of providing reassurance for those Anglican clergy who wanted to adopt full-blown Tractarian principles and remain loyal to the Church of England. If the task could not be accomplished successfully, it would indicate that the Church of England's doctrinal formularies were flawed and that it was not a natural evolution within historic Christendom. Newman attempted the task, but ended up torturing the language of the Articles to make them take on meanings which seemed removed from their natural sense. Fundamentally, the Thirty-Nine Articles were imbued with the spirit of sixteenth-century Protestantism; the moving spirit behind them had been Thomas Cranmer, and they had not been drafted specifically in order to demonstrate the historic roots of Anglicanism within the early Church.[27] Yet this was the task that Newman was now demanding of them. Tract 90 was published amid great controversy. Newman's bishop, Bagot of Oxford, declined to condemn him, but he ordered that the publication of Tracts should cease.[28] Newman ceased to be an effective leader within Anglicanism, and his passage into Roman Catholicism took place in 1845, at which point the Oxford Movement was deemed to have come to an end.

In many respects, the attraction of the Catholic revival within Anglicanism, and indeed its lasting impact, was as much cultural and aesthetic as theological, and it was these strands which were relatively little affected by the ending of the Tracts and the conversion of Newman. The aesthetic strand, which is connected to the wider European Romantic movement, can perhaps be said to date from the publication of Keble's hugely popular volume of verse, *The Christian Year*, in 1827. Keble's poems provided suitable reading for all the Sundays of the year, together with the major festivals and saints days, thus drawing Anglicans' attention to the existence of Christian time, played out over a year that began on Advent Sunday and concluded in the following November. He was very much the poet of pastoral England, and his verses are full of shady glades, green lanes and violets that bloom unseen. Had he been a painter rather than a poet, his work might have resembled that of Thomas Gainsborough. Isaac Williams also wrote poetry, although the fuss created by the publication of his Tract on reserve resulted in him being denied the Oxford poetry professorship in succession to Keble.

A more enduring legacy than poetry was architecture. Because so much of it has survived and is visible in towns and cities, it is this with which the Catholic revival – both Anglican and Roman – has come to be most clearly associated. Nigel Yates has argued that ecclesiologists and ritualists, who expressed their ideas by re-ordering existing churches, building new ones and introducing a greater degree of ceremonial into worship, existed, together with the Tractarians, as separate, but connected groups within the high churchmanship of the 1830s and 1840s, and that they did not emerge later, as has sometimes been supposed.[29] Yates also argues that the attraction of ritualism was as much psychological as theological, and that it appealed to those who were seeking a return to a vaguely understood medieval golden age, as well as to those who saw it as expressing a more properly Catholic doctrine of the Church.[30] The general rage for the Gothic revival was clearly important here, with societies being founded in 1839 at both Oxford and Cambridge to promote the building and re-ordering of churches in the Gothic revival style.[31] In addition to a greater emphasis on the altar and on richer and more ornate decoration and fittings, such buildings were characterized by a preference for open pews. These replaced the traditional high-backed or box pews, and were designed to eliminate social distinctions among the worshipping community, as well as to make the worshippers more conspicuous, and therefore reduce the likelihood that they would sleep, gossip, fidget or flirt.[32]

Although many clergy were actively involved in church building and restoration, it is worth emphasizing the role which the newly important architectural profession played in transforming Victorian churches.[33] Some Tractarian laymen were undoubtedly attracted to careers in architecture, a profession that was beginning to offer great possibilities for the hardworking, the ambitious and the talented. Whilst William Butterfield and George Gilbert Scott, the great show-piece architects, remain the best known, there were other local architects at work, whose lives remain obscure even when their buildings live on. Christopher Neville, who was patron and vicar of Thorney in Nottinghamshire, employed Nockalls Johnson Cottingham to restore his church. Cottingham was a Gothic revivalist who was later to design the reredos at Hereford Cathedral.[34] Later Neville admitted to his diocesan bishop that his own indifference to architectural matters had resulted in his paying insufficient attention to the details of the project. Suddenly he found the persuasive architect about to transform his church in a manner which did not reflect his views. Among the many alterations, 'I find he proposes to place the commandments on the Communion Table in what he calls a *triptic*, a word I never saw, or heard. The outer leaves or doors are to be opened during service and shut afterwards, and the whole highly ornamented and gilt.'[35] The bishop advised against the adoption of Cottingham's plan, and Neville seemed relieved. He described himself as the last clergyman in the diocese to whom could be ascribed Romish or Tractarian views.[36]

At Fosbury in Wiltshire the architect was Samuel Saunders Teulon. On 30 September 1856, the bishop of Salisbury, Walter Kerr Hamilton, who was the first Tractarian to be promoted to an English diocese, noted in his diary, 'A district has been made out of Shalbourn parish in Tidcombe … Mr Teulon is Architect. House and Church have cost abt. £4000 – the Church has no chancel – It is one long building – but the East End is made what Mr Teulon calls a Ritualist Chancel, by rising two steps and placing the seats stall ways. The Effect is very good and suits our Service.'[37] Here again, it seems to have been the architect rather than the local clergy who took the initiative in setting the tone for the building. Nevertheless, once established in newly Gothic churches, the clergy generally seem to have adapted quite readily to different liturgical conventions. A higher level of ceremonial followed naturally in a re-ordered church, and older customs, such as bringing in communion wine in a bottle, or a loaf of bread on a crockery plate, seemed to be verging on profanity.[38] The numbers of clergy associated with Tractarianism in the middle of the nineteenth century were not very large, perhaps less than 5 per cent of the total number of Anglican clergy, but their influence was to prove out of all proportion to their size, in promoting a revival of a particular type.[39]

Roman Catholic expansion

Catholicism did not receive any further state sanction after Elizabeth's accession in 1559, but it was far from eliminated from England and Wales. Some people, particularly in the north west, chose the option of outward conformity to the Church of England whilst maintaining their own Catholic beliefs and practices, thus earning the soubriquet of 'church papists'. The policy of the Elizabethan settlement was, as Alex Walsham puts it, to make the Church of England 'a nursery in which the masses were gently weaned, not roughly snatched, from popery'.[40] The result of this slow weaning was that many were able to continue with their religious inclinations relatively free from disturbance, as long as they were perceived as posing no threat to national security. The Toleration Act of 1689, although officially excluding Roman Catholics (and Quakers) from its protection, in fact created an environment in which all types of voluntary religion could thrive. There is no evidence of any Catholic chapels being closed by any public authority in the period from 1689 to the advent of legal status for Catholics in 1791.[41] For most of the eighteenth century, Catholics were allowed to carry on their affairs unmolested and were largely ignored, although there were occasional serious flare-ups, such as the Gordon Riots of 1780, in which 285 people died in London. The Gordon Riots had been sparked by a demand that the Catholic Relief Act of 1778 be repealed. The demand was unsuccessful, and a further series of Relief Acts were passed in the late eighteenth century, which paved the way for the Catholic Emancipation Act of 1829.

By the mid-nineteenth century, Catholicism in Britain had grown considerably, from under 100,000 in 1800 to 750,000 in 1850.[42] Although still tiny within the overall population, amounting, as we have seen, to only 4 per cent at the time of the 1851 religious census, it was this perception of rapid growth, combined with the foreignness, both perceived and actual, of the Catholic faith and its adherents, that was sufficient to ignite what was to be the last large outbreak of popular anti-Catholic protest in England in 1850. The catalyst was Rome's decision to establish in England and Wales a diocesan structure with a hierarchy of 12 bishops. This relatively uncontroversial procedure was disastrously presented to the British people by the man appointed to be the first cardinal archbishop of Westminster, Nicholas Wiseman. Wiseman referred to it as an opportunity for him to 'govern' London and the Home Counties. Although Wiseman undoubtedly intended this in a purely spiritual sense, this subtlety was lost on the English press. Already whipped up into an editorial frenzy by the setting up of the Catholic hierarchy, Wiseman's appointment was denounced as a gross act of papal aggression. In the ensuing weeks, which culminated in an orgy of burnings in effigy on Guy Fawkes' night on 5 November, Catholic clergy and properties were attacked and the police were required to restrain Protestant mobs. But the protests died away as suddenly as they had arisen. From the later 1850s, Catholics in England (there were still very few in most of Wales) began to be accepted as a natural (albeit a seldom encountered and therefore slightly mysterious) feature of the religious landscape. There remained, however, a strongly anti-Catholic tone in much Protestant preaching and literature. By 1900 the Catholic population was heading towards 2 million, and the foundations had been laid for Roman Catholicism to emerge as the major alternative to the Church of England in the twentieth century.

Catholics in nineteenth-century England were not a homogeneous group, but this was also true of Anglicans and many of the larger Nonconformist bodies. More attention, however, seems to have been given to the internal dynamics within Catholicism, and more theories seem to have been built upon conclusions arising from these analyses.[43] There were three significant groups. First, there was the existing English Catholic community, whose antecedents went back to the eighteenth century or earlier. Secondly, there was a very substantial number of recently arrived immigrants, mainly from Ireland. Their numbers had been building up since the 1820s, and increased very heavily in the second half of the 1840s, as people sought escape from starvation in the wake of the Irish potato famine. Thirdly, there was a small but influential group of converts from Anglicanism. The first three cardinal archbishops of Westminster each emerged from one of these constituencies. Nicholas Wiseman had an Irish grandfather and was born in Seville to a

Spanish mother, and having spent most of his career in Rome, can be seen as embodying the 'foreign' element which the English Protestant psyche found so troublesome. Henry Manning, who succeeded Wiseman in 1865, was a former Anglican clergyman, who had been a Catholic for just 14 years when he became archbishop of Westminster. Herbert Vaughan, who succeeded Manning in 1892, came from an old-established English Catholic family with its roots in the English/Welsh border. These three archbishops all did a great deal to shape Catholicism in nineteenth-century England and Wales. Under their influence, it emerged as a doctrinally orthodox, well-organized, highly disciplined and increasingly well-resourced community, with a specific identity which set it apart from Protestantism. This identity was forged both by the creation of Catholic institutions, such as schools, social clubs and welfare societies, and by the encouragement of Catholic devotions, such as to the Virgin Mary, to the Sacred Heart of Jesus and to the pope. This institutional and devotional revival in the Catholic life and practice of England and Wales also occurred more or less simultaneously in Ireland, the USA and parts of continental Europe. Making all this possible was an increasingly purposeful army of Catholic priests, many of whom laboured in unpleasant conditions in the cities. Several scholars have noted that these men rarely survived to a great age, and they remain very much the neglected foot soldiers in the expansion and consolidation of nineteenth-century English Catholicism.[44] The number of Catholic priests in England increased from 826 in 1851 to 3,298 in 1900.

The road to religious equality

The story of Christianity in nineteenth-century England and Wales is from one point of view the story of rights and privileges being transferred from the dominant Anglican establishment to members of other religious bodies, and indeed latterly to those who professed no faith at all. This served to ease tensions which, had they remained unaddressed, would probably have had serious political and social consequences. Anglicans had to adjust to the fact that their monopoly on privilege was being steadily dismantled and that hitherto Anglican institutions were being secularized. At the same time they had to contend with a whole range of internal tensions, crises and revivals. These included institutional reform and reorganization, Evangelical and Anglo-Catholic revival and scientific and theological enquiry. In England, Anglicans had to adjust to becoming simply one among several Christian denominations, albeit still the most powerful one, and still formally and legally established. In Wales, Anglicans had to accept that they were significantly outnumbered by Nonconformists and that disestablishment, the campaign for which began in 1870, would almost certainly

occur – in fact, it was delayed until 1920. Equally, Protestant Nonconformists and Roman Catholics had to adjust to the fact that if they still felt
discriminated against, this was less likely to be on account of hostility to
their religious view, and more likely to be the result of discrimination on
the basis of class prejudice, gender or lack of education. Big milestones on
the road from toleration to religious equality were the repeal of the Test
and Corporation Acts in 1828, the Catholic Emancipation Act in 1829, the
Reform Act of 1832 and the reform of the municipal corporations in 1835.
All these measures allowed non-Anglicans a greater degree of involvement
in the political process, and challenged the domineering oligarchies who
had hitherto considered themselves as having a God-given right to run
everything.

From the mid-1830s, Dissenters launched campaigns against the contin-
uance of a number of significant social disabilities, or what they termed
'practical grievances'.[45] There were five major ones. First, in order to safe-
guard the civil rights of their children, they were obliged to take their
babies to be baptized by an Anglican clergyman. This was because the state
registered births only in the baptismal registers of parish churches, which
meant that baptismal certificates functioned in the way that birth certificates do today. Secondly, they were obliged to marry in an Anglican church
– only Quakers and Jews were exempt. Thirdly, if the lack of a municipal
or Dissenters' cemetery meant that there was no alternative to the church
graveyard, they were obliged to be buried according to Anglican rites – the
alternative being the ignominy of burial without words. Fourth, they were,
like their Anglican neighbours, liable to pay church rate, a local tax which
was raised in order to maintain the fabric of the parish church. Fifth, they
were excluded from the grammar schools and from taking degrees of the
universities of Oxford and Cambridge, and had little opportunity to take
degrees anywhere outside Scotland.

This had serious implications for their future career choices, and explains
why so many went into manufacturing. At Oxford it was necessary to
subscribe to the Thirty-Nine Articles on entry; at Cambridge the statutes
were a little less draconian – it was possible for Nonconformists who were
prepared to put up with compulsory college chapel attendance to embark
upon courses of study. They were, however, prevented from taking their
degrees, as this required assent to the Thirty-Nine Articles. When King's
College London and Durham University opened their doors in 1831 and
1836 respectively, they too required compulsory subscription. Meanwhile
the avowedly secular University College London, the so-called 'godless
college in Gower Street', which was founded in 1826, was not empowered
to give university degrees until ten years later. In Wales, St David's College

Lampeter, which opened in 1827 as a strongly Church college (but not a theological college) with an emphasis on training the Welsh clergy, never explicitly banned Nonconformist students from its lecture rooms. It did not, however, gain degree-awarding powers until 1852.

Between 1836 and 1906 the Dissenters' grievances were gradually rectified. In 1836, the Civil Registration Act introduced the civil registration of births, marriages and deaths, and made it possible for chapels to be licensed for marriages for the first time. Nevertheless, the fact that under the Act notification of Dissenting marriages had to be made to the Poor Law Guardians, and they were thus dubbed 'work-house marriages', created a secondary grievance, which was particularly felt by the upwardly mobile.[46] In 1880, the Burials Act permitted Nonconformists to be buried in their own graveyards with their own form of words. Church rate was a wound that festered from the 1830s to the 1860s. From the mid-1830s, certain Nonconformists were imprisoned for their refusal to pay. One of the most celebrated cases was that of William Baines, a Congregationalist shopkeeper from Leicester. His refusal to pay the church rate levied in the parish in which he resided, St Mark's Leicester, led to his being incarcerated in prison for seven months in 1840–41. A massive campaign of public support was launched, spearheaded by Edward Miall, who was the minister of the chapel which Baines attended. Baines's national notoriety focused attention on what was just one of a number of similar cases. Miall's campaign was designed to organize Dissent into a powerful body which would succeed in securing disestablishment and the total separation of church and state. His political radicalism injected energy into the campaign; he advocated votes for all men, secret ballots, payment of members of parliament, annual parliaments, repeal of the corn laws and a general destruction of the powers of the Church, squires and aristocracy. To further these ends, Miall founded the Anti-State Church Association, which was later renamed the Liberation Society.

The battle over church rate had the effect of producing a bitter and intensely public annual showdown between the Church and Dissent. It was the grievance that affected the most Dissenters the most frequently. As Timothy Larsen has noted, 'most Dissenters most of the time were not looking for a place to bury an unbaptised daughter, or the prestige of an Oxford MA', but the injustice of taxing one man to support another man's religion was something which could enrage all who were friendly to Dissent.[47] It was also a disaster from the Anglican point of view. If a rate failed to be set, then there was no source of income from which the parish could draw for necessary repairs to the church fabric. If a rate was set, the Dissenters had no alternative but to pay up or risk prison. As the sums demanded were usually small, it was more a matter of principle than financial hardship. When no rate was levied, bell ringers, choir, organist and sexton had to be dismissed, and the congregation had to hope that the roof would not fall in while they were at worship in the increasingly dusty church. Sometimes churches had to be closed in the interests of safety. This was what occurred at St Mary's Nottingham, which, as we saw at the beginning of the chapter, was closed for months on end in the early 1840s because the tower was judged to be so unstable that the whole structure had become unsafe. It was a brave incumbent who took legal action against his Dissenting churchwardens, although this did happen at Llanelli in 1837, when the vicar, Ebenezer Morris, took the wardens, an Independent and a Unitarian, to court, for 'failing to fulfil their duties'. The court action resulted in their imprisonment.[48] When wardens refused to set a rate, or parishioners refused to pay, raising money by public subscription was the measure most frequently adopted as the century wore on, particularly after the Braintree church rate case, which dragged on through eight different courts from 1837 to 1852, and finally established that a rate was only legal if a majority of the vestry agreed to it. Church rate did not finally become voluntary until 1868.

Education

The advantages which the established Church had as the virtually unchallenged provider of education at elementary, grammar school and university levels proved to be even more long drawn out and equally as contentious as the church rate controversies. In 1843 Nonconformist ire was aroused with the introduction of Graham's Factory Bill which, if enacted, would have passed the education of factory children into the complete control of the Church of England. In what amounted to an uncharacteristic display of defiance by the usually apolitical Wesleyan Methodists, the Wesleyans threw their strength behind the rest of Nonconformity, and the government was forced to abandon the Bill. The Anglican stranglehold on education was so contentious because it meant that Nonconformist parents had to choose between their children's education and their religious principles. Although Quakers and Methodists founded some schools of their own, most town grammar schools and the ancient universities remained the exclusive privilege of Anglicans until mid-century. In 1854 Nonconformists were at last admitted to Oxford degrees, and this was extended to Cambridge in 1856. They were not, however, to be admitted into university teaching posts or college fellowships until the 1870s. It can be argued that, with their large numbers of chaplains, deans and Anglican theologians, both the ancient universities retained a strongly Church of England ethos until well into the twentieth century. It was not uncommon for a young man to go up to Oxford or Cambridge as a Congregationalist or a Methodist, and to emerge three years later as an Anglican.

Forster's Education Act of 1870 was a defining moment in the shift in the balance of power away from Christian organizations of all sorts, and towards the state as the primary provider and financer of schools. As such, it was an important reference point in the secularization of England and Wales. By 1870 the majority of Nonconformists had ceased to believe that the schools of any particular denomination should be paid for by that denomination alone; this had been their earlier position, known as the voluntary principle. They had now accepted that schools were expensive and that only with the help of the state could an adequate system of elementary education be provided for all children. Nonconformists therefore welcomed the overall principle of the 1870 Education Act, which established non-denominational Board schools in places where no other adequate schools existed. Under the Cowper-Temple clause which was appended to Forster's Act, any 'catechism or religious formulary' distinctive of a particular denomination was to be excluded from the syllabus in the new Board schools. Nonconformists failed, however, in their attempt to prevent the possibility of poor children being sent, at the expense of the ratepayers, to church schools, where such existed.

Tensions between Nonconformists and Anglicans on the education issue flared up again in the 1890s, when some ultra-high-church Anglicans on the London School Board flouted the Cowper-Temple clause by trying to impose openly doctrinal elements on syllabuses and Trinitarian tests on teachers. The high churchmen lost, but the incident raised the temperature of the debate. Things came to the boil again in 1902, when Balfour's Education Act abolished school boards and gave control of schools to local authorities. Denominational schools were now permitted to receive rate aid, on condition that a third of the managers of such schools were publicly appointed. Anglicans had long sought such rate aid, which would obviously be of most direct benefit to them, as they controlled far more schools than any other denomination. Nonconformity reacted furiously, and in England a passive resistance campaign was organized, led among others by the Baptist John Clifford. By 1906, 70,880 summonses had been issued for non-payment of rates, goods had been distrained and auctioned, and in 176 cases non-payment and refusal to allow distraint of goods had ended in periods of imprisonment. The controversy did not subside until 1906, when a new Liberal government moderated the terms of the 1902 Act.

In Wales, opposition to the 1902 Act took a very different form. Rather than individual passive resisters withholding that part of their rates that was considered likely to be used for educational purposes, the protest took place at an institutional rather than an individual level. The campaign was organized by the leading Welsh politician and future prime minister David Lloyd George, and resulted in 14 of the 16 Welsh local educational authorities simply refusing to implement the Act.[49] The government retaliated with the Education (Local Authority Default) Act, intended to circumvent local revolts. The Act was passed, but little enforced. Had the government not fallen in 1906, it is difficult to know how they would have resolved matters in the light of the virtual shut-down of the schools system by most local authorities. Thus the 1902 Education Act had two different meanings on either side of the England–Wales border. In England, the Act was the last, curiously anachronistic, occasion in which one Christian group – the largely Anglican magistracy and political establishment – could contemplate prosecuting another Christian group on account of the strength of their religious views. In Wales, it played out differently, and with a seemingly less bitter legacy and certainly a less heavy footprint on the historical record. By 1902 Nonconformists had become the Welsh political establishment, and Welsh Anglicans maintained a much lower profile during the course of the dispute.[50] Bitterness between Welsh Anglicans and Nonconformists certainly existed, but remained at this time focused on the campaign to disestablish the Welsh Church.

Anglicans, Nonconformists and Catholics at the end of the nineteenth century

In order to illustrate the variety of English and Welsh Christianity, this chapter has dealt mainly with Nonconformists and Catholics, and only with the Anglo-Catholic wing of the Church of England. This has tended to present the Anglican establishment as an embattled entity, watching nervously from the sidelines whilst its traditional privileges were systematically stripped away. This does not, however, do justice to what was a dynamic religious body which responded positively to many (though by no means all) of the changes thrust upon it, and which could still command the support of one in four of the English population in 1851, something which could be said of no other institution in Victorian Britain.[51] In Wales, the strength of Nonconformity, the disestablishment campaign and conflict arising from issues relating to tithe payments meant that the Anglican Church was less warmly received. It was, however, very far from being the culturally alien entity that it has sometimes been caricatured as being, and it was well supported by a network of Anglican societies and institutions and by a large number of energetic and Welsh-speaking clergy.[52]

The final decades of the century also witnessed the emergence of Anglicanism as a self-consciously worldwide communion, to some extent coordinated (although definitely not controlled) through the decennial meeting of the Lambeth Conference. The first Lambeth Conference took place in 1867 under the chairmanship of Archbishop Longley. An initial expectation among some participants had been that the Communion should become a more centralized bureaucracy, in which the Conference would function as a pan-Anglican synod, giving authoritative rulings upon matters of common concern. In fact, Anglicanism became a loosely federated family of provincial synods, without any strong central framework. Within this family the Archbishop of Canterbury assumed more of the status of a respected senior relative (and inevitably related more distantly to some branches of his family than to others) than of an authoritative holy father.[53] The Lambeth Conference did, however, make some progress towards providing a framework for embryonic ecumenical discussions. The most significant late nineteenth-century Lambeth moment was the publication of the Lambeth Quadrilateral in 1888 (sometimes called the Chicago–Lambeth Quadrilateral in deference to the fact that the formula had been devised at the General Convention of the Episcopal Church of the United States of America in Chicago two years earlier). The Quadrilateral provided a formula which from an Anglican standpoint was seen as summarizing the essentials for a reunited Christian Church. The four elements were that, first, all Christians needed to accept the Old and New Testaments as containing all things necessary for salvation, secondly, the Apostles' and Nicene Creeds, thirdly, the two sacraments of baptism and Eucharist, and fourthly and most controversially, the historic episcopate. From a Free Church perspective, it was the episcopal element that would prove the greatest stumbling block when the Chicago–Lambeth Quadrilateral was used in ecumenical discussions.

By the end of the nineteenth century, the Church of England had changed considerably from how it might have seemed when Joshua Brooks surveyed the scene on the morning of the 1851 religious census. It had completed a very substantial administrative reform in which parishes and dioceses had become smaller and more manageable, money had been redirected to poorer areas, clergy had been deployed more effectively and new roles had been found for lay people. It was in the process of accepting the implications of at least some aspects of critical thought – for example in relation to biblical criticism as applied to the Old Testament – and it had revised its position on matters such as hell and eternal damnation to accommodate more liberal perspectives. Although it was still firmly wedded to the liturgical use of the Book of Common Prayer, in many churches the outward appearance of its services was changing, as they moved in a more Catholic direction. By the first decade of the twentieth century, practices such as the eastward position (the priest standing with his back to the congregation for parts of the Eucharist), the mixed chalice (wine and water) and the use of lighted candles in daylight – which only a few years earlier had been seen as the mark of extreme Anglo-Catholicism – had been adopted in over a fifth of the Anglican churches in England and Wales.[54] In terms of its numerical strength, Anglican fortunes at the end of the nineteenth century are harder to evaluate. The number of ordinations continued to rise until 1886. Baptisms, confirmations and Easter communions were all increasing. But the number of marriages celebrated in Anglican churches was falling, and there is also evidence of a considerable drop in attendance at Sunday worship, particularly in urban areas.

The Church of England had perfected its internal pluralism to the extent that (in places) it could look almost indistinguishable from Roman Catholicism, and (in other places) it could look and sound very similar to Congregationalism or Methodism, or (elsewhere again but less frequently) to Unitarianism. Although there were obvious and very distinctive theological differences between Nonconformists and Catholics, it can be argued that they shared a common identity as Dissenting denominations within an Anglican establishment, and that typically they were vibrant communities shaped by the powerful forces of religious revival.[55] Amongst all three Christian communities – Anglican, Catholic and Nonconformist – there had emerged some significant areas of overlap, common interest and shared experience, despite the very powerful elements of competition and suspicion that remained.

By the end of the century, Nonconformity was undoubtedly more middle class than it had been at the beginning. Even the membership of the Salvation Army was to become gradually dominated by the lower middle classes, as those who had been 'gloriously saved' began to put their chaotic lives in order and to tread the inexorable path towards greater stability and well-being. The children of Salvationist families, and indeed those born into similarly puritanical households, tended to be imbued with middle-class values from their earliest days, thus contributing to an upward mobility of Protestant Christian culture.

In Nonconformity, changing tastes in architectural styles reflected both the upward mobility and the technological adventurousness of many congregations. In the early part of the century, urban Dissenters in search of prestige buildings had imitated the establishment by building warehouse-like chapels with Grecian fronts, or wholly Grecian chapels like Carr's Lane Congregationalist in Birmingham. But soon the Unitarians, as advanced in architectural taste as they were in theological ideas, introduced the Gothic style (borrowed ironically from the Roman Catholic architect A.W.N. Pugin) for buildings like the Mill Hill chapel, Leeds (1848). Congregation-alists and Methodists quickly followed, evolving what Clyde Binfield has termed 'Dissenting Gothic'.[56] By the 1870s, both bodies were experiment-ing with other styles – Romanesque, Perpendicular, Norman towers, doors and windows. From the outside, some chapels looked almost indistinguish-able from Anglican churches, as did the Wesleyan Methodist chapel at Chapel Allerton, Leeds. Internally, too, the stark simplicity associated with old Dissent yielded to the Victorian desire for style and comfort: padded seats, effective heating, carpets, stained glass, prominent organs, elaborate pulpits, galleries supported by the most slender wrought-iron columns so as not to obscure the view of the preacher; all proclaimed that the Anglican monopoly on worship had decisively come to an end and that the Noncon-formist alternative could be considerably more comfortable.

In Wales, urban Nonconformist architecture, particularly as displayed in the chapels of the Welsh Independents and the Calvinistic Methodists, was usually much grander than its Anglican counterparts, proclaiming that it was the members of these denominations who were the real leaders of Welsh society. Welsh Nonconformists preferred classical styles to Gothic, probably because classical was cheaper and perhaps also because they had stronger prejudices against the Catholic associations of Gothic architec-ture. In contrast, Welsh Anglican churches tended to be more formulaic in their design; typically they were solid stone rectangular buildings, with bell turret and single bell.

Most Catholic churches continued to be cheaply run buildings with school rooms, hidden away in inconspicuous side streets. The grand build-ings tended to reflect the wealth of individual donors, such as the 16th Earl of Shrewsbury, but there were far fewer of these, partly because the commu-nity was so much smaller, but also because Cardinal Manning discour-aged the building of elaborate churches, preferring instead that the money should go into schools. It was Cardinal Vaughan who took the decision to begin building Westminster Cathedral, in the Byzantine style, in 1895. Another large Catholic church dating from a slightly earlier period (it was consecrated in 1890) was Our Lady and the English Martyrs, located on a prominent crossroads in Cambridge and funded by a former ballet dancer, the widow of a very wealthy button manufacturer. It replaced an earlier, smaller church on a less conspicuous site, and architecturally it more resem-bled a miniature cathedral than a church in a town in which only about one in a hundred people were Roman Catholic. Its size and grandeur provoked considerable Protestant hostility. Its most striking external feature was its spire, which was designed to be slightly taller than the tallest pinnacle of

King's College, and to match the height of the magnificent Ely Cathedral, at the centre of the Anglican diocese some 15 miles away. Our Lady and the English Martyrs was always a little too big for its purpose, but it was a most potent symbol of late nineteenth-century Catholic confidence in this most Anglican of towns and most Nonconformist of counties.

CHAPTER 2

Protestant Europe

The religious division of Europe

In 1839 the rural population of Protestant Zurich overthrew the liberal government after an attempt was made to appoint the German theologian David Friedrich Strauss to a professorship at the University of Zurich.[1] Some four years earlier, Strauss had published what would become one of the nineteenth century's most controversial books about Jesus, *Das Leben Jesu*, in which he portrayed him as an entirely human figure and the world of the Gospels as lacking all elements of the supernatural. Swiss Catholics might also have been expected to be as outraged as Protestants about the possible arrival of the unorthodox Strauss in their town, but no alliance between Catholics and Protestants took place because of the deep political gulf that existed between the two communities. The story of Strauss and the Zurich chair illustrates something about the power of popular protest in the face of the problem of avant-garde Protestant theological opinion in its nineteenth-century form, but it also tells us something about the complexities of Protestant and Catholic Europe. Zurich may have been the first state to renounce its allegiance to Rome, in 1520, but by the nineteenth century, Switzerland was emerging as a nation with a large Catholic population. It was one among several European countries the mixed religious nature of which meant that it was impossible to assign either to the Protestant or the Catholic side, and it suffered a brief civil war, in which religion was a crucial factor, in 1847.[2] After the foundation of the Swiss nation state in 1848, five of the 25 cantons were clearly Protestant and nine were Catholic. The remaining 11 were mixed. Between 1850 and 1900 the percentage of Catholics to Protestants in Switzerland barely changed, with a Catholic population of 40.6–41.9 per cent, although they may have been perceived as increasingly numerous because of a gradual migration of Catholics into what had previously been exclusively Protestant areas.[3]

Other countries with similarly mixed Protestant and Catholic populations were Germany and the Netherlands. In the Netherlands, the religious affiliation of the population at the end of the nineteenth century was 35.2 per cent Roman Catholic and 48.6 per cent Dutch Reformed, with other Protestant denominations making up a further 11.5 per cent.[4] Rather than different religious communities living in different geographical areas, a phenomenon known as 'pillarization' has been identified. This describes a state of affairs in which the Dutch became divided along vertical 'pillar' lines rather than horizontal 'class' lines. In 'pillarized' Dutch society, although people of different ideologies or denominations lived in close physical proximity to each other, they in effect led parallel lives with no social connection. This was made possible because each 'pillar' of society, whether a Church or a political ideology, provided a full range of organizations to support its own members. The existence of a Dutch Association of Catholic Goat Breeders perhaps illustrates the extreme to which this mentality could be taken.[5] National life was prevented from fragmenting completely by a network of formal and informal structures which kept the pillars in place. Michael Wintle has argued that this form of 'vertical pluralism' began to emerge in the nineteenth-century Netherlands and assumed its most fully developed form between the 1920s and the 1950s. The Catholics and the orthodox Calvinists provided two of the pillars of Dutch society – the other two were formed by the socialists and the liberals.[6]

By the beginning of the nineteenth century, the religious map of Western Europe had been more or less settling into its modern form for the previous hundred years. As we have seen, the Dutch republic, although officially Protestant, was split, Switzerland was split, and what would become Germany was split between a largely Protestant north and a largely Catholic south. France, Poland, Spain, Portugal, Ireland and the territories that are now called Belgium, Italy, Austria and Hungary were Catholic by majority. Britain and Scandinavia were Protestant, although Britain, which ruled Ireland, was having to contend with a very large and increasingly well-organized Irish Catholic population. Throughout nineteenth-century Europe, Catholics and Protestants lived alongside each other with varying degrees of ease and accommodation. As Mary Heimann puts it, 'The post-Reformation division of what had once been Christendom into two mutually suspicious and antagonistic ideological blocks is now so familiar that we may easily forget how unnatural religious disunity seemed to Europeans at the time. Neither the Catholic nor the Protestant side believed that truth was divisible, or that religious differences among Europeans were anything less than a scandal.'[7] For nearly two centuries after Luther and Calvin, Europe had existed in an intermittent state of religiously motivated warfare, interspersed with cold war and attempts at diplomacy. By the early years of the eighteenth century, however, it had become clear that a stalemate in the wars of religion had been reached; Protestantism would clearly not be obliterated any more than Catholicism would reform itself in a Protestant direction. Catholics and Protestants would have to begin the very slow process of learning to live together. Meanwhile, the existence of rival versions of religious truth in close physical proximity has often been cited as a major factor in Europe's turn away from Christianity – another important marker in the road towards secularization.

Even in those places such as Scandinavia and Scotland which might seem unambiguously Protestant, or Spain or Savoy which might seem unambiguously Catholic, there had always been small populations who had failed to follow the majority faith and who had sometimes encountered hostility or persecution as a result. In the nineteenth century, the size of minority religious populations grew substantially and religious pluralism became an everyday reality in much of Europe. This was for two main reasons: emigration and increasing levels of state tolerance of religious difference. Thus in Glasgow in 1778 there had reputedly been only 20 Catholics. The number rose to 2,300 in 1808, and the first resident priests since the Reformation arrived in the city. The advent of cheap steamboat travel from Ireland swelled numbers still further, and in 1831 there were 27,000 Catholics in Glasgow, which represented some 13 per cent of the population.[8] The Glasgow experience was replicated in many other Protestant-majority areas, and was particularly assisted by the high mobility of the Irish. Scandinavia, meanwhile, created the legal frameworks to accommodate non-Lutherans. Norway, which, in common with the rest of Scandinavia, had had strict laws linking religious profession with citizenship, relaxed these in 1845 so that it was possible to be a Norwegian citizen without being a member of the Lutheran Church, and to practise non-Lutheran forms of worship. Gradually the compulsory enforcement of baptism, confirmation and communion was abolished, and a similar development occurred in Denmark after 1849. Sweden and Finland moved more slowly, and full freedom of religion was only granted in Finland in 1922.[9] This chapter considers the nature of Protestantism in three very different nineteenth-century contexts, Scotland, Germany and Scandinavia.

Scotland

In some respects, Protestantism in Scotland had more in common with its Calvinist cousins in Switzerland and the Netherlands than it did with the types of Protestantism found elsewhere in Britain, where, as we saw in the previous chapter, it most often took the form of low-church Anglicanism and various types of Methodism. Scottish Presbyterianism was part of the Reformed tradition, and as such it identified its chief fathers-in-the-faith as

John Calvin of Geneva and John Knox, a disciple of Calvin who had been the leading figure in the Scottish Reformation.

During the nineteenth century, Scotland was indisputably a deeply Protestant country, with a religious culture that was quite different from the rest of the United Kingdom.[10] Even if some of the recent claims made by Scottish nationalists about the supposedly nationalist aspirations of nineteenth-century Presbyterians can be shown to be rather far-fetched,[11] it remains true that much of what makes Scotland different from the rest of the British Isles is derived from its religious tradition. Indeed, after the Treaty of Union of 1707, in which Scotland became absorbed into the British state, losing its own political and economic independence, it was the distinctive form of Scottish religion, together with the legal and the educational systems, which became one of the most highly significant vestiges of the national consciousness. Arguably the loss of Edinburgh's political power after 1707 enhanced the power of the Church of Scotland's General Assembly, which met annually and devoted itself to the consideration of a range of social and economic as well as religious matters. The General Assembly gave the Church of Scotland the opportunity to speak publicly to whoever would listen; the Church of England had no equivalent forum at this period. In certain other respects too, Scotland had long exhibited more in common with some other parts of Protestant Europe. For example, in the post-Reformation period, levels of mass literacy in Scotland had come nearer to reaching the high levels achieved in Scandinavia than to England, where fewer people could read. In quantity and quality, Scottish schools and universities had long outstripped what was available south of the border.

Scotland had become a Presbyterian nation in 1690. Previously there had been an extended struggle for control of the Church between Presbyterians and Episcopalians. The scars from this struggle, together with the underlying convictions of Reformed theology, had produced a very strong dislike of bishops, and the enormous influence of John Knox (who had been dead since 1572) had been resurrected in order to link episcopacy with popery. Presbyterian doctrine had hardened against anything seen as tinged with popery, which included prayer books, liturgies and the celebration of religious festivals, including Christmas, which Presbyterians prohibited. In the seventeenth century, a covenant theology had emerged which placed the Presbyterian Church and its individual members in a direct contract with God.

Five years after the 1707 Treaty of Union, the British parliament reintroduced patronage to Scotland. This entailed an individual lay person or corporation, in their capacity as owner of the right of presentation, having the power to select and install their choice of minister in a parish church; it was the system that operated within the Church of England. In England the use (or abuse) of the patronage system could sometimes arouse unfavourable comment, but as a mechanism for promoting clergy to parishes it was not generally controversial. Theological differences in Scotland meant that patronage was a much more sensitive issue; indeed it became the most contested question in Scottish religion between 1690 and 1874, when it was permanently abolished. It had been first abolished in 1690 before the Act of Union, as it conflicted with the crucial Presbyterian concept of 'the call', in which parishioners signed an invitation to a favoured candidate for a vacant pulpit. It also ran counter to the fundamentally democratic manner in which Presbyterianism operated, from the parish up to the national level. Ordinary male parishioners were heavily involved in the lives of their parishes, as we shall see shortly in respect to teind payment and the kirk session, and they expected their involvement to extend to the choice of minister. Leaving the choice in the hands of an individual patron belonged to the world of Episcopalianism; it was not the Presbyterian way. Not surprisingly, in 1712 the Church of Scotland's General Assembly had opposed the reintroduction of patronage, but had been mollified by being told that local presbyteries would have the power to overrule a presentation. Until 1730 there were few disputed presentations. But controversy and sometimes violence did become more widespread after that date, when church courts started to back patrons in the face of popular opposition. This resulted in the defection of four ministers in 1733 to form the Secession Church, causing the first of what was to become a number of splits, and beginning the process by which Scottish Presbyterianism began to fracture into a number of different denominations.

In 1647 the Church of Scotland had adopted the Westminster Confession of Faith, which became the definitive statement of Presbyterian doctrine in the English-speaking world. It remained the doctrinal statement to which practically all of those who had seceded from the Church of Scotland continued to adhere. There was little in doctrinal terms to separate the established Presbyterian Church from the Secession Church, or from the Relief Church, which came into being in 1761. Dissent arose as a result of more Evangelical elements pitting themselves against the more 'Moderate' party, who were often rationalists who saw themselves as the Christian face of the Scottish Enlightenment. There were also differences about the extent of the church–state relationship, focused most particularly over the patronage question. For the Moderates, patronage seemed a useful tool for ensuring that the clergy remained compliant and like-minded. For the Evangelicals, it could seem to be the work of the devil, involving the interference by men of sometimes dubious principles in the sacred work of the Gospel. Initially those who dissented from the establishment were not opposed to the principle of a state church, only to the prevailing party which governed it. But from the end of the eighteenth century there was a gradual and inexorable shift to a 'voluntaryist' position – the belief in the separation of church and state. This put the established Church under constant pressure, so much so that by the second quarter of the nineteenth century it had reached breaking point.[12]

As the strength of Evangelicalism increased, so patronage disputes intensified, and large numbers left the established Church to form congregations of the Secession Church or, less often, the Relief Church. By the 1820s, around 29 per cent of the total Scottish population and around 32 per cent of the population of the Lowlands were Presbyterian Dissenters, and many had defected very recently from the state Church.[13] The scale of loss was enormous, far surpassing the level of Anglican losses to Nonconformity in early nineteenth-century England. In 1820 the formation of yet another Presbyterian denomination, the United Secession Church, out of groups of eighteenth-century seceders from the Church of Scotland, signalled a further pulse of energy for Dissenting Presbyterianism. The established Church, rather than being purged of its Evangelical elements to the extent that its churchmanship became distinctively non-Evangelical, as might have been expected, retained a very significant Evangelical constituency, which began to destabilize it from within. In 1834 they succeeded for the first time in ousting the Moderate party from control of the General Assembly. Between 1834 and 1843, the Moderates and the Evangelicals within the established Church engaged in an intense and bitter struggle known as the Ten Years' Conflict, in which the dominant Evangelicals vainly sought government legislation and support. An evangelical Veto Act passed by the 1834 Assembly permitted congregations to veto a patron's choice of an 'intruded' pastor, but the civil courts rejected the alternative 'call' as having no legal foundation. Parliament's repeated refusal to pass modifying enactments and the government's rejection in 1842 of an Evangelical 'Claim of Right' to spiritual independence from the state made schism inevitable. On 18 May 1843 the Evangelical party under the leadership of Thomas Chalmers dramatically walked out of the General Assembly in what was known as the Disruption. Chalmers took with him 38 per cent of the clergy and between 40 and 50 per cent of the Church's lay adherents, and with them he constituted the Free Church of Scotland.[14] It was, as Callum Brown put it, 'the most spectacular church schism in Britain since the Reformation'.[15]

Although a dramatic gesture in the manner of its execution, the Disruption had been carefully planned, which meant that all over Scotland, ministers immediately left their manses, and elders and congregations left their parish churches, to meet on the following Sunday in a variety of alternative venues which included farmyards, public halls, barns and open hillsides. The event was to become illustrative of the impossibility of maintaining a church–state relationship when the state insisted on acting in a way which a large body of Church members found intolerable, but it also attests to Scottish Presbyterianism's great vitality and resilience. Within four years the Free Church of Scotland had built an astonishing 730 churches, each with an adequately housed and paid minister, together with 500 schools, a feat which must surely rank as one of the greatest achievements of any religious community in the nineteenth-century world. The Disruption resulted in two Churches which were both genuinely national (although the Free Church was particularly strong in the Highlands, and the Church of Scotland in the south) and both Presbyterian. As John Wolffe puts it, 'The Church of Scotland split in 1843 as a result of the paradoxical conviction of the founders of the Free Church that integrity of witness as a national church required, under the current circumstances, the renunciation of formal connections with the state.'[16] If anything, the Disruption and its aftermath enhanced Scotland's status as one of world's foremost Protestant nations.

Scotland's best-known nineteenth-century churchman was Thomas Chalmers, who became famous not only for being instrumental in the Disruption but also for trying to usher in what he termed the 'godly commonwealth', by making the parish the central focus for welfare and education as well as for religion.[17] The idea of the godly commonwealth had existed in Presbyterianism in the sixteenth and seventeenth centuries, standing for an ideal in which a covenanted nation acknowledged no separation between church and state but endeavoured to create a new community based on conformity to the word of God.[18] Just at the point when attempting to bring such a vision into reality might have seemed an idealistic impossibility, which took no account either of the realities of urbanization or of the liberalizing tendencies of an increasingly democratic and plural society, Chalmers attempted to inaugurate the godly commonwealth in Glasgow.

Born in 1780 and brought up in rural Fife, Chalmers had had a powerful evangelical conversion. His first experiment was as minister of the rural parish of Kilmany, where it occurred to him that what was needed was the transformation of the parish into a microcosm of the godly commonwealth. This he sought to achieve through preaching, Scripture-based education, systematic visiting, poor relief and harnessing resources for community rather than individual benefit. When he became minister of the St John's parish in Glasgow in 1815, he transposed his activities into an urban key, successfully striving for the abolition of assessment-based poor relief (it was replaced by self-help and communal philanthropy), the endowment of new parish schools and a vigorous evangelical ministry conducted by a large team of lay visitors. Chalmers became convinced that what he had achieved in Glasgow could become a blueprint for turning the whole of the British Isles into a federation of self-regulating Christian communities. He believed that even the 'warm-hearted Irish Catholics' could be won over to it if they were treated fairly over Catholic emancipation and poor relief.[19] Chalmers was clearly overwhelmed by what he saw as the extent of his success, and he became hopelessly idealistic about the possibilities for extending it more widely. Above all, Chalmers needed large amounts of government cash in order to make his scheme work. The money was unforthcoming, as this was the beginning of the period when the British government was turning away from funding religion, and this applied as much to Scottish Presbyterians as it did to English Anglicans. Chalmers's disillusionment over this became one factor in his willingness to break with the established Church in 1843. He viewed the Disruption, not as a secession, but as 'a tragic severing of the relationship between the true Church of Scotland and a British state which had broken its pledge to preserve the Church's integrity'. David Hempton makes a perceptive comparison between Thomas Chalmers and John Keble. Although they were far removed theologically and culturally, Chalmers and Keble shared a fundamental commitment to the virtues of the rural parish as the instrument of society's regeneration, and 'both marched against the formidable armies of utilitarianism and Liberalism'.[20] Keble, of course, never split from the Church of his birth, whereas Chalmers went on to make the Free Church of Scotland a truly national denomination.

Well before the influence of Chalmers, Presbyterianism had had a major impact on ordinary people at parish level, and this continued in different ways throughout the nineteenth century. In pre-industrial lowland Scotland, people had had to interact with the established Church not just devotionally and educationally, but also economically and judicially.[21] Economically, although the local church and its school were supposed to be managed by the local landowners known as the board of heritors and financed by the landowning 'teind-holders', the burden of this tax was often passed on to the tenantry. They were expected to contribute to church finances out of the produce of their occupation – oatmeal, barley, fish or whatever – in a manner similar to what occurred elsewhere in the British Isles in the eighteenth century.[22] Tenants, or their servants, were also expected to turn a hand to repairing the church thatch and harvesting the minister's glebe.[23] In return, children were provided with schooling, and financial provision was made for those of the parish's poor who were judged to be of good character. The judicial influence of the Church of Scotland was as important as the financial one. It remained stronger for longer in Scotland than elsewhere, and somewhat inevitably produced a subculture which seemed to link Scottish religion with moral censoriousness and a prurient interest in the affairs of one's neighbours. From 1560 onwards, the ruling committee of the parish church, the kirk session, had grown in power so that it effectively became the magistrates' court in criminal law, with more serious cases being referred to the civil system. Until about 1850, investigating allegations of fornication and adultery were the staple of the kirk sessions, although they were capable of being interested in almost any misdemeanour. 'With fornication cases regularly taking a year – and sometimes several years – to complete, many kirk sessions were continuously engrossed with the sexual exploits of parishioners.'[24] The vision of the (male) church elders gathering to pour over the details and pass judgement on the offenders (with women usually judged most harshly and fined most) has lingered in the Scottish imagination as encapsulating hypocrisy masquerading as religious influence.

By the mid-nineteenth century, the kirk sessions began to lose their power over society at large and to retreat into passing judgement only on wayward members of their own congregations. Nevertheless Scottish churchmen continued to exert enormous influence, particularly in the supposedly secular context of local government in spheres such as the drinking laws, poor relief and education. Their actions revealed that they saw little or no distinction between their role as public servants and their role as enforcers of puritan values. In 1904 Glasgow councillors were censoring pictures from art galleries in the city.[25] In rural areas, it remained common for late nineteenth- and early twentieth-century parish councils to consist of the minister and a cross-section of farmers, and for them to continue behaving very much like a kirk session. In one parish near the Borders, the parish council was constituted in this way. It stopped payments to claimants who were known to buy drink, and demanded that the parish medical officer '"clear himself of the scandal" of adultery, in a manner redolent of an eighteenth-century fornication case'.[26] Teetotalism remained stronger in Scotland for longer, with an (admittedly largely unsuccessful) attempt to introduce prohibition in the period immediately after the First World War.[27] The Sabbath was also far more strictly observed in Scotland than elsewhere in the British Isles, an attitude which derived directly from the Westminster Confession. Ironically Sunday trading was never regulated in Scotland as it was south of the border because it was never felt necessary – 'no-one till the 1970s had dared open a shop'.[28]

Callum Brown has argued that Scottish Presbyterians became steadily more strongly churchgoing as the nineteenth century progressed, and that rates did not slow down until some time between 1890 and 1914. The 1851 religious census, although unfortunately not as accurate for Scotland as it is for England and Wales, seems to indicate that the Church of Scotland and the Free Church both had 32 per cent of churchgoers, and that Presbyterian churchgoing in Scotland was an enormous 90 per cent of the total worshipping population. Non-Presbyterian churchgoers can be analysed as 5 per cent Roman Catholic (but 16 per cent in Glasgow), 3 per cent Episcopal, 1 per cent Methodist and 1 per cent 'other'. One of Brown's most interesting conclusions is that rates of churchgoing were actually higher in urban, industrial areas than in rural parishes. This argument contradicts the position which has frequently been offered by proponents of the secularization thesis, which is that that as societies have become more urbanized, churchgoing rates have dropped. A link between urbanization and higher rates of churchgoing has also been noted in Ireland, where David Hempton observed that 'orthodox religious practice was consistently higher among urban dwellers and the better educated than among the Irish labouring poor in the west of the country'.[29] Brown concludes that 'in Scotland urbanization was not a cause of decline in churchgoing in the mid-nineteenth century, but that towns with long-term high population growth had a partial tendency to lower churchgoing, probably because church building failed to keep pace with demand for pews until 1850'.[30] Although badly wounded by the Disruption, the Church of Scotland began to claw back in the second half of the century; membership data for the Presbyterian Churches reveals that by the 1890s the Church of Scotland accounted for 53 per cent of Presbyterian worshippers, the Free Church for 30 per cent and the United Presbyterian Church for 17 per cent. However, this general trend needs to be balanced with a recognition that Presbyterian Dissent was very much stronger in the West Highlands and Hebrides, where the established Church had become exceptionally weak.[31]

Scottish Presbyterianism in the last years of the nineteenth century and the early years of the twentieth was marked by the sudden onset of declining support and attempts at reunion.[32] In 1894 the Free Church and the United Presbyterian Church (which had been formed in 1847 by a union between the Secession and Relief Churches, and thus represented old-style Dissenting Presbyterianism) entered negotiations which resulted in reunion between them in 1900, and the formation of the United Free Church. A determined Highland minority, who refused to accept any relaxation of the traditional tenets of Calvinism, stayed out of the union and designated themselves as the Free Church Continuing, becoming popularly known as the 'Wee Frees'. In 1909 negotiating committees from the Church of Scotland and the United Free Church began to discuss union. Conscious of the diminished differences between them in theology, and the increasing number of Scots who claimed no connection with any Church at all, they explored the possibility of reunion on the basis of a Church which was recognized as 'national' rather than 'established', in continuity with the Church of Scotland, but free of state intrusion in its affairs. Historical continuity, spiritual freedom and national outreach were all identified as the most desirable elements. Various acts of parliament were passed to bring this about, and in 1929 the Scottish Presbyterian Churches united, with only a small group of United Free Church members (in the end 25,000) seceding as the United Free Church Continuing. Since 1929 the Church of Scotland has been the spiritual home of more than 90 per cent of Scottish Protestants.

Protestant Germany

The religious history of Germany in the nineteenth century is made complicated by two factors. First, as we noted at the beginning of the chapter, Germany was one of those places which contained large numbers of both Protestants and Catholics. Secondly, Germany did not exist as a unified country until 1871. Up until that time, the German territories consisted of a large number of independent states, in varying relationships with each other, and with varying church–state relationships and religious complexions. Until the beginning of the nineteenth century, these states had been linked by little more than the loose political framework which had been provided by their increasingly tenuous inclusion in the Holy Roman Empire. All this changed when Napoleon's forces began to overrun the territories of the Holy Roman Empire from 1792, and he finally abolished it in 1806, replacing it with the Confederation of the Rhine, which consisted of 16 German states and the Grand Duchy of Warsaw. In the following year, Prussia, the large Protestant state in the north east of the German territories, also came under the influence of Napoleon.

After the fall of Napoleon, the Congress of Vienna, held in 1815, was responsible for redrawing the map of Europe. The German Confederation was established in place of the Confederation of the Rhine. It comprised 38 states (39 after 1817): 34 monarchies and four free cities. All these component parts retained their heads of state and their own independent legal and administrative systems. There were some strange anomalies, with some German-speaking populations excluded, and some non-German minorities, such as Italians and Czechs, included. Furthermore the British monarch remained ruler of Hanover until 1837, and Luxemburg and Schleswig also had foreign sovereigns. One of the most significant beneficiaries of the Congress of Vienna was Prussia, which became much larger through the acquisition of the Rhineland and Westphalia.[33] The idea was to create a buffer between France and Russia, but a spin-off of Prussian expansion was that it produced one of Europe's most powerful economic and industrial regions. The German Confederation germinated the seeds for what would become a powerful new nation, although this did not finally come about until the proclamation of the Second German Empire, which occurred in 1871, when the king of Prussia was offered the hereditary crown of a united Germany.

The intermixing of Catholics and Protestants in the German territories at the beginning of the period produced what Nicholas Hope has described as 'a plural Christian order which defied accurate description, especially at a time when boundaries of church and state were changing almost day by day'.[34] This had been further increased by the territorial reorganizations of 1815, which had introduced an even higher level of denominational pluralism. As the century progressed, however, the rise of Protestant Prussia, the increasingly weakened position of the Catholic southern German states and the exclusion of Catholic Austria from further involvement in German affairs after 1866, meant that the newly united Germany was much more Protestant than its predecessor German Confederation had been. Protestants now comprised roughly two-thirds of Germany's population. Indeed, some Protestants were swift to declare that the 'Holy Roman Empire of the German Nation' had now been replaced by 'the Holy Protestant Empire of the German Nation'.[35] As if to underline the shift, in the 1870s, when the Prussian Otto von Bismarck became Germany's first chancellor, the persecution of Catholics became one of the central features of government policy (see Chapter 3). By the final quarter of the century, 'cultural Protestantism', expressed in an enthusiasm for German institutions ranging from unification to literature, had become a powerful force among the middle classes. As David Blackbourn puts it, 'Most middle-class Protestants would have applauded Schiller's comment about Berlin's destiny as the capital of Protestantism, even though few of them went to church in Berlin by the 1880s. That was not the point. German culture *was* Protestant.'[36]

Martin Luther had been the great sixteenth-century German reformer, but German Protestantism was far from being straightforwardly Lutheran. Reformed (Calvinist) Churches had predominated in some areas, and the religious pluralism brought about by the post-Congress of Vienna re-mapping of 1815 had made it seem sensible in some territories to bring the Lutheran and the Reformed Churches together. Protestants in Baden, Nassau and the Hesses created new, united state Churches in the post-Napoleonic era. In Prussia, the Lutheran and Reformed Churches were joined together by royal command of Frederick William III, a devout member of the Reformed Church who was pained that he could not partake in the sacrament with his Lutheran Queen Louise. The result was a Church which became very closely allied to state policy, a state of affairs which was acceptable to the theologians at Berlin University but less so to the country pastors. Elsewhere the Churches of the predominantly Reformed Prussian Rhineland and Westphalia shunned union, and received their own Church constitution in 1835. In Catholic-majority Bavaria, multiple models of Protestant Church organization co-existed.[37] By the middle of the century, however, there was a stronger movement towards ensuring parity for the three major Protestant denominations of Lutheran, Reformed and Union Churches, and towards ironing out theological differences. *'Evangelisch'*, meaning 'Protestant', rather than 'Evangelical' in the English sense, began to be used officially to describe all three Churches from 1846. It helped them to develop a shared sense of Protestant identity.

Another major component of German Protestantism was Pietism, which had developed in the late seventeenth and early eighteenth centuries in reaction against what Pietists saw as Lutheranism's over-intellectualization and over-identification with state policy. Pietists emphasized Luther's ideas on the sufficiency of Scripture and the personal nature of faith. They stressed conversion and religious experience, in a way which would link them with the evangelical revivalists of the eighteenth century and beyond, but which would put them at some distance from Luther's original emphasis on the objectivity of grace as conveyed by word and sacrament.

A major centre of Pietism had developed at the University of Halle, founded in 1694 near Leipzig and put on the map in its early years by the Pietist theologian and missionary advocate, August Hermann Francke. Another, rather different, Pietist stronghold was established at Herrnhut from 1722, where Moravian Hussite refugees who were fleeing from the Catholic Habsburg re-conquest of Moravia and Bohemia, established their first settlement. They did this under the patronage of Count Nikolaus Ludvig von Zinzendorf, a pupil of Francke and the son of the Saxon ambassador to the Habsburg court in Vienna, and as such an unlikely sponsor for a radical Protestant movement. Life at Herrnhut captured people's imagination, and John Wesley was much influenced by a visit he made to it in 1738. The emphasis was on communal prayer and pastoral care, order and ascetical simplicity. Women put away their jewellery and dressed in specific colours depending on their age and marital status. Marriages were sometimes arranged by drawing lots. The Moravian Sunday was occupied with worship from five in the morning until nine at night.[38] But Moravians, and Pietists more generally, did not allow themselves to become overwhelmed by their desire for personal spiritual experience. They were

subject to Enlightenment influences as well as to revivalism. Their disciplined asceticism was combined with a humanitarianism expressed through
social welfare and evangelism. Pietists organized orphanages, cared for the
sick and engaged in ambitious foreign missionary ventures. Crucially, the
influence of Pietism was not limited to those wishing to pursue a strict way
of life in a Moravian community. By the end of the eighteenth century, the
influence of Pietist theological education and worship was being felt very
broadly among the clergy and in the Lutheran parishes, across Scandinavia
as well as in Germany. It appealed to those who wanted a religion that was
about ordinary life as well as about academic theology.

Although the influence of communities such as Herrnhut had begun
to waver by the beginning of the nineteenth century, across the Lutheran
world the broader legacy of Pietism, now more generally re-baptized as
Awakening, continued to be strongly felt. By 1830 an awakened, evangelical
mood was visible in most German lands and in the Scandinavian states.
Indeed, in the post-1815 world, the Pietist critique of increasing state interference was one of the factors putting Lutheranism under the greatest pressure. It was the Pietist clergy who were most critical of the government
tendency to treat them like policemen in preaching gowns. They began to
style themselves as 'neo-Lutheran' in contrast to the newly merged Lutheran
and Reformed Churches, of whose compliance with state policy they disapproved. But paradoxically, it was the Pietists whom the state was often the
most keen to promote, particularly in Prussia, where government officials
favoured Pietists because they considered that they would oppose revolutionary tendencies and be forces for conservatism.[39] In the longer term, the
state's position was vindicated, for in the second half of the century the
assumption became widespread that the Church was a bulwark against the
forces of the political left. The Church, with Pietists included, had become
another pillar of the ruling elite.

If Pietism, and an increasingly close identification with the state, were
two of German Protestantism's key features, the third was the influence
of Enlightenment rationalism. Pietism and rationalism had a somewhat
complex relationship, one sign of which had been the loss of Pietism's
historic stronghold at Halle, when that University was taken over by rationalist thinkers. The most famous legacy (and export) of nineteenth-century
Protestant Germany was undoubtedly its philosophical and theological
ideas. Education and the universities flourished in the Protestant states, and
there were more and larger theology faculties in Germany than anywhere
else in the world. It followed that theology was a high-status profession,
with professors among the best paid in society. Ordinary Germans held
learning in great respect, and looked to the theology faculties to provide

them with a rational, plausible, modern account of Christianity. The professors were happy to oblige, and there emerged an influential tradition of liberal Protestant theology which toned down the supernatural elements of Christianity, emphasized the humanity of Jesus and began to explore the range of textual problems presented by Scripture. German theologians had no difficulties in seeing themselves as the sons of the Enlightenment, for in Germany, unlike in France, Spain or Italy, the Enlightenment had been dominated by religiously minded men, whose primary concern was to rid the churches of intolerance and an excessive preoccupation with theological controversy.[40]

The German intellectual climate also produced many thinkers who were to have a profound affect on the modern world, although in ways which often left the Christian origins of their thought far behind. The two towering figures were Immanuel Kant and Friedrich Hegel. Kant, who died in 1804, belonged to the eighteenth century but had huge significance into the later period because of his role as an Enlightenment thinker. Kant defined Enlightenment as the courage to use one's reason to think independently and critically, refusing to accept the tutelage of another's authority. He also stressed that one could only 'know' reality through human categories internal to the mind.[41] Like many of those who followed him, Kant was sceptical about the supernatural elements in religion, the existence of miracles and the value of prayer. Although his view of the world was very different from views likely to be held by European thinkers today, it is easy to see how his perspectives helped to secure his place as one of the founding fathers of the modern Western intellectual tradition.

Hegel, who originally entered the University of Tübingen with a view to the Lutheran ministry, became a youthful disciple of Kant. He continued to regard himself as a Lutheran, but became absorbed by the intellectual problems posed by philosophy, ethics and history. Hegel emphasized the constant process of development within history and intellectual movements; no idea was static and therefore eternally valid. Everything was in a flux of movement in which an idea (a thesis) became challenged by an antithesis, and in the ensuing conflict the two became reconciled in a synthesis, and then the process began again. This was a theory of knowledge that Hegel believed had wide application across the sciences and the humanities. It was indeed widely taken up; after his death, in 1831, a group of so-called 'Young Hegelians' emerged who developed Hegel's ideas in a variety of different directions.

German Young Hegelians included Karl Marx, Ludwig Feuerbach and Bruno Bauer. Marx became the most famous, although his political and social theories had no immediate impact on the German people. Indeed, his time would not come until the twentieth century, when his ideas were taken up by revolutionary political leaders in all corners of the globe. Marx broke decisively with Hegel by developing a strictly materialist view of history; he had no time for Hegel's notion that the force that was at work behind it all was a 'world spirit'. The most important reality, for Marx, was the economic one: that men had to work in order to provide themselves with food and shelter before they could engage in any form of 'higher' political or social activity. A materialist conception of history focused on the everyday lives and labours of ordinary human beings. It endeavoured to show that the repeated pattern was the exploitation of one social class by another.

Feuerbach, like Hegel, gave up his theological studies in order to pursue philosophy. He took the ideas of his mentor further by recasting them in a manner which was openly hostile to Christianity. For Feuerbach, Christianity was illusory, because he denied the possibility of transcendence, and he believed it to be repressive in its material outworking in the world. Christianity was an imaginative necessity which man had created in order to endorse the importance of his own species. Feuerbach influenced Nietzsche and Marx, and thus the philosophical tradition of atheism in Europe. His most famous work, *Das Wesen des Christentums*, was translated into English by George Eliot as *The Essence of Christianity*. George Eliot, who also translated Strauss's *Das Leben Jesu*, the book that provoked the riot mentioned at the beginning of the chapter, became one of the most important conduits for the transmission of German religious thought into the English language, although she is better remembered as a major Victorian novelist. Her experiences translating German theology led her decisively away from her Evangelical roots and into agnostic free thought.

Bruno Bauer, meanwhile, adopted a position that was even more extreme than Strauss's, attributing the Gospel story to the imagination of a single mind rather than to the earliest Christian community, as Strauss had maintained. In 1842 he was deprived of his teaching post at Bonn University. The German Protestant theological faculties may have seen themselves as in the vanguard of intellectual progress, but there were limits to what they would tolerate.

Not everything in the German Protestant intellectual world led people to atheism or extreme scepticism. There was another tradition, the father of which was Friedrich Schleiermacher, who stands out as the most significant of the early nineteenth-century German theologians. Schleiermacher was influenced both by Kantian rationalism and by Pietism. He had been raised by parents who had converted to the Herrnhuter Brethren, and so had experienced at first hand Moravian spirituality and education. He had studied at a Moravian seminary and at the University of Halle. He gained a reputation as a rousing preacher during the Napoleonic period, and had been strongly critical of Frederick William's decision to unite the Reformed and Lutheran Churches, realizing the loss of spiritual authority that would ensue from allowing the Churches to become so entirely at the mercy of the royal will. He was also much influenced by the Romantic movement, which provides the background for the thoughts which inform his best-known book, *Religion: Speeches to its Cultured Despisers*. It is a book, rather like Coleridge's *Aids to Reflection*, which if read today can seem surprisingly modern in its tone and concerns. Schleiermacher argued that in order to have an appreciation of religion, one needs a sense and taste for the infi-nite. It is a matter of feeling and intuition, rather than a matter of assent to dogma. Religion provokes in the believer a feeling of absolute dependence. Schleiermacher's prioritization of feeling over rationalism is indicative of his Pietist roots. He proved hugely influential for several generations of German theologians, including Albrecht Ritschl and Adolf von Harnack, who represented successive developments in German liberal Protestantism. Ritschl emphasized the importance of the apprehension of theological state-ments by a believing community. Harnack sought to peel away the layers of centuries of interpretation in order to uncover the original meaning of Christian texts. After a reaction against Schleiermacher (and indeed liberal Protestantism as a whole) in the early twentieth century, led by the Swiss Reformed theologian Karl Barth, Schleiermacher is once again enjoying something of a modest revival in his reputation.

By 1900 the German Empire was striving to be a world power economi-cally and militarily. However, in terms of theology, it had already achieved that status. At the beginning of the nineteenth century, its universities had been in disarray owing to the Napoleonic Wars, and, in theology at least, their influence was limited to their immediate state Churches. In 1900 Germany dominated theological research, with scholars such as Harnack attracting followers from all over the world. Germany set the theological agenda throughout Europe and America, either in its style of rationalist theology being adopted as the new 'critical' way, or by being seen as the enemy within the gates, as in some factions of Presbyterianism within the United States. But whatever theologians felt about the merits of German theology, throughout the world they were using a German-produced edition of the Greek New Testament, that of Eberhard Nestlé, and it is an edition which continues to be used today.

Scandinavia

To conclude this chapter on Protestant Europe, we shall consider briefly developments in nineteenth-century Scandinavia. Scandinavia provides the best example of how a virtually monolithic Lutheran region tried to come to terms with the realities of the modern world and particularly with the rise of nationalism. Since the Reformation, all the Nordic Churches had been organized as Lutheran state Churches, the government of which was also an integral part of the government of the state. The default setting for all citizens was Lutheranism, and although there had been Moravian activity in Sweden from the 1730s, and also in southern Norway, other types of Protestant Nonconformity and Roman Catholicism only made a very limited appearance later in the nineteenth century. In the first half of the nineteenth century, Scandinavian Lutherans would have been conscious of their common membership of the northern European Lutheran world, and of having been subject to many of the same influences that had affected some of the German areas, in particular Pietism and Awakening. The sense of being members of national Scandinavian Churches was something which does not seem to have developed until later.

Scandinavia had had a long history of internecine warfare and conquests of territories, and in the period from the Reformation to the time of the Napoleonic Wars it had evolved into two extremely hostile multinational states, West- and East-Norden. West-Norden consisted of Denmark-Norway (Denmark controlling Norway), Iceland, the Faeroe Islands and the Duchy of Schleswig-Holstein (now in Germany). East-Norden consisted of the kingdom of Sweden, which included Finland, and the western part of Pomerania (also now in Germany). In the political re-balancing which occurred in the post-Napoleonic period, Denmark was forced to pay the price for having backed Napoleon by conceding Norway to Sweden. Sweden remained in control of Norway until 1905. Denmark lost Schleswig-Holstein to the German Confederation following its defeat to Austria and Prussia in 1864. It retained control over Iceland until 1918, whilst Greenland and the Faeroe Islands remained Danish possessions, although they were granted home rule during the twentieth century. Sweden meanwhile had lost control of Swedish Pomerania in 1807, and of Finland to Russia in 1809. This led to the development of Orthodoxy as a small but important element within Finnish Christianity, the only significant non-Lutheran form of religion to be found in Scandinavia at this date. West-Nordic Lutheranism was more low church, with a strong integration of church and state. East-Nordic Lutheranism was higher; in Sweden, for example, there was more emphasis on the role of bishops and archbishops. West and East used different liturgies and hymns, and there were differences in church order. The two Lutheran traditions had therefore evolved in considerable isolation from each other.[42]

The Church of Sweden was unique among the Lutheran Churches in attracting interest from supporters of the Oxford Movement. This was because some of them considered it to have true Catholic credentials because of its unbroken line of episcopal succession, which had existed since the Middle Ages. The other Nordic Churches could not demonstrate this unbroken succession, and so held little interest for high-church Anglicans. For them, the Swedish Church seemed to be their only fully acceptable Scandinavian sister, and Sweden became a fascinatingly unique example of a Protestant Church that was able to make a water-tight case for its catholicity. It helped the Tractarians to develop their theory that Protestantism and catholicity could exist side by side. For the clergy of the Church of Sweden, the 'discovery' of an unbroken sequence of bishops was hardly news. Some of them regarded the developing Anglican high-church obsession with it as 'superstitious and anti-biblical', in the words of G.W. Carlsson, the chaplain to the Swedish embassy in London.[43] Although other Church of Sweden clergy tended to share Carlsson's views on episcopal succession, some found elements of the Tractarian message more congenial, particularly as they sought to stem the demands of revivalists who were seeking greater lay participation, or, as the clergy saw it, encroachment, in the clerical domain. Archbishop af Wingård of Gothenburg was keen to make his priests aware of the spiritual importance of the priesthood and of ministry as a vocation, not delegated by the congregation, but given from above, by God.[44] To his credit, perhaps, he chose not to emphasize the Oxford Movement's stress on episcopacy. Nevertheless, from the 1850s, there began to be a new emphasis in the Swedish Church both on the role of the priesthood and on the spiritual and liturgical (as opposed to the cultural, educational and political) functions of bishops. The Swedish Church developed early and strong relationships with the Anglican Communion. It remained different in tone and character from the other Nordic Churches.

We have seen that throughout Scandinavia, the nineteenth century was a period in which countries either tried to hang on to their territories, as in the case of Denmark and Sweden, or to assert their national identity and independence, as in the case of Norway, Finland and Iceland. Lutheranism tended to be exploited in ways which permitted it to serve these agenda. Dag Thorkildsen has argued that in Norway, the powerful quest to recover and propagate a Norwegian national identity led to the virtual abandonment of traditional religion. The role of Christianity was reduced to being part of the historical and cultural heritage represented by St Olav and Trondheim Cathedral. Norwegian values became based on what could be gleaned from retelling the ancient Nordic myths, celebrating national industries and landscapes and developing the Norwegian language. As part of this process, Norwegians reacted strongly against their existing education system, the main purpose of which had been to teach Lutheran doctrine. Under Pietist influences, Norwegian church primary schools had been widely founded during the eighteenth century under the control of the local pastor. They taught reading and the Bible, and expected every pupil to learn by heart Luther's catechism, a total of 759 questions and answers. Pupils were expected to pass an examination in the catechism before confirmation, and those who failed were prevented from owning property, marriage, testifying in court or earning an adult wage. Failure produced public shame, and risked permanently infantilizing the unsuccessful. Whilst the Norwegian system indicated both the dangers of reducing Christianity to a test paper, and of making civil rights and responsibilities a reward for demonstrated religious knowledge, it also led to a rising chorus of demand for educational reform, in which limiting the role of the Church and broadening the curriculum were seen as essential components. A law passed in 1860 established the first 'folk high schools', which replaced the study of Luther and his catechism with the study of Norway and its culture.[45] Christianity was not squeezed out completely, but religion took its place in the secular curriculum alongside other subjects. Meanwhile church activity was more likely to take the form of Awakening-inspired hymn singing and preaching than formal Luther study, a development that was furthered by the continuing influence of Hans Nielsen Hauge. The influence of Hauge, who had led the Norwegian revivalist movement until his death in 1824, continued to be felt for the rest of the nineteenth century, owing to the leadership of his successor, Gisle Johnson. Hauge's sufferings and imprisonment, which had resulted from his infringement of the law against lay preaching, led to his having martyr status among the Norwegian laity. The Haugian revival in the Norwegian Church encouraged high levels of lay-led activity, an interest in mission and a strongly Pietistic atmosphere.[46]

The most influential figure in the Norwegian folk high-school movement was the Danish theologian, educationalist and politician N.F.S. Grundtvig. He had pioneered the idea in Denmark in the 1840s, and the schooling system was adopted elsewhere in the Nordic lands, developing for Scandinavia an educational programme that was in advance of what was available elsewhere in Europe and providing one of the foundations for its subsequent economic prosperity. Grundtvig's educational philosophy was that of a nineteenth-century nationalist; his ideas were similar to those espoused by reformers in other small countries who felt oppressed by their more powerful neighbours. Grundtvig believed that education should awaken the Nordic spirit of the Nordic people, and provide them with knowledge which could enhance their skills and enjoyment of life; he opposed the teaching of Latin and German, and supported colleagues who caused controversy by speaking Danish on formal occasions. Theologically he had reacted against the rationalism that he encountered as a student and then a pastor in Copenhagen. He wanted to find a new basis for faith which did not depend on its being shored up by the Danish civic establishment. To do this he alighted upon the Apostles' Creed rather than the Bible. In 1825 he claimed to have made the 'unparalleled discovery' that Christ was alive and was the 'living Word' of the Apostles' Creed, as used in the Danish baptismal and communion liturgy. He began to see a connection between baptized Danes and an unbroken chain of the baptized leading back to the early Church.[47] Grundtvig's focus on the sacraments has led to him being seen as the founder of a new, 'higher' church movement within the Danish Church, but he is more accurately viewed as a major figure in the pan-Scandinavian Awakening.

Søren Kierkegaard was the other major theological figure in nineteenth-century Scandinavia, and in certain respects a counterbalance to Grundtvig. He too had studied at Copenhagen, where he spent most of his life, which was marred by personal unhappiness and lack of recognition of his philo-sophical abilities, because he wrote in Danish. He attempted to move West-ern thought beyond Hegelianism, and his theological writings revealed deep psychological insight into the Christian understanding of redemp-tion, which has been a factor in ensuring their continued popularity to this day. In 1854, the year before his death, Kierkegaard made himself hugely unpopular by attacking the Danish Church for its comfortable, establish-ment ethos. He voiced strong disapproval of what he saw as Grundtvig's extremely nationalistic ecclesiology, which seemed to have baptized Danish-ness as a Christian doctrine. Kierkegaard chose to launch his attack after reading an obituary notice for J.P. Mynster, the highly respected and much loved bishop of Zealand. The obituarist had described Mynster as 'a genu-ine witness to the truth … a link in the holy chain of witnesses to the truth, which extends throughout time from the days of the Apostles onwards'.[48] Kierkegaard exploded at what he saw as this blasphemy. How could a well-heeled Danish bishop be compared to the Apostles and martyrs who had suffered persecution for their faith? Not surprisingly, Kierkegaard's attack provoked a strong reaction, not only among Mynster's many supporters but also among the Grundtvigians. The Grundtvigians had a high view of their Christian duty to serve the society in which they lived and believed that they should thank God for life's good things, and enjoy them. They were appalled by Kierkegaard's apparent call to asceticism as the only authentic form of Christianity. The entire movement inspired by Grundtvig became opposed to Kierkegaard. But, as Lars Österlin points out, Kierkegaard was really articulating an existential, philosophical comment rather than an ecclesiastical reform programme.[49]

Thorkildsen has argued that Awakening, or revival, was the key component in moving Scandinavia into the modern age. This was partly through its influence on the creation of a modern educational system, but also, as productive and self-disciplined revivalists became wealthy and successful, through forging a middle class where none had previously existed. A link has often been made between eighteenth-century Pietism and nineteenth-century Awakening, and the connection seems strengthened by the fact that in Scandinavia the authorities frequently resorted to invoking eighteenth-century anti-Pietist legislation to clamp down on nineteenth-century revivalist activities.[50] In reality, however, Awakening in its nineteenth-century form was a new development, and was led by people who had been shaped by the very different post-Enlightenment, post-revolutionary, pluralist world. As we have seen, Scandinavian-style Awakening was a remarkably flexible concept, able to incorporate Grundtvigian ideas about creed, Church and sacraments, and about the importance of secular, nation-based education, with teaching about agricultural improvements, and to mix them with an emphasis on lay preaching, domestic prayer and a puritanical aversion to dancing, music, cards and smoking. As fiddlers burnt their fiddles, the trend was for singing simple, recently composed hymns in the appropriate language of the nation. Above all, there was within the Awakening a yearning for religious freedom and a desire to end the obligation to use the services of the parish clergyman. The Lutheran monopoly, which had once seemed so firmly rooted throughout the Nordic regions, could not survive the pressures for religious pluralism. Inevitably, when the Nordic authorities sought to repress revivalist movements, it led swiftly for demands for liberal political rights such as freedom of assembly and freedom of religion. As Thorkildsen concludes, revivalism in Scandinavia spelled the end of the religious unity of the state, and finally opened what had been a previously monochrome religious society to the realities of modern pluralism. Ironically, then, it was religious revivalism that contributed significantly to the secularization of Scandinavia.

CHAPTER 3

Catholic Europe

Catholicism in the age of Napoleon

As the nineteenth century dawned, the Roman Catholic Church was staring in the face destruction and humiliation in its European heartlands. France, which had previously been the leading European Catholic state, with more Catholics than any other country, and with a Church which had been powerful and autonomous, had abandoned the faith of its fathers. The recently deceased pope, Pius VI, had been subjected by French revolutionary forces to kidnapping and to the type of ritual abuse reserved for recently deposed dictators. Priests, religious and lay people in their thousands had either abandoned Catholicism, been murdered, or had gone into hiding or exile in order to continue in their faith. The convulsive forces of the French Revolution had left every fibre of European Catholicism shaken, and much of it obliterated. The crucial assumption which had underpinned the formation of early modern Europe, that a state would be sympathetic to a particular form of religion, had been smashed to pieces. The Catholic states of Europe either wanted to get rid of the papacy or they wanted to reduce it to a purely ceremonial role. Catholicism was facing its greatest challenge since the Protestant Reformation.

The French Revolution had begun in 1789 and its impact continued for decades. The wealth of the Church had been an immediate target, as had the disparity between the poverty of many of the ordinary clergy and the lavish lifestyles of certain ecclesiastical dignitaries. The result was a massive confiscation and sell-off of ecclesiastical property and the suppression of religious orders. As the forces of atheistical, republican revolution began to spread beyond France, the presence of the papal monarchy, strategically located within the papal states towards the centre of the Italian peninsula, posed an obvious obstacle to the growing imperial ambitions of the French Republic.

Giovanni Angelo Brashci, who as Pius VI was pope during the crucial period from 1775 until 1799, lacked an army or a militia. He was a soft target for the young General Napoleon Bonaparte's revolutionary forces, as they marched in to annex Lombardy and the most prosperous parts of the papal states, namely Ravenna and Bologna, in 1796. As well as military protection, Pius lacked political acumen. A few years earlier he had dithered and prevaricated as revolution swept through France. His delay in condemning both France's adoption of the Civil Constitution of the Clergy (which entailed the election of priests and bishops and the reorganization of parishes and dioceses) and its abolition of annates (the payment of the first year's revenue from a benefice or diocese to the pope) had initially led to the belief that he might eventually offer some form of endorsement to the new order. In fact, Pius had no intention of doing this, and his initial silence had stemmed from the fact that he hoped to avoid pushing the French Church into schism; in particular he had wanted to avoid provoking France into the type of ecclesiastical split which had become permanent in sixteenth-century England. Pius's sympathies were entirely with the counter-revolutionary side, and he condemned the execution of Louis XVI as an act of murder. The pope was in an extremely weak position when Napoleon's forces arrived in the papal states, and he was forced to agree to an armistice on 20 June 1796, which involved the Vatican handing over large sums of money, works of art and manuscripts in order to prevent Napoleon marching straight on to Rome. Under pressure, Pius also agreed to issue instructions to French Catholics to remain loyal to the revolutionary government, and to recognize the Republic. But he refused to reverse his earlier, belated condemnation of the Civil Constitution. In September, he ended the armistice and began to form a citizens' militia to defend Rome.

Napoleon responded by occupying the rest of the papal states, his forces plundering churches as they went, with the Marian statue at Loreto being sent to Paris to the Museum of Egyptian Antiquities. Terrified that Napoleon would occupy Rome itself, Pius was forced to make a peace at Tolentino in February 1797. This entailed a doubling of the payments to France and the signing away of papal possessions in Avignon and elsewhere. It was the first time that a pope had been forced to part with his ancient temporal endowments. Once again he was outmanoeuvred. Napoleon's forces marched into Rome, occupying the eternal city on 15 February 1798, 23 years to the day after Pius's coronation. The Vatican palace was ransacked, resistance suppressed with brutality and a pagan altar erected outside St Peter's basilica. Pius, who was 81 and terminally ill, was placed under house arrest in Siena. But fearing that he might become a focal point for resistance to French rule, it was decided that he must be removed from Italy. The paralysed pontiff was sent on a desperate journey across the Alps to France, where he died at Valence on 29 August 1799. He was buried by a schismatic constitutional priest, and his death was recorded by the local prefect as 'Citizen Braschi, exercising the profession of pontiff'.[1]

Three months after Pius VI died, Napoleon, who was still barely 30 years old, became First Consul and Head of the French Republic. In the years that followed he forged an empire which at its height, around 1812, stretched from Seville in the west to Warsaw in the east, and from the southern tip of the Italian peninsula to Danzig in the north. There were large Catholic populations throughout the Napoleonic Empire, all of whom experienced the trauma of being governed according to the principles of republican France. Napoleon's expansionist fortunes changed decisively when he attempted to push further east into Russia. His men were unprepared for the ferocity of the Russian winter, and many perished in the snow. Napoleon was driven back into France, obliged to abdicate in 1814, and then finally crushed in the following year at Waterloo. In 1815 the map of Europe was re-drawn at the Congress of Vienna. Although his empire collapsed, many of Napoleon's ideas about the role of government and the Church lived on and lie at the root of some manifestations of European secularity.

To contemporary observers, it had seemed plausible that the death of Pius VI might have marked the end of the papacy – the extinction of another European royal line. However, at almost the same time that Napoleon was becoming First Consul in November 1799, a papal conclave to elect Pius's successor, funded by the Austrians, was meeting in Venice. It remained deadlocked for three months, and then finally elected the 'Citizen Cardinal of Imola', Barnarba Chiarmonte, who had preached a well-publicized and lengthy sermon on Christmas Day two years earlier, in which he had said that democracy was not contrary to the Gospel and that God favoured no particular form of government. Napoleon had been delighted by these utterances, and it was noted that the cardinal's notepaper was headed with the inscription 'Liberty, equality and peace in our Lord Jesus Christ'.[2] Meanwhile Napoleon was adjusting to the idea that if he were to rule Europe successfully, he would have to find some accommodation with the Church, and that ecclesiastically legitimated good order was preferable to religious anarchy, of the sort that had developed in France. It was, he thought, better to control the clergy than to fight with them.[3]

Initially at least, Napoleon found the new pontiff, Pius VII, very much more congenial than his predecessor. Negotiations began for a concordat between the Holy See and France, which was finally signed on 16 July 1801, and which would govern relations between the two powers for a century. It also provided a pattern for the papacy's relations with other nations in the years that followed. The Concordat severely curtailed the freedoms of the Church, and it was evident that there was to be nothing approaching a return to the situation that had pertained in the pre-revolutionary period. Catholicism was acknowledged as the religion of the great majority of the French people, but implicit in this was the (to the papacy) odious notion that it was merely one religion among others. Although the free and open practice of Catholicism was permitted, the French Republic took control of many practical matters relating to appointments and treated the clergy like civil servants, as paid officials. Land that had been seized during the Revolution remained under French control, and clergy became salaried officials, ordered to pray for the Republic and the First Consul. Napoleon tied the hands of the pope still further by unilaterally adding 78 Organic Articles to the Concordat. These insisted among other things that civil ceremonies must precede church weddings and that the French government must approve all papal pronouncements before they were published. But the Concordat permitted the papacy to save some face. It was, crucially, a negotiated agreement between two powers rather than a term of surrender imposed by the victor on the vanquished. It acknowledged that the papacy did have authority and the right to concede certain privileges. It also permitted a slender olive branch to be extended to the French Church, thus avoiding a permanent schism between Rome and France, which would undoubtedly have further undermined the position of the Vatican.[4]

The Concordat of 1801 represented the high point in Napoleon's dealings with Pius VII. Thereafter, the relationship between the two men swiftly deteriorated. In 1804 Napoleon had himself declared hereditary emperor of his new empire by the French state. But as the transformation from ambitious general to hereditary monarch proved a difficult act to accomplish, he knew that he needed the presence of the pope to lend both mystique and legitimacy to the coronation, although he remained quite determined to place the crown upon his own head. Pius obediently agreed to travel to Paris, and to widespread surprise he found himself mobbed by adoring crowds on the journey. It seemed that everybody wanted a papal blessing, and, in a particularly telling gesture, many who had been married under the civil regime stretched forth their hands to have their wedding rings blessed. It was the nineteenth century's first visible expression of the development of a cult of the pope, which would become a notable phenomenon as the century progressed. Napoleon was naturally alarmed about this surge of popular support for Europe's religious leader. Once in Paris, he tried to humiliate him, although the pope retaliated by refusing to be present at the imperial coronation unless Napoleon underwent a Christian marriage ceremony with his consort Josephine beforehand.

Relations deteriorated further in the following year, when Napoleon began to style himself King of All Italy. With no reference to the pope he placed his brother Joseph on the throne of the Kingdom of Naples. Napoleon was determined that the pope should give up temporal power once and for all and that such authority as might remain in him would be purely spiritual. Once more, in January 1808, French forces marched into Rome, and once more the pope was bundled out of the city and into exile, following the same route which had been forced upon his predecessor 11 years earlier. The pope was taken to Savona, on the Italian Riviera, where he was kept in isolation in the hope that he would become compliant. Pius responded by reverting to behaving like a poor monk, whilst refusing to institute any of the bishops that Napoleon nominated. This was a serious matter, as very many European sees had fallen vacant. In the Kingdom of Naples, for example, nearly 100 of the 131 sees were vacant by 1815.⁵ Cutting out the pope entirely, Napoleon began to turn to the bishops in Paris, first to grant him a divorce from Josephine, and then, summoning a council of the imperial bishops, to attempt to persuade them that they, rather than the pope, might institute new bishops. This ploy was partially successful, and a group of bishops set out for Savona to obtain Pius's support for the innovation. When this proved insufficiently fulsome, Napoleon demanded that the pope be brought to Fontainebleau, although by the time he had arrived the emperor had already set out for Russia, and the two men did not finally meet face to face until 19 January 1813, at which point Napoleon already knew that his dreams of massive expansion into Russia were in tatters.

For six days at Fontainebleau Napoleon battered the pope with his anger, until the weary pontiff finally agreed to the total surrender of his temporal power and to the institution of bishops by metropolitan bishops if the pope declined to act. Pius immediately regretted his signature on the scrap of paper which Napoleon declared to be the Concordat of Fontainebleau. Meanwhile Napoleon's own grasp on power was slipping. In January 1814 he offered the pope full restoration to Rome and a peace treaty. On 12 April Napoleon abdicated, and on the 24 May Pope Pius VII made a triumphal re-entry to Rome. When the Congress of Vienna redrew the map of Europe in 1815, the papal states were restored almost in their entirety. This, according to Eamon Duffy, was the 'single most important fact about the nineteenth-century papacy';⁶ the struggles with Napoleon had made it plain that if the pope was to have any chance of being unhindered in his spiritual ministry, he also needed the security which came from being an independent temporal sovereign. Yet the papal states cut a swathe across the centre of Italy, and incorporated Rome, its natural capital. Thus the continued existence of the papacy's temporal power became the biggest obstacle to the ambitions of the Italian people for a unified nation, just as it had been some years earlier to the expansion of the Napoleonic Empire throughout the Italian peninsula.

The Church in the post-Napoleonic era

One of Pius VII's first actions in 1814 was to restore the Jesuits. This religious order had been suppressed by Pope Clement XIV in 1773, who had succumbed to pressure from the rulers of Spain, Portugal, France and Austria, in what Duffy identifies as the papacy's most 'shameful hour'.[7] From their foundation in 1540, the Jesuits had been central in taking Catholicism to the world beyond Europe, and, as we shall see in Chapter 5, they were to play a major part in Catholic missionary activity in the nineteenth century. But as well as being missionaries and linguists, the Jesuits were thinkers and educators. The Church needed them, but it needed a great deal more besides. All over Europe, the Catholic Church was in a weakened and debilitated state. Churches had been destroyed and the numbers of clergy had dwindled. The general absence of bishops had meant that those clergy who remained had been very much left to their own devices. Many people had lost the habit of regular religious practice. New ideologies which tended to be inimical to Catholicism, such as liberalism and nationalism, had gained much ground. Politically, although France and Austria remained significant players after 1815, and although Catholic kings returned to Paris, Madrid, Naples and Turin, the balance of power had shifted decisively to the Protestant nations, Britain and Prussia, and to Orthodox Russia. Despite all this, the number of Catholic Christians in Europe vastly outnumbered non-Catholics. It was estimated that there were about 100 million Catholics to 40 million Protestants and 40 million Orthodox.[8]

As the papacy was no longer an office of international political significance, it needed to cast itself in a new role. As if to assist in this process a crop of new thinkers emerged, including Joseph de Maistre, Félicité de Lammenais, Henri-Dominique Lacordaire and Charles Montalembert. These men held varying views at different points in their careers and had some significant influences upon each other; they were also part of bigger intellectual currents and particularly Romanticism. Although initially favoured, they gained little papal approval for their efforts. This resulted in the papacy becoming more isolated from the mainstream of Catholic thought than needed to have been the case. Indeed, Lammenais was condemned by Pope Gregory XVI in his encyclicals *Mirari vos* in 1832 and *Singulari nos* in 1834. Earliest in this intellectual line was de Maistre, who published in 1819 a treatise on the nature of the papacy, *Du Pape*, which emphasized the importance of the papal office as the paradigm of all monarchical powers and the source from which all other authorities flowed.[9] The work was clearly a reaction against the horror and anarchy of revolution and against the influences of the Enlightenment. De Maistre argued that since the sixteenth century, the papacy had been weakened by those who questioned its authority, and that the urge to question, once embarked upon, became insatiable. What was needed was a strong and authoritative Church, which would bring the political benefit of a cohesive society in which authority, embodied in a human king, would be respected. The essential first step was the restoration of papal authority, and he moved from this position to advocate papal infallibility. De Maistre's theories had enormous impact. The book became a crucial landmark on the road which led the Catholic Church towards the magnification of the papal office and the position that became known as Ultramontanism.

Ultramontanism, the idea that authority should be vested 'over the mountains' in Rome rather than within Catholic Churches at national or diocesan level, was to emerge as the single most influential new tendency within nineteenth-century European Catholicism. Influenced by de Maistre, Lammenais also developed his ideas about authority at this time, publishing his *Essai sur l'indifférence en matière de religion* in 1818. His argument that for knowledge of the truth, a person is dependent upon the community and that the essence of Christianity is a (political) freedom guaranteed by the papacy, attracted a fervent band of Ultramontanist supporters. Later he campaigned more stridently for the separation of throne and altar, believing that the French Church under the restored monarchy of Charles X was in a hopelessly subordinate position. He fell foul of orthodox Catholic thinkers, however, who objected to his denial of the supernatural. It was what was perceived as the dangerous logic of Lammenais's teachings on freedom that led to the papal condemnations, after which Lammenais left the Church. He ended his life having abandoned Catholicism. Whereas Lammenais had wanted to support the political aspirations of those large Catholic populations who lived under Protestant rule in Belgium, Poland and Ireland, all Gregory XVI had felt able to do was to condemn any resistance to those in authority, whether Catholic or Protestant. It was a position which identified the papacy as an extremely conservative institution, insensitive to the realities of life for Catholics in much of northern Europe.

Lacordaire and Montalembert, who had both cooperated with Lammenais in the production of his newspaper *L'Avenir* ('The Future') suppressed their liberal views after the publication of *Mirari vos*, although they did not altogether abandon them. Montalembert, who was a layman, put his energies into campaigning for freedom for French schools and for Catholic principles in political life. Lacordaire, meanwhile, remained much in demand as a speaker and set about reintroducing the Dominicans into France. Both of them were strongly of the opinion that the laity should be encouraged to play a more active role in the day-to-day affairs of the Church.

The mid-nineteenth-century papacy: Pius IX

The condemnation of modern thinking which Gregory XVI had accomplished in *Mirari vos* set the tone maintained by his successor, Pius IX, although this was not immediately apparent after his election. Indeed, he had been elected as a compromise candidate who was not thought likely to continue with the extreme conservatism of his predecessor. Elected in 1846, it was initially thought that the unusually young (he was 55) Cardinal Giovanni Maria Mastai-Ferretti was open-minded, conciliatory and not hostile to political liberalism. Indeed, as a champion of the Italian people, it was hoped that he might be willing to take a lead in Italian unification (*Risorgimento*). Initially the omens were good. Pius IX (Pio Nono as he was frequently called) introduced street lighting, public health measures, agricultural reforms and plans for railways into the papal states, all necessary nineteenth-century innovations which his predecessors had blindly resisted. He also developed a particularly pastoral vision of the papacy, which involved a simpler style of life, frequent preaching, confirming children, visiting schools and hospitals and taking part in Masses all over Rome. One of his earliest acts as pope was to declare an amnesty for former revolutionaries in the papal states. He was congratulated by the Protestant statesmen of Europe and America. It even began to seem possible that the pope might become president of a federation of Italian states.[10]

But Pius was not in fact the progressive liberal that his actions made him appear. He had a tendency to send out conflicting signals, doing one thing whilst believing another. He also found himself caught out by the speed of European politics, and just two years into his pontificate the Continent became convulsed by the revolutionary events of 1848. Two Catholic nations, Italy and Austria, were at war. Pius made a speech indicating that he could not support Italy militarily against Austria, nor could he give credence to the notion of a federal Italy headed by the papacy. He saw himself as a priest first, and only secondly as a temporal ruler.[11] Pius's popularity plummeted, and he went from being the most popular to the least popular man in Italy. After the assassination of the papal states's prime minister on 24 November 1848, Pius fled into exile, disguised as an ordinary priest. He took refuge just over the border from the papal states in Gaeta, in Neapolitan territory. He did not return to Rome until April 1850, and for two decades thereafter had to rely on the presence of French and Austrian troops to maintain him in power. Meanwhile the Italian forces of national unity, who had run Rome as a republic during his absence, became increasingly hostile and committed to a policy of fiercely anti-clerical secularism. Clearly, the writing was on the wall for the temporal power of the papacy. In 1860 Pius lost two-thirds of the land of the papal states to the Kingdom of Piedmont and for the rest of the decade it was evident that the papacy's temporal authority was shrinking back towards the city of Rome itself. In July 1870 the Franco-Prussian War broke out, and the French forces needed to mobilize every soldier at their disposal. This meant that the French contingent who had been stationed in Rome to defend the pope were removed to other duties. The way was clear for the Italian nationalist forces under King Victor Emmanuel to march into what remained of the papal states, and on 20 September Rome was overrun. Within a year it would be declared the capital of a unified Italy. In the settlement that followed, the papacy was given exclusive use of the Vatican, the Lateran and the papal country residence at Castel Gandolfo. The pope was offered, but did not accept, generous financial compensation for the lost papal territories. He was given the right to appoint all the bishops in Italy. It amounted to a perfectly reasonable basis on which to establish a new relationship between church and state in the changed circumstances of unified Italy. Pius IX, however, was mortified, adopting a position of permanent protest and styling himself as the Prisoner of the Vatican.

The conservatism which Pius had adopted in the years after his exile in Gaeta had made him particularly sympathetic to those strands of Ultramontanism which emphasized the importance of maintaining the papacy's temporal authority and its spiritual pre-eminence. Above all, the advocates of Ultramontanism were creating a largely self-contained, almost hermetically sealed intellectual context within which the papacy should operate, which did not depend in any significant way on support from the modern world. Politically this was expressed in concordats with the Catholic nation of Spain (1851 and 1859) and Austria (1855) and in the re-establishment of episcopal hierarchies in the Protestant strongholds of England and Wales (1850), the Netherlands (1853) and Scotland (1878, and completed by his successor, Pope Leo XIII). Pius also developed further the Catholic infrastructure in those parts of the New World which were being settled by European and particularly Irish immigrants.[12] This Ultramontane spirit, more than anything else, was the legacy of Pius IX's pontificate to the Catholic world in the century which followed, up until the Second Vatican Council in the 1960s.

Whereas initially Pius had seemed to be pursuing policies that were the opposite of those of Gregory XVI, after 1850 his pronouncements suggested that he was falling in step with his recent predecessors. This was seen most famously in his encyclical of 1864, *Quanta cura*, to which was attached the *Syllabus errorum*. Angered that Montalembert had been urging a reconciliation between the Church and democracy, Pius decided to strike a blow to liberal Catholicism with a forceful denunciation of what he saw as the evils of the modern world. However, in a move which underlined the extent to which the intellectual world of the papacy was constructed from its own past, he was careful to point out that everything that he condemned had been condemned in earlier papal pronouncements. Of the 80 propositions which he condemned, the most famous in the *Syllabus errorum* was the anathematization of anyone who thought that the 'Roman Pontiff can and ought to reconcile and adjust himself with progress, liberalism and modern civilisation'. Across Europe, the *Syllabus errorum* was greeted with horror; it was burned in Naples, its publication in France was banned for a short time, and a similar action was contemplated in Austria. For liberal Catholics, there was a not unreasonable fear that the continuation of pronouncements in this vein could lead to the suppression of Catholicism all over Europe. As Sheridan Gilley has put it, the *Syllabus* 'did not properly distinguish between the northern European liberalism which gave a new freedom to the Church to open churches, schools and monasteries, and the Latin liberalism which closed them down'.[13] Montalembert's ally, Bishop Dupanloup of Orléans, laboured hard to demonstrate that the *Syllabus* needed to be understood in the context of earlier papal pronouncements, and not read literally.

Meanwhile the desire to aggregate ecclesiastical power to Rome, felt to be in the best interests of the Church by the pope and many of his supporters, continued unabated. There was a new emphasis on the promotion of causes which, it was hoped, would make the Church more disciplined and cohesive, for example, the founding of several new seminaries in Rome for different national groups.[14] Nothing illustrated the policy of privileging the Roman above the regional more clearly than the new emphasis on taking the cream of the crop of young men from their home nations, where they would previously have expected to have attended a diocesan seminary, and transporting them to the wholly different world of Rome for the years of their training. The mother houses of the regular religious orders were also now encouraged to site themselves in Rome. Meanwhile, wherever they were in the world, priests were urged to wear clearly identifiable clerical dress and to avoid looking like laymen. This period marked the beginning of the clerical collar, which in the twentieth century would even be adopted by extreme Protestants.

Pius also began to encourage particular expressions of devotion, particularly to the Virgin Mary and to the Sacred Heart of Jesus. In 1854, precisely ten years before the publication of the *Syllabus errorum*, the pope had defined the doctrine of the Immaculate Conception. This had clarified Catholic teaching by declaring that Jesus's mother had herself been conceived free from the stain of original sin. In the years that followed, a number of Marian appearances were recorded in various European locations, and at Lourdes in France in 1858 she appeared, helpfully declaring that she was indeed 'the Immaculate Conception'. Not surprisingly this served as a further boost to Pius's spiritual authority. All over Europe, ordinary Catholic households began to reflect the devotional trends of the period with the acquisition of new, often mass-produced artefacts, such as images of the Sacred Heart, statues of the Virgin Mary and portraits of Pio Nono himself. He was the first pope in history whose image was subject to mass reproduction; unlike several of his immediate predecessors, he was free of obvious physical blemishes, and so could adorn the homes of the faithful as a handsome and authoritative white-clad figure. The cult of the papacy was coming into its own.

Above all else, Ultramontanism began to express itself in the desire to see a declaration of papal infallibility. Like the doctrine of the Immaculate Conception, papal infallibility was a doctrine that had been widely accepted over a long period of history, but never formally defined. In particular, the extent to which the utterances of a pope should be taken to be infallible was the subject of much contention. Did infallibility extend only to the most formal of papal statements, or did the pontiff live in a permanent state of inspiration? And how should one resolve the obvious risk of one infallible pronouncement appearing to be in contradiction to another? In 1867 the pope declared that he was summoning a general council of the Church, to commence in two years' time, with the intention of tackling what he saw as the two greatest dangers facing the Catholic world, namely unbelief and rationalism. He also had plans, which were to remain wholly unrealized, to attempt to heal the breach between Catholicism and the other branches of Christianity. For his most ardent supporters, however, it seemed to be a heaven-sent opportunity to define the doctrine of papal infallibility once and for all.

As what would become known as the First Vatican Council approached, the bishops who would attend (700 in total) found themselves grouping into those who favoured a formal definition of infallibility and those who were against such a definition (the group known as the inopportunists). When the Council opened on 8 December 1869 it became clear that the infallibilists, led by the Englishman Henry Manning, were in the majority but that there was a massive weight of international opinion behind the inopportunists, led by the German Ignaz von Döllinger. The Pope, who had begun the Council with a certain degree of detachment on the matter, became increasingly angry with the liberals and convinced of his own infallibility. The final decree, when it emerged from the pen of Archbishop Cullen of Dublin, drew back from the fully blown infallibilist position, separating the papal teaching from the papal personage, and making it clear that the pope's teaching could only be said to be infallible under certain strict conditions. In particular, he had to be speaking *ex cathedra* – in his specially solemn and official capacity. Furthermore, his infallible teaching had to be on a matter of faith or morals, and of concern to the whole Church. This ended anxieties about infallible papal entanglements with political questions, or about ill-judged interventions in passing theological debates. But the decree also articulated for the first time a status for the pope at a much higher level than that of the bishops. 'Henceforth, bishops would be regarded as the mere lieutenants in the hierarchy of the Church, with the Pope as commander-in-chief.'[15]

The final vote on the infallibility debate took place on 18 July 1870. Almost all of the inopportunists – about 80, mainly northern Europeans – had left Rome the previous day to avoid having to vote against it. On the following day, the Franco-Prussian War broke out, and the First Vatican Council was put into a state of what turned out to be indefinite adjournment, as the remaining bishops scrambled to leave Rome before the Italian nationalists invaded. Although the forced abandonment of the Council was hardly auspicious, the matter of papal infallibility had at least been resolved, albeit under the most extraordinary of political circumstances. Extravagant speculations about the extent of papal infallibility had been dealt a fatal blow. Moreover, only once in the subsequent period has the papacy drawn on its infallible teaching office, and that was in the definition of the Assumption of the Virgin Mary, another doctrine that had been accepted by most Catholics since the Middle Ages, in 1950.[16]

Catholicism and the rise of nation states

After 1870, all over Europe there emerged liberal regimes that were hostile to the papacy, and appalled by the assumption of papal power that had taken place at the Vatican Council. As broad national groupings became unified into new countries, and as anti-clerical republican governments became the norm in Catholic countries, a new priority began to be that each state should establish for itself a clear national identity. It became vital that the Piedmontese and the Neapolitans should also believe themselves to be Italians, and that the Bavarians and the Westphalians should also understand themselves to be German. New states needed to create loyal citizens who would be willing to smooth over regional differences and if necessary bear arms in defence of national boundaries. Religion was an important element in the cementing of national identity, and Protestant religion was seen as a particularly effective form of glue. As we saw in Chapter 2, Lutheranism had a strong tradition of identity with the nation state, particularly in Scandinavia. Protestantism as a whole was more tolerant of liberalism, democracy and modern innovations of various sorts. Catholicism, by contrast, was seen as conservative, reactionary and anti-nationalist. Above all, Catholics were believed to owe a primary loyalty to the occupant of the Vatican, which was likely to cut across their duties as national citizens. As European governments swung in a more Protestant – or in Catholic countries more secular – direction after 1870, there was a considerable backlash against the Catholic citizenry. Furthermore, in countries where the Catholic Church had traditionally played a large role in providing education, health care and welfare, the state was now pushing the Church aside as it became heavily involved in such provision for the first time. There was scope for conflict at both local and national level.

On the pope's doorstep, the new Italian government remained estranged for a decade, with the pope issuing excommunications of everyone who had cooperated in the capture of Rome. Catholic Austria repudiated its concordat, whilst the newly unified Germany emerged as a predominantly Protestant nation under its new chancellor, Otto von Bismarck, after the defeat of France in the Franco-Prussian War. Bismarck launched an intensive persecution of German Catholicism known as the *Kulturkampf*, meaning the struggle between cultures (the progressive and the clerical). Even though opposition to infallibility had been led by a German archbishop, and some German Catholics, the German government used the infallibility issue as a stick with which to beat German Catholics generally.

The *Kulturkampf* lasted throughout the 1870s and was spearheaded by Paul Falk, who was appointed Minister of Public Worship and Education with the explicit brief of defending the rights of the German state against the Church. Falk swiftly ensured that all schools were opened to state supervision and inspection, and that no Catholics might serve as school inspectors. In 1873 the May Laws extended the possibility of state veto over all clerical appointments, and opened seminaries to state supervision. Civil marriage was introduced, and preachers could be subject to prosecution if their sermons were judged to contain political content. In 1875 all members of religious orders who were not involved in running hospitals were expelled from Germany; the Jesuits, Redemptorists and Lazarists (Vincentians) had been removed three years earlier. By 1878 only three of eight Prussian dioceses still had bishops, 1,125 of 4,600 parishes were vacant, and nearly 1,800 priests had been imprisoned or were in exile.[17] In terms of its intended aim of eradicating Catholicism from Germany, all this persecution was a resounding failure. It was perhaps the early penetration of Ultramontanism into German Catholicism that made it so imperviously resistant. Catholics responded to persecution with vocal protest, and by flocking to Germany's

Marian shrines at Marpingen and Kevelaer.[18] They also responded by developing a stronger sense of lay Catholic German identity, seen both in the massive support given to the Centre Party, which articulated the Catholic political presence in Germany up until 1914, and in the spectacular growth of Catholic religious, sporting and social organizations which marked the final decades of the nineteenth century. Bismarck acknowledged the failure of his policy privately, and was able to find an exit from it when his adversary, Pius IX, died in 1878. Pius's successor, Leo XIII, was outwardly more conciliatory, which made it possible for Germany and the Vatican to call a truce in the *Kulturkampf.*

In France, the issue was not one of forging a new nation from a variety of smaller states, as in Italy and Germany, but of limiting the space of the Church in a nation where secularism was becoming institutionalized. Although, as James F. McMillan has shown, the French Church recovered remarkably well in the period from the Napoleonic era to about 1880, with steadily rising numbers of ordinations and admissions to religious orders, by the 1860s there was an increasingly vocal republican and freethinking voice which wanted to affirm its commitment to the organization of society on a totally secular basis.[19] The French translation of Darwin's *Origin of Species* (1862), German biblical criticism and Ernest Renan's humanistic *Vie de Jésus* (1863) all served to drive a larger wedge between traditional French Catholicism and those who saw themselves as in some sense the intellectual heirs of the Revolution.[20] In France, free thought turned to militant atheism rather faster than was the case elsewhere, and where moderate Christian positions were maintained, they could be strongly overlaid with anti-clericalism.

These perspectives were given new prominence after the establishment of the Third Republic in 1879, which sparked off France's own version of a *Kulturkampf.* Education was the unsurprising target for secular reformers, and a range of legislative measures restricted the involvement of religious orders and prohibited the giving of religious instruction. By the early 1890s, around half of the nuns and brothers who had taught in the nation's primary schools had been removed. The Third Republic also began to legislate for divorce and for Sunday working, and to develop an elaborate secular ritual, with particularly grand funerals for republican heroes. Anti-Catholic feeling heightened in the wake of the affair of Captain Dreyfus, which involved a Jewish army officer being falsely accused of selling secrets to the Germans. The Church was seen to be complicit in Dreyfus's wrongful conviction, and the anti-clerical backlash which resulted was sufficient to open up the road which led to the eventual separation of church and state in France.

In 1904 France broke off diplomatic relations with the Vatican, and in 1905 the Separation Law revoked the Napoleonic Concordat which had regulated the affairs of the Church for the previous century. Henceforth the state no longer paid the salaries of the clergy (or of pastors or rabbis). It was intended that Church property be sequestered by the government and transferred to representative bodies of parishioners all over France. However, the refusal of the Pope (Pius X) to cooperate in this meant that the French Church could not, until 1924, exist as a legal entity capable of taking ownership of its property, and it lost many of its buildings as a result. By the early twentieth century, the French government and the Vatican were once again in an ugly stand-off, in which the French Church was to be the major loser. The Ultramontane position proved rigidly limiting when dealing with the unfolding realities of the European secular state.

Irish Catholicism and its global impact

At the opposite pole to French Catholicism, particularly in terms of its relationship to the state, and its influence on the people, was Catholicism in Ireland. In 1797 the French traveller de Latocnaye attended Mass in Lismore, County Waterford, and remarked that he 'could hardly find room to stand, both church and cemetery round it being full of people'.[21] Although the level of Mass attendance in early nineteenth-century Ireland has been a matter of some dispute,[22] by the beginning of the twentieth century Irish Catholics had achieved the highest level of religious practice of any Christian community in the world. Furthermore the role of the Irish in spreading Catholicism across the globe was unsurpassed by any other nation. During the course of the nineteenth century, and particularly as a result of the famine in the 1840s, Irish Catholics – laypeople, priests and members of religious orders – emigrated in huge numbers to Britain, the United States, all over the British Empire and particularly to Canada and Australia. There they set up parishes, schools and missionary endeavours of many sorts. It has been noted that at the First Vatican Council in 1869–70, some 73 bishops of Irish birth were present (about 10 per cent of the total) and about 150 of Irish descent (some 20 per cent of the total).[23] Thus Irish Catholicism punched far above its weight, with its global influence out of all proportion to the size of the nation. As Adrian Hastings observed, 'If Ireland had turned Protestant in the sixteenth century as did Scotland, the whole religious picture of Britain, America and Australia would be very different, and indeed that of all the countries affected by the modern Irish missionary movement.'[24] The refusal of the majority of the Irish to accept Protestantism has been one of the most overlooked factors in the modern shaping of Christianity.

After centuries of struggle with the religion and politics of mainland Britain, Irish Catholicism might have been expected to have developed in

a largely separate world from its continental European cousins, but Nigel
Yates has argued recently that this was not in fact the case. He suggests that
the Irish clergy shared a very similar social background to that of the clergy
in those parts of Europe where Catholicism was either the established or
the majority religion. In Ireland as in Europe, they also tended to be very
local to the diocese to which they were ordained, and to share many of
the same preoccupations, particularly of their French counterparts.[25] By the
early years of the nineteenth century, Irish Catholicism was finding a clear
voice under the leadership of Daniel O'Connell, the father of Irish constitutional nationalism and the founder of the Catholic Association, which
articulated the political aspirations of Irish Catholics. Except in the north
east and the eastern coastal counties, Ireland was undoubtedly a Catholic
nation. In 1861, the religious allegiance of the people was divided 77.7 per
cent Catholic, 12 per cent Anglican and 9 per cent Presbyterian.[26]

But Ireland was remarkably different from those other staunchly Catholic countries in Europe where there was little opportunity to exercise
religious choice, and where secular creeds, including socialism, commu-
nism and scientific materialism flourished as alternatives to the Catholic
worldview. Although Catholicism was the numerically superior creed in
nineteenth-century Ireland, and although it was experiencing a growing
sense of self-confidence, it did not tend to see itself as ascendant; that was
a state of mind which centuries of having to operate within the penal code
had prevented. Furthermore the Anglican Church of Ireland remained the
established Church until 1871, and once the Church was disestablished,
Ireland was left as one of the few nations in Europe without a national
religious establishment. Ireland was ruled from London from 1801 until
1922, and for the first 28 years of this period there was not even a Catholic
Emancipation Act, although it had been widely and wrongly assumed by
Irish Catholics that emancipation would follow swiftly after the union.[27]
These circumstances slowed the speed with which Catholics gained control
of Irish institutions.

Moreover, whereas in the early decades of the nineteenth century relations between Irish Catholics and Protestants had been reasonably good,
with neither community seeking to interfere in the other's affairs, by the
1820s the Irish evangelical revival had undermined this situation. As Patrick
Corish put it, 'at this stage in Irish history politics settled into a pattern of
religious sectarianism, rather than class conflict'.[28] Irish Protestants began
to see their Catholic neighbours as the necessary recipients of aggressive
evangelism, if they were to have any chance of being rescued from their
soul-imperilling beliefs. Catholics had to respond to the onslaughts of
organizations such as the Hibernian Bible Society and the Irish Society for

Promoting the Education of the Native Irish through the Medium of their own Language. The response came with Ultramontanism in its Irish form, the so-called 'devotional revolution' which brought about a stronger, more militant sense of Catholic identity by means of better organization, stronger discipline and intensified devotional life.[29] The polarization between Catholic and Protestant was intensified by several other factors. The first was population loss, exacerbated by the famine of 1845–49, in which more than 1 million died and more than 1 million emigrated, and, as the emigration continued after the famine had ended, the population was reduced from over 8 million in 1841 to under 4.5 million in 1921. The second was the Ulster Revival of 1859, which, as we shall see in Chapter 6, was part of a pan-global evangelical revival. Thirdly, as in Germany and France, reports of appearances of the Virgin Mary occurred in the second half of the century. In Ireland it was at Knock, County Mayo, in 1879. These events served to heighten the religious consciousness of both Irish Protestants and Irish Catholics, and the sense of separation between the two communities.

Until recently, a powerful historiographical tradition attributed the process of altering the religious consciousness of Catholics to the arrival from Rome of Paul Cullen, who was archbishop of Armagh from 1849 to 1852, and then Dublin from 1852 to 1878, a period in office which largely coincided with the pontificate of Pius IX. In 1865 Cullen became Ireland's first cardinal, and, in addition to his duties in Ireland, he was also responsible for recommending the appointment of most of the bishops of the Irish diaspora.[30] This made him one of the most powerful churchmen in the second half of the nineteenth century. Lately, however, the significance of Cullen in bringing about reform to the Irish Church has been questioned. Nigel Yates has pointed out that Cullen's two immediate predecessors as archbishop of Dublin, John Thomas Troy and Daniel Murray, were far more influential than had previously been supposed, as were some of the other bishops, particularly Francis Moylan, William Crolly, James Warren Doyle and John MacHale. These bishops had adopted a democratic and collegial approach to Church government, based on regular meetings which had begun in the mid-eighteenth century and become important annual events from 1823. Thus pastoral reform and devotional change were both firmly on the agenda before the arrival of Cullen, although it is he who has been given most of the credit for bringing them about. When Cullen arrived he was immensely critical of the situation in Ireland, and sent reports back to Rome which effectively rubbished the efforts of his episcopal colleagues; these reports have become part of the historical record. Although Cullen was similar in social background to the other bishops, he differed from them in having been absent from Ireland for many years and having acquired in

Rome an uncritical enthusiasm for Ultramontanism.[31]

It was Ultramontanism, a doctrine which including increasing the power of the pope's representatives over the other bishops, which permitted Cullen to become as powerful as he did. He was able to influence appointments in a manner which reflected his views, and in 1850 he used the Synod of Thurles as an opportunity to abolish the regular meetings of the bishops. Thurles differed from other clerical meetings in that the decrees which it issued were binding once they had been approved by Rome. Although historians who have seen Cullen as pivotal to the transformation of Irish Catholicism have tended to emphasize the Synod of Thurles as the key event in bringing change to the Church, much of what was approved was simply the implementation throughout Ireland of the disciplinary regulations that the reforming bishops had been enforcing in their own dioceses for decades. Yates concludes that, 'The Cullen revolution ... was more a revolution of tone than of substance, but its impact both on the Irish Roman Catholic Church and on ecumenical relations in Ireland was such that it continued to set the agenda for his successors for the best part of a century after his death in 1878.'[32] Certainly by the time of Cullen's death, Catholicism had assumed the shape which it would retain until the large-scale decline in practice, which in Ireland dates only from the 1980s.

The late nineteenth-century papacy: Leo XIII

The final decades of the nineteenth century were marked by a shift from the 'political Catholicism' which had in varying ways been a feature of life in many of Europe's Catholic nations to a 'social Catholicism' which attempted to discover the social conscience of the Church and to provide a Catholic alternative to what it perceived as the growing menace of socialism. The pontificate of Leo XIII (1878–1903) has been characterized as 'Ultramontanism with a liberal face',[33] and although Leo certainly had more time for the modern world than had his predecessor, it would be wrong to portray him as an out-and-out liberal or as a man of avant-garde opinions. Nevertheless he is probably best remembered for issuing the encyclical *Rerum novarum* in 1891. This encyclical, the first to articulate the Church's social teaching, arose out of the annual deliberations which a group of Catholic social thinkers had been having at Fribourg over the previous seven years. In it, Leo XIII sympathized with the plight of the poor, condemned those who would oppress them and indicated that socialism provided no solution to the tyranny of oppression. He told the wealthy that they had wide-ranging responsibilities as well as rights, and governments that the state had a duty to protect its workers. In particular, the right to a living wage and to trade union membership was defended, together with its logical consequence – the right to strike. Leo preferred that Catholic trade unions be founded, seeing them as a desirable feature in a landscape that included Catholic schools and political parties.

Rerum novarum also struck some conservative notes, in particular by arguing that inequalities were a natural part of the social order and that acceptance of the status quo, rather than class war, was the appropriate response. As a contribution to late nineteenth-century Christian social thought, *Rerum novarum* was not exceptional. What was extraordinary was its provenance as a papal encyclical. There seemed to be an extraordinary boldness about a pope who was speaking out against the economic and human pressures of the industrial world. Because of its papal authorship, the document was hailed as the 'Magna Carta of Social Catholicism' and became the cornerstone for all subsequent Catholic social teaching. Many Catholics felt emboldened to take the teachings further and to focus their efforts upon the plight of the working classes of the industrialized regions. The response of the political left to such endeavours was to view them as cynically minded attempts to undermine the class-consciousness of the proletariat. Karl Marx commented that, 'The scoundrels are flirting with the workers' question whenever it seems appropriate.'[34] Although it might have seemed odd that the late nineteenth-century Catholic Church should have rather suddenly interested itself in such matters, the pressures on its pan-European core constituency were not something that could have been ignored indefinitely. The 'Catholic worker' was to remain an important person on the European landscape.

Leo XIII's other major legacy to the Catholic world was his firm recommendation that its theologians study the voluminous writings of the thirteenth-century thinker Thomas Aquinas. The directive was enshrined in the encyclical *Aeterni patris* of 1879, and in 1880 Aquinas was declared to be patron of all Catholic universities.[35] Although the recommendation that theologians should attend to so major a figure as Aquinas might have seemed an uncontroversial proposal, what Leo intended was not 'an open-ended encounter with historical and philosophical texts, but … a new standard of orthodoxy'.[36] Leo wanted to impose Thomism across the Catholic world as part of the Ultramontane project. The reasoning was that theologians who were quarrying from a single, giant, internally consistent theological resource were more likely to formulate a body of modern scholarship that was consistent and cohesive. Furthermore Aquinas represented a towering Catholic source against which orthodoxy could be tested. Its canonization as a source permitted the simultaneous condemnation not only of those philosophical giants such as Kant and Hegel, whose ideas underpinned the worldview of many Protestant intellectuals, but also some Catholic thinkers who had fallen out of papal favour, such as Antonio Rosmini.[37] The adoption of neo-Thomism permitted the presentation of theology as a body of timeless truths which left no room for the consideration of current theories about the Bible, or science, or history, which were exercising so much of the time and attention of Protestant and some Catholic thinkers. It provided fertile soil for the anti-modernist movement to put down its roots, which came to a head when Leo's successor, Pius X, castigated modernism in his decree *Lamentabili* and his encyclical *Pascendi*, both of 1907. Denouncing modernism as 'a compendium of all the heresies', Pius comprehensively condemned many of the most notable of Catholicism's late nineteenth- and early twentieth-century thinkers, including George Tyrrell and Alfred Loisy. A strange collective paranoia overtook those with positions of authority within the Church, in which they became obsessed with sniffing out and putting down any infringements of Catholic orthodoxy. As Atkin and Tallet put it, 'No one was immune from suspicion. Teachers in seminaries had their letters opened, students were denounced on the basis of essays, even priests who rode bicycles were mistrusted for embracing modern technology.'[38] The future John XXIII, Angelo Roncalli, was investigated for some remarks he made about faith and scientific research at the seminary in Bergamo.

The Roman Catholic Church ended the period in a state of intellectual paralysis, from which it would not fully recover until John XXIII convened the Second Vatican Council in the 1960s. Nevertheless it had, during the nineteenth century, faced up to and fought off some extraordinary challenges, including the humiliation of the papacy, political oppression, mass migration, famine, industrialization and disestablishment. In the nineteenth century, the Roman Catholic Church proved itself to be an extraordinarily resilient institution, with millions of dedicated members.

CHAPTER 4

The United States and Canada

The legacy of Protestant Europe

At the beginning of the nineteenth century, Christianity in the United States of America was most commonly Protestant in theology and European in origin. Methodists, Baptists, Presbyterians, Congregationalists, Episcopalians, Lutherans and German and Dutch Reformed Christians had for the previous 200 years been steadily creating the backbone of American Christianity, although there remained vast tracts of land in the west which the Protestant Gospel had yet to reach. When Europeans first began to travel to America in organized groups from the early seventeenth century, their effect had been to weave a fragmented tapestry in which different denominations created the dominant fabric of the eastern colonies in which they settled. There were Anglicans in Virginia; Congregationalists in Massachusetts, Connecticut and New Haven; Baptists and Quakers in Rhode Island; Quakers in Pennsylvania; Dutch Reformers in New York and New Jersey; and Roman Catholics in Maryland, Pennsylvania and New York. All of these colonies, however, contained people of a different weave, who either identified with minority Christian traditions or who had little interest in religion. There was always a tension between the ideal of religious freedom which had been at the forefront of the minds of the colonists, and the practical reality, which for many involved a desire to maintain the doctrinal purity of the majority group with the concomitant need to exclude those who were seen as theologically heterodox.[1] Full-blown religious liberty with a profound theological undergirding was in reality limited to places like Rhode Island and Pennsylvania. Nonetheless, as time went on, expediency and toleration became the order of the day everywhere.

The American Revolution (1775–83) had represented a crisis for Churches that were institutionally linked to a European parent. The Dutch Reformed Church had declared its freedom from Dutch control in 1755 at an early point in the revolutionary era; but particularly affected by the war were the Anglicans and the Methodists. The Anglicans had had the ignominy

of being closely identified with the losing side, and were more or less shat-
tered by the end of the war – two-thirds of the rectors of Virginia left their
parishes, and other states ended up with less than a handful of Anglican
clergy. Many of the wealthiest Anglican laypeople also made a hasty departure. But the Church did not collapse completely. From out of the wreckage
emerged Samuel Seabury as the first bishop of what became the Protestant
Episcopal Church of the United States of America.

The Methodists also found themselves in a complicated predicament.
Although Methodism had developed independently in America, the catalyst had been the preaching tours of the Wesleys and George Whitefield,
and so it was clearly part of the revival movement which had developed
within the Church of England. Furthermore, John Wesley's attempts to
persuade Americans that they should be grateful for Britain's beneficent
rule, published on the outbreak of the Revolution as *A Calm Address to Our
Own American Colonies*, had done little to endear him to those with patriot
sympathies. On the outbreak of war, all of Wesley's English preachers
returned to England, with the exception of Francis Asbury, who became
the leader of post-independence Methodism and a major figure in the
second Great Awakening. In 1784 Wesley, together with two other Anglican priests, took the momentous step of ordaining three of his preachers
'to go and serve the desolate sheep in America'. When the three arrived
in Baltimore, they met up with Asbury and decided that they would form
themselves into an Episcopal Church, with superintendents (who became
known as bishops), elders and deacons. They also ensured that they were
completely independent of Anglicanism. Thus American Methodism came
into existence just at the moment when its English parent was beginning
to slow down, in part as it grappled with the implications of the departure
from Anglican Church order signalled by Wesley's American ordinations,
and also with the not unconnected issue of the future of Methodism in
the post-Wesley era. Throughout the next century, the Methodist Church
would become the chief agent in the spread of evangelical Arminianism in
the United States of America, and in the first half of the nineteenth century
it would be unrivalled as the United States's largest denomination.[2]

The revolutionary era left Americans with a strong sense of the equality
of all denominations and of the unworthiness of attempting to compre-
hend all people within a single Church. Their attitudes in these matters
were markedly different from those of their European cousins. Already by
1800, many different types of Christianity were in existence and very few
received any favourable treatment from state legislatures.[3] The constitution
prohibited religious tests for public office and the First Amendment stated
that 'Congress shall make no law respecting an establishment of religion

or prohibiting the free exercise thereof'. Yet in fact, in every state with the exception of Rhode Island, religious tests of one kind or another were required for state offices.[4] It was taken for granted that the state would not ignore religious matters. A complete unravelling of the church–state connection was seen as unnecessary because there was no sense of anti-clericalism or hostility to an all-powerful institution. Visiting in 1831–32, the French Catholic Alexis de Tocqueville noted that it was the religious aspect of the United States that was the first thing to strike his attention, and the longer he stayed the more he perceived the political consequences which arose from this. 'In America, one of the freest and most enlightened nations in the world, the people fulfil with fervour all the outward duties of religion … In France, I had almost always seen the spirit of religion and the spirit of freedom marching in opposite directions. But in America I found they were intimately united and that they reigned in common over the same country.'[5] De Tocqueville concluded, on the basis of discussions with clergy of many denominations, that it was the separation of church and state that made this possible, together with the clergy's willing abstention from politics and public appointments. Religion might be less powerful in America than in certain European nations, but he believed that its influence was more lasting.[6] The bewildering array of denominations, and their limited engagement in public life, could certainly have been interpreted as a sign of powerlessness by an early nineteenth-century European, but in America these things were viewed positively. The Church was seen as an inclusive entity, in which, within limits, each communion should be respected. Religious diversity was a sign of vitality. The complex internal market of religious faith and the spirit of proto-ecumenism which it could on occasion engender would baffle Europeans. Even as late as the early years of the twentieth century, the German theologian Dietrich Bonhoeffer remarked that 'it has been granted to the Americans less than any other nation on earth to realise the visible unity of the Church of God'.[7] But perhaps he had failed to see that the 'visible unity' of all Christians had never really captured the American religious imagination.

The growth of Roman Catholicism

The nineteenth century witnessed the increasing Americanization of those Churches of European origin, as the customs, languages and theological nuances of the early generations of settlers began to be smoothed away. As a balance to this, however, all the European denominations received large and regular infusions of new blood, often in the form of German or Scandinavian language speakers. The changing ethnicity of the new arrivals tells its own story. It has been estimated that in 1790, the national groupings of the population of the United States broke down in the following way: English 61 per cent, African 19 per cent, Native American 8 per cent, Scottish 5 per cent, German 4 per cent, Irish 1 per cent, Dutch 1 per cent, all others 1 per cent.[8] By 1850 this had shifted to people from Ireland 42.8 per cent, Germany 26.0 per cent, England and Wales 13.7 per cent, Canada and Newfoundland 6.6 per cent, Scotland 3.1 per cent, France 2.4 per cent, all others 5.4 per cent.[9] From this it is clear that the Roman Catholics faced the greatest challenges from immigration, as almost all of the Irish and many of the Germans were of Catholic background. Forty million immigrants entered the United States between 1800 and 1920, of whom about one-quarter were Roman Catholic. The number of Catholics rose from 25,000 laity and 23 priests (a total of 1 per cent of the population) at the time of the nation's founding in 1776, to 12 million and over 15,000 priests (14 per cent of the population) in 1906.[10] Alexis de Tocqueville had observed the trend in the 1830s: 'America is the most democratic country in the world, and it is at the same time (according to reports worthy of belief) the country in which the Roman Catholic religion makes most progress.' But he noted shrewdly that 'if you consider Catholicism within its own organisation it seems to be losing; if you consider it from the outside, it seems to be gaining'. De Tocqueville chided his co-religionists for tending to 'lapse into infidelity',[11] but faced with the amazing array of religious choice offered in the New World, it was hardly surprising that many of those coming from monochrome Catholic societies were enticed by other possibilities.

In addition to the European immigrants, there was a significant pre-existing Spanish Catholic population in the south west and far west of the country, and the Mississippi valley contained large numbers of French Catholics. The interior of the country was sparsely populated by Catholics at the beginning of the century, and the clergy found dealing with those that they did encounter a challenge completely unlike anything for which they had been prepared in Europe. The European Church, and the Vatican authorities, seemed to have very little insight into the rough and tumble that the Church faced on the frontier. Difficulties also arose from tensions between priests of different nationalities, and particularly the French and the Irish – there was a surplus of French priests, whilst the Irish remained in short supply. As early as 1818, seven different national groups were represented among the clergy in the archdiocese of Baltimore, and it was a major challenge for bishops to try to meld these men into an American Catholic Church. Because this was a priority, it is clear that many bishops had reservations about taking priests from Europe, even when they faced manpower shortages. This is seen in the many negative replies which John Hand, the founder of the Missionary College of All Hallows, Dublin, received to the letters he wrote to the 16 American bishops in 1842. Hand offered to send them young priests, trained at his new institution, which was being set up specifically to provide missionary clergy for dioceses in the English-speaking world beyond Ireland. Many of the American bishops declined to have Irish priests because, in an attempt to create an indigenous clergy as quickly as possible, they were investing heavily in training their own clergy in their own seminaries; they also claimed that Europeans would fail to understand the manners and morals of American Catholics. Later on, however, as the influx of Catholics continued, some of the bishops of the more poorly resourced, newly founded urban dioceses became more willing to take men from All Hallows, although they remained anxious that the employment of large numbers of Irish clergy would subject the Church to continuing anti-Irish hostility.[12]

Meanwhile, and much to the alarm of a nation which saw Protestantism as at the heart of its identity, by 1860 Roman Catholicism had edged ahead of Methodism as the nation's largest denomination, with 3.5 million members. This had been preceded by an anti-Catholic backlash orchestrated by 'nativist' Americans, in which the Irish were a particular target and which resulted in mob violence and the birth of a new, but short-lived, political party. The most violent incidents were in Boston in 1834, when an Ursuline convent was burnt to the ground, and in Philadelphia ten years later, when 13 people lost their lives and over 50 were wounded in three days of rioting. The anti-Catholicism sparked by the nativist controversy was the moment at which religion and American politics became most deeply entangled. In 1849 the Order of the Star-Spangled Banner was founded in order to defend America's destiny as a 'chosen' Protestant nation and to protect it from the 'despotic' power of Rome. Its membership was limited to American-born Protestants without Catholic wives or parents, and its objective was to oppose the election of Catholics and foreigners and to remove them from office where possible. Officially known as the American Party from 1852, because of their secretiveness they were popularly designated as the 'Know-Nothings'. By the mid-1850s they were gaining landslide election results, but their decline was almost as rapid as their rise. It seemed that the American people had little enthusiasm for their cult of secrecy, and the foundation of the Republican Party in 1854 provided a more comfortable political home for those with nativist sentiments. The rising conflict between north and south on the slavery question would swiftly prove to be a greater challenge than the American Protestant fear of Catholic foreigners.[13]

The impact of the prevailing 'congregational' culture of America was such that at an early stage in its expansion, Roman Catholicism had developed democratic tendencies that were not seen in the Catholic Church elsewhere in the world. One particular issue was the practice which became known as 'trusteeism', which involved individual congregations of Catholics organizing themselves and calling a priest, in the Protestant manner. At a time when money was short and when episcopal authority was weak or non-existent, 'trusteeism' was the best means to provide a Catholic pastoral ministry for those who wanted one. It also meant that the priest who arrived would speak the right language and be acceptable to the congregation. As the episcopate began to expand, strife between bishops and trustees became a particular feature of early nineteenth-century Catholic life. Bishops, newly imported from Europe, were astonished to discover that priests might attack them openly and enjoy the protection of their trustees.[14] As the century progressed, Catholics continued to behave with sturdy independence, and the Vatican, which classified the United States as a mission territory until 1908, had to struggle with what seemed to be the rapidly growing and unruly American cuckoo in its nest. Matters came to a head with the 'Americanism' crisis of the last two decades of the nineteenth century. This centred on the American hierarchy's desire to promote Catholicism by making it seem more 'American' in the eyes of the Protestant majority. It was a challenge to do this against the background of the *Syllabus errorum*, and the decree on papal infallibility, which, as we saw in Chapter 3, had set the Catholic hierarchy on a path of confrontation with the modern world. There was also the related question of the extent to which Catholicism could be allowed to depart from European norms in order to become 'something else' in the New World. As we have seen, Church leaders hoped that such an adaptation to American culture would assist in transcending the unwanted European import of hostilities between different national groups, particularly between the Germans and the Irish and the French, thus forging a genuinely American Catholicism, in which English was the only viable language that could be used in the parish. Pope Leo XIII responded in two encyclicals, *Longinqua oceani* (1895) and *Testem benevolentiae* (1899), which emphasized the undesirability of advocating the American style of church–state relations as the model for the rest of the world, and the impossibility of altering Church teaching in order to accommodate local conditions. The American hierarchy were caught between a rock and a hard place, and had to do their best to accept graciously this somewhat unwanted instruction. That American Roman Catholics had been criticized by Rome for being too 'American' would have come as a great surprise to many American Protestants, who doubted the Catholics' entitlement to be regarded as Americans at all.

Developments in evangelical Protestantism

For American Protestants, the Great Awakening was simultaneously a significant element in the European legacy and a decisive part of the creation of a new American religious culture. In a nation which had been largely founded by people who were seeking an arena in which to express separatist and puritan sentiments, it was not very surprising that revival should be a major force for religious change. People who inwardly knew that true religion could never be equated with mere Church membership or outward conformity would hardly settle for anything less than a quest for ever more intense forms of spiritual revelation. Thus it was that the Great Awakening, which had begun in the 1720s, entered a decisive second phase in the 1790s and continued for several decades into the nineteenth century. A third period of revival took place in the final quarter of the nineteenth century and lasted into the early years of the twentieth. American revivalism also made a major impact on the British Isles (see Chapter 6). Its impact on America itself was to give that nation a religious culture which was, at least up until the time of the Civil War, unambiguously evangelical in tone.

In the early nineteenth century, many thousands of Americans had their first decisive encounter with Christianity at a camp meeting, or when a visiting preacher entered town. If their faith had begun to fail them when the tents were dismantled or the preacher moved on, there was always the possibility that it would be renewed when the next preaching season came round. The intensity of religious experience might be cyclical, but the realities of human experience were not. Life was harsh and full of uncertainty; weather and crops were unpredictable, loved ones were often separated by great distances and perhaps unlikely to be seen again in this life. Death was certain and its timing unknown. This created an urgency for trying to attend to religious matters in the times between the preachers' visits. The American Bible Society and the American Tract Society made strenuous efforts to provide reading material for their target group, which was unconverted Americans. In just three years between 1829 and 1831, the American Bible Society printed and distributed more than 1 million copies of the Scriptures, when the nation's entire population was not yet 13 million. The Tract Society, which specialized in publications that were brisk, understandable and entertaining, printed over the same period an average of five pages for every person that was in the United States. There was also a massive explosion in other forms of religious print, with nearly 600 Christian magazines being launched in the period between 1790 and 1830, some of which went on to be supported by a large circulation.[15] These developments were made possible because of rapid advances in paper and print technology, and they allowed Protestant evangelicals to shape the thought of their fellow Americans to an extraordinary degree.

Evangelicals had further opportunities to influence their compatriots through the key role they played in the development of all levels of American education. The American Sunday School Union was founded in 1824, with the objective of a Sunday school in every town, and it was a major religious force for decades. As a national organization, it was able to direct Sunday school teachers into unevangelized frontier areas, and as a publisher it was able to provide materials for the lessons. Before the growth of public education, it proved crucial in providing teaching for those students for whom no other opportunities existed. The missionaries of the non-denominational Sunday School Union established well over 70,000 new Sunday schools during the nineteenth century. Towards the end of the century, they pioneered the 'uniform lesson plan', which involved Sunday school teachers from different denominations in a locality meeting together mid-week to prepare the following Sunday's teaching. Evangelical influence was also much in evidence in the very small number of higher education colleges that existed in antebellum America. With the exception of the few colleges founded by Catholics, almost all other institutions were sponsored and staffed by Protestant evangelicals.[16]

By the middle of the century, a few lone theological voices were questioning America's dependence on evangelical revivalism. These included Horace Bushnell, a Congregationalist from Connecticut, who had been influenced by Schleiermacher and Coleridge, and John Williamson Nevin and Philip Schaff, who both taught at the German Reformed Seminary in Mercersburg, Pennsylvania. Whilst Bushnell favoured an evangelical Christianity that was more centred on the domestic environment than on revival, Nevin and Schaff favoured a Reformed Christianity that would rediscover its German theological roots. None made much impact on his contemporaries, although all pinpointed an aspect of the American Christian experience that would be highlighted, and indeed celebrated, in the twentieth century. In the 1840s and 1850s most American Protestants could not think beyond the next revival and were suspicious of any form of European thought that did not conform to the 'commonsense' categories associated with the Scottish Enlightenment.[17]

New religious movements

In a vast, rapidly changing nation, in which waves of revivalism pulsated periodically through not very stable communities, the stage was set for the birth of some distinctively American new religious movements. Some of these developed into worldwide Churches, the main ones being the Disciples (or Churches) of Christ, Seventh Day Adventism, Christian Science, the Church of Jesus Christ of Latter-Day Saints (the Mormons) and the Jehovah's Witnesses. Others, particularly those which were really experiments in Christian community living and which embraced celibacy, became extinct. Most of these movements had links with evangelical revivalism and courted the same constituency, in some cases offering their followers 'the next step', or providing specific teachings about the end of the world or the origins and purpose of the American nation. Adventism, the belief that Jesus would soon return to the earth and begin a period of personal rule, often reckoned to be going to last for 1,000 years, was a major ingredient found in most nineteenth-century new religious movements. Adventism prompted feelings of joy and anxiety. On the one hand, enticing Jesus to return to the earth seemed to provide the panacea for all pain and misfortune. On the other, being part of the cosmic countdown could produce huge psychological pressure, particularly when the Day of Judgement was not simply identified as being 'soon' but as taking place on a specific day, so many years, months, weeks and days in the future. Whatever else it did, the widespread belief that the world was about to end tended to threaten the authority of America's emerging religious institutions. As Sydney Ahlstrom put it, 'The cry went up against hierarchies, seminary professors, dry learning, "hireling ministers," unconverted congregations and "cold formalism" ... Farmers became theologians, offbeat village youths became bishops, odd girls became prophets.'[18] Here we shall look at just three of the most influential of these new religious movements. They are the Millerites (from which Seventh Day Adventism would emerge), the Shakers and the Mormons.

The Millerites

William Miller was a farmer who became addicted to studying in his local library at Poultney, Vermont. He went through an extended Deist phase, but was converted in a Baptist revival. Thereafter he applied his rationalist spirit to his study of the Bible. For Miller, the Bible was the King James Version, with the annotations of the seventeenth-century Anglican archbishop of Armagh, James Ussher. Ussher's annotations were based on his dating of various biblical events; he had been trying to reconcile the datings provided by Eusebius and Jerome, and he famously concluded that creation had taken place in 4004 BC. Using Ussher's dating as a starting point, Miller put aside the commentaries which he had previously used and decided to try to understand the biblical text for himself. Working carefully over the Book of Daniel, he calculated that the world was due to end 'around the year 1843'. 'I was thus brought ... at the close of my two-year study of the Scriptures, to the solemn conclusion that in about twenty-five years from that time [1818] all the affairs of our present state would be wound up.'[19] Initially tentative about sharing his conclusions more widely, Miller did not overcome his fears of making his views public until 1831, and when he did so he was assisted by his brilliant publicist, Joshua Himes. Himes provided a great deal of finance, and supervised the distribution of 5 million copies of Millerite publications in the period leading up to 1843.[20] Without him, it is likely that Miller would have remained just another obscure preacher foretelling the end of the world, offering the revival to end all revivals. Miller was clear that he wanted people to stay in their Churches and not to come out and form a new denomination. With this in mind, he found the unresponsiveness of evangelical ministers to his message surprising; he believed that all he was doing was communicating an important theological truth, which would be plain to anybody who studied the problem in a 'scientific' way; he believed strongly in the human ability to understand Scripture.

If Miller and Himes failed to make much headway with the clergy, they had more success in attracting a varied cross-section of American society. These were not, on the whole, the dispossessed, but included bankers, lawyers, craftsmen and farmers, people who, if they chose to stop work because the world was about to end, could have a significant impact on the economy. As David L. Rowe puts it, 'Millerites were not fascinating because they were so different from everyone else, but because they were so like their neighbours.'[21] It has been estimated that somewhere between 10,000 and over 1 million Millerites awaited the second coming of Christ, first on 21 March 1843 and then again on 22 October 1844. When Christ failed to appear on the second date, the movement collapsed, and the Great Disappointment ensued. Miller, who had always been reluctant to be nailed down to a specific date (something which had been foisted on him by some of his more ardent supporters) responded pragmatically: it was not the Bible or his method of interpreting it that had been at fault, but rather the unreliable findings of biblical scholars and historians.[22] For his followers, the Disappointment caused spiritual turmoil and, for those who had left their employment, material suffering, but it did not necessarily also destroy faith. Very soon it was concluded that Christ had indeed appeared on the appointed day, and had 'cleansed the temple', but that the event had taken place in heaven. Further scriptural study led to the conclusion that the Sabbath should be observed, as the Jews did, on Saturday, not on the 'popish' Sunday. The most important leader to emerge from among the post-Disappointment Adventist groups was Ellen White, a woman who combined visions and prophecy with considerable organizational skill, and very clear views about diet and health. She believed that abstinence from certain foods could bring the individual closer to Christ. One of her disciples was John H. Kellogg, who advocated the consumption of cold cereal as a breakfast food. Under Ellen White's leadership the Seventh Day Adventist Church emerged as a worldwide denomination with distinctive emphases on education, health, fitness, the avoidance of meat, alcohol and caffeine, the Saturday Sabbath and evangelical Christianity. In 1903 the Church moved its headquarters from Battle Creek, Michigan, to Washington DC, at which point it had an American membership of more than 50,000. By 1994 it had a worldwide membership of 8.3 million, of whom fewer than one in ten lived in North America.[23]

The Shakers

Quite a few ex-Millerites coped with the Disappointment of October 1844 by joining the Shakers, a group which, in the 1840s, was at the height of its growth, with a membership of around 5,000. The Shakers, properly known either as the 'United Society of Believers in Christ's Second Appearing', or 'The Millennial Church', had been founded by Ann Lee, who was originally from Manchester, England, in Watervliet, New York, in 1776. Initially influenced by the Shaking Quakers in Bolton, the emigration of Ann Lee and her tiny band of followers had been prompted by their conclusion that Christ's second coming had already taken place, in the form of a woman, and that Ann Lee was that woman. Ann was thus the female principle in Christ, as Jesus was the male principle. Ann, whose experience of childbirth had been hellish, and followed by the loss of all of her four babies, also concluded that sexual relations were the root of all evil. Sex was the means through which sin had entered the world, and in order to overcome sin it was necessary to give up sex. To put into practice their controversial ideas, the Shakers needed the space and freedom of the New World. Once in America, however, they adopted the communitarian lifestyle only as a result of economic necessity, and initially made no converts at all. But when a Baptist revival flared up nearby, the Shakers found that their time had come. They began to attract people whose spiritual instincts had been aroused, but not satisfied, in standard evangelical revivals. They concentrated on picking up new members from places where revivals had just occurred, and the movement grew. After Ann Lee's death, two leaders, one male and one female, took over, and together they developed a highly disciplined and regulated form of community living. It was a strange mixture of monasticism (community living, compulsory celibacy, a strong emphasis on obedience and authority); revivalism (they spoke in tongues and their name derived from the intense shaking or spinning which overtook them during their ecstatic worship, although later it referred to the ritualized communal dances performed during services); progressiveness (equality for women and an innovative approach to agriculture, medicine and design); and heterodoxy (the belief that Mother Ann was the female Christ and the denial of the Trinity, on the grounds that this was too male an expression of the Godhead).

For the ex-Millerites, the attractiveness of joining Shaker communities probably rested in the opportunity it gave them to be with fellow Adventists who had lived through their own version of the second coming and come out the other side. Shakers were seen as calm people who had given up the emotional roller-coaster of expectation and disappointment, revival and decline, in order to achieve a stable lifestyle. Shaker communities were noted for their good order and for the peace which seemed to have settled upon members. The standard of living was high because they were successful as farmers and craftsmen, their most famous legacy being the furniture and household objects which later generations would seize upon as the essence of American simplicity and good taste. Although the 'gift to be simple' in a safe environment was an obvious attraction, for the ex-Millerites the disadvantage of joining the Shakers was the enforced adoption of celibacy, which was an obvious trial for happily married couples. Lawrence Foster has argued that this was the major reason why ex-Millerites who joined Shaker communities frequently did not stay for more than a few years. Even one of the most ardent early converts, Enoch Jacobs, who had laboured hard to advocate Shaker theology to his ex-Millerite brothers and sisters, in the end walked out of the community at Union Village, Ohio, declaring that he would 'rather go to hell with Electa his wife, than live among the Shakers without her'.[24] The reality of celibacy proved to be a much greater stumbling block for married converts than the belief that Ann Lee was the female principle in Christ. It also explains why the Shakers never became a national denomination and were little more than a remnant by the end of the nineteenth century.

The Mormons

Like Lee and Miller, Joseph Smith also saw himself as a prophet of the last days. The Church of Jesus Christ of Latter-Day Saints, which he founded, would, like Seventh Day Adventism, also become a worldwide denomination. From around 138,000 in 1890, the Church in the United States had grown to around 5 million by the end of the twentieth century, and to about 10 million worldwide.[25] But Mormonism did not simply seek to prepare its followers for the end of time: it provided a creation myth and Old Testament history for modern America. Smith offered a further scriptural revelation in the Book of Mormon, 'Another Testament of Jesus Christ', a work printed to look like and (superficially at least) to sound like the Old Testament.

Mormonism was therefore intended to supersede orthodox Christianity, in the way that Christians believed Christianity had superseded Judaism. The Book of Mormon tells the story of the descendants of a small group of Hebrews who apparently escaped Jerusalem just prior to the Babylonian invasion (600 BCE) and sailed for the 'promised land' of the west coast of America: first the Jaredites, who extinguished themselves through fighting, and then the Nephites and the Lamanites, who built elaborate cities and engaged in missionary activity, but also succumbed to feuding. After his crucifixion, Christ appeared to them in America and organized a church. Peace and harmony broke out, but after several centuries conflict returned and in approximately 421 the evil Lamanites (the ancestors of the American Indians) destroyed the good Nephites. According to Mormon beliefs Moroni, the last prophet of the destroyed group, buried the records of his people until such time as they would be needed as 'a new and additional witness that Jesus Christ is the Son of the living God'. The scene was therefore set for Joseph Smith, a farm worker and treasure hunter in New York State, to find the records written on metal plates after an angelic visitation from Moroni in 1823. In time Smith translated the plates (which were then swept away by the angel) and the Book of Mormon was published in 1830.

For non-Mormons, the Book of Mormon is the elaborate imaginative creation of an apocalypticist who was finely tuned to the concerns of his day, and also steeped in the language and concepts of the King James Version. Indeed, Smith sought to model himself on the Old Testament patriarchs that he so admired (which was why he advocated polygamy – he scandalized American society by having possibly as many as 48 wives, although Mormon historians contend that many of these were wives in name only, 'sealed' to Smith in a future life).[26] In fact, very few Mormon men were ever polygamists, unable to cope with the strains of supporting multiple families, and the Mormons officially abandoned the practice in 1890 (polygamy had been outlawed by the Supreme Court since 1879).

When public opinion became increasingly hostile to Smith and his religion, and in search of land on which to found their New Jerusalem, Smith and his followers left New York and began their exodus journey, the long trek west, which brought them eventually, and after extraordinary hardship, to Utah. On the way, the Mormons developed communities at, and were then systematically driven out from, Kirtland Ohio, Jackson County Missouri and Nauvoo, Illinois. In Nauvoo, Smith was declared king of the Kingdom of God and became head of the military. He received a new series of revelations which took Mormonism even further from its Christian roots. In 1844 he announced that he would stand as president of the United States, and destroyed the opposition press in Nauvoo. Meanwhile disaffected ex-Mormons were all too ready to regale a horrified public with tales of polygamy, corruption and megalomania. A series of events was triggered which resulted in Smith being murdered on 27 June 1844. The leadership of the movement then passed on to Brigham Young, an ex-Methodist from Vermont. It was Young who supervised the development of Salt Lake City and the process which eventually saw Utah being granted statehood. It has continued to be the Mecca for Mormons all over the world. The denomination itself quickly developed as a conservative, white, family-orientated, middle-class, essentially American form of religion, although today around half of the world's Mormons now live outside the United States, many in Mexico and further south.

African-American Christianity

In the seventeenth and eighteenth centuries, Africans were brought as slaves to work on the plantation islands of the Caribbean and on parts of the North American mainland. Although the practice of keeping slaves was abandoned in the northern colonies after the American Revolution, slavery in the southern states continued until 1865. The majority of those in captivity in America were, at the time of arrival, practitioners of African Traditional Religions of various types, although it has been estimated that up to 20 per cent of them were Muslim and that they continued as best they could to practise their faith at least until the second generation.[27] A question for the plantation owners who now controlled the African slaves was should they be converted to Christianity? Opinions divided on whether or not this was in the interests of the plantation owners. Some took the view, particularly in the earlier period, that the 'heathenism' of the Africans justified their enslavement; if they became Christians the rationale of slavery would be undermined, as they would become 'nearer' to their Christian owners. Plantation owners relied on their own skin colour, ethnicity and religion to distinguish them from their slaves, and they had no wish to blur what they saw as an intrinsic distinction. They feared that as Christians, their slaves would become rebellious and haughty, revelling in the spiritual equality which they would learn that they shared with their baptized owners.

The Bible did not offer slave owners a clear answer, providing them with some texts which they found helpful and others which they found unsettling. Indeed, during a South Carolina legislative debate in 1834 over the prohibition on teaching slaves to read and write, one contributor noted that anyone who wanted slaves to read the *entire* Bible belonged in 'a room in the Lunatic Asylum'.[28] The lack of clarity gave rise to a larger problem for Protestant America: the Bible was their only source of religious authority, and yet on this most pressing of issues its testimony was ambiguous. Where did that leave biblical authority? The Apostle Paul had felt that baptism transcended the divisions between slaves and the free, but he did not condemn the institution of slavery, which was central to the maintenance of the Roman Empire.[29] Slave ownership had found approval among the ancient Israelites, with texts such as Exodus 21 and Leviticus 25 providing guidance on how slaves should be treated. If any generalization could be extrapolated from the biblical texts, it was that under the slave system masters had duties and responsibilities too; obedience had to be met with fair treatment. This exegesis helped to shape what became the prevailing view, which was that slave owners had a duty to provide for the spiritual needs of their slaves and to direct them towards Christianity. In the pre-Independence period, it was, however, the British government and the Church, rather than the slave owners, who took the initiative. In an attempt to lessen the anxieties of some slave owners, some of the Society for the Propagation of the Gospel missionaries required that adult candidates for baptism first sign a statement which declared that they were seeking baptism 'merely for the good of their soul' and were not trying to free themselves from the duty and obedience that they owed to their earthly master.[30]

Conversion, of course, meant different things to different types of Christians. To the Anglican missionaries of the SPG, it meant explaining Christianity by catechizing through a question and answer mode. It required those being catechized to learn and repeat fixed responses to specific questions, so that, like the Norwegian Lutherans, they could absorb the central tenets of Christianity in their minds. To traditional New England Congregationalists, it meant explaining the principles of Calvinist belief, including the difficult notion that God had only chosen some for election, although under the influences of the 'New Divinity' many were moving towards the view that Christ's atonement was unlimited and 'sufficient for all'.[31] To the evangelicals of the Great Awakening, conversion meant a moment of personal 'awakening', an intense response of being convicted of sin followed by complete surrender to God. This form of conversion was a matter of feeling, not intellect; it did not require the convert to be able to articulate all the right answers or to be among the elect. Not surprisingly, the evangelical Arminian form of conversion was more successful than anything else in introducing Christianity among the slave plantations. Those slaves who embraced Christianity (and many did not) warmed most to the Methodists and Baptists, the two denominations which did more than the others to support slaves and to allow them to participate in worship on something approaching their own terms. At a time when some eighteenth-century religious leaders had regarded slavery as a natural part of the status quo, John Wesley had denounced it, not for reasons of economic pragmatism, but with a bold assertion of the natural rights of all people to pursue freedom, holiness and happiness.[32] In 1758 he baptized two African-American slaves. Methodists continued to petition against slavery, although, as we shall see, black Methodists became increasingly frustrated by bi-racial worship and by attitudes of white superiority. In the 1840s Methodism tore itself asunder over one of its bishops, James O. Andrew, who exercised episcopal oversight while owning slaves.[33] Baptists, meanwhile, had a particularly positive approach to permitting blacks to preach, an attitude brought about in part by the flexibility of their ecclesiological structures.[34] Albert J. Raboteau has argued that 'it would be difficult to overestimate the importance of these early black preachers for the development of an African-American Christianity. In effect, they mediated between Christianity and the experience of the slaves (and free blacks), interpreting the stories, symbols and events of the Bible to fit the day-to-day lives of those held in bondage. And whites – try as they might – could not control this interpretation or determine its "accuracy".'[35] The activities of black preachers in the south, were, however severely curtailed in the antebellum period, when all gatherings of blacks began to be viewed with alarm. At a denominational level, the Baptists too split over the slavery question in the 1840s – the schism which produced the Southern Baptist Convention, which by the early twentieth century had become the largest Protestant denomination.

It has been argued by William E. Montgomery (and others) that another reason for the success of evangelical Christianity among the black population was that it most naturally paralleled some of the features of African religion, and that it fostered feelings of self-worth that were not conveyed by Anglicanism or New England Puritanism.[36] Whilst this is undoubtedly true, it is also worth bearing in mind Charles Joyner's point that African-American Christianity was not a form of evangelical Protestantism but something altogether new. Once in America, Africans encountered a huge variety of other Africans from tribes with whom they had previously had no contact. What emerged in America was essentially a new African culture rather than any particular African culture. When this blended with Protestant evangelicalism, it produced the unique and creative synthesis known as African-American Christianity.[37] It was really quite different from white religion, although evangelical revivalism provided a context that was more tolerant of emotionally charged experiential forms of worship, where the emphasis was on music, singing, shouting, dancing, and sometimes spirit possession and ecstatic states.[38]

Albert J. Raboteau argues that, theologically, enslaved Christians turned some of the central motifs of American Protestant Christianity on their head. Ever since the first white European settlers had journeyed across the

Atlantic, they had seen themselves as the exodus of a new Israel, liberated from the bondage of Egypt and led to the Promised Land of milk and honey. For black Christians, the imagery was reversed. Africa had been their land of milk and honey. Their traumatic passage across the ocean had brought them to a new Egypt, where they, the old Israel, suffered bondage under a new Pharaoh. For these reasons black Christians alighted upon the exodus story as having central relevance, as their hope became fixed on divine deliverance from slavery. In 1864 a white Union Army chaplain working in Alabama commented unfavourably upon the slaves' fascination with the Book of Exodus. 'Moses is their *ideal* of all that is high, and noble, and perfect, in man. I think they have been accustomed to regard Christ not so much in the light of a *spiritual* Deliverer, as that of a second Moses who would eventually lead *them* out of their prison house of bondage.'[39] If this was the case, it was also clear that their identification as the children of Israel gave them a special sense of a close relationship with God, and that when slaves sang of 'being bound for the Land of Canaan' they were not necessarily using a metaphor for heaven but could mean actual escape to the free north, or Canada.

African-American Christianity developed quite differently in the north and in the south up until the Civil War, because of the different paths which the northern and southern states took over slavery. In the north, blacks had originally participated in white churches and inter-racial worship. They were permitted to preach to blacks and, very occasionally, to whites as well. However, as blacks became increasingly unhappy at being treated as second-class citizens, the incentive to form separate black churches became greater. One of the most famous spurs to this process was an incident which took place around 1787, when a former slave, Richard Allen, and other black members, withdrew from St George's Methodist church in Philadelphia after another worshipper, Absalom Jones, was dragged from his knees during prayer because he was not sitting in the black section of the building. This set in motion the process by which Jones became minister of the first black Episcopal congregation in the country which set itself up as St Thomas's, Philadelphia, in 1794. It also led Allen to found the African Methodist Episcopal Church, which became a major national denomination, in 1814. Jones and Allen had also founded in Philadelphia the Free African Society, which was America's first organization created for blacks by blacks and which became a prototype for other such fraternal organizations.[40] By the 1830s other northern blacks were successfully organizing churches for themselves. In the south, blacks had significantly fewer opportunities to found their own churches, although a few did come into existence, such as the First African Baptist Church of Savannah,

Georgia. The African Methodist Episcopal Church set up some congregations, particularly in border areas, but it tended to be something of an elite Church amongst mainly free southern blacks. Most of the enslaved who took up Christianity found themselves participating either in black congregations in white-controlled churches, where the theological message centred on obedience to masters, or in informal folk churches, with little contact with denominational structures or established religious traditions. This situation continued up until the end of the Civil War.

In the immediate pre-Civil War period, for a growing number of northerners, the abolition of slavery became a moral crusade, the outcome of which would determine the destiny of the nation. For a growing number of southerners, even those who had previously been ambivalent about the moral status of slave-holding, it increasingly began to be seen as a way of life that was worth defending. They argued that slavery was a means of bringing blacks from heathenism to Christianity, and that it was intrinsic to a Christian society, which was being threatened by the secular forces from the north. As we have seen, in the period from the late 1830s to the 1840s, many of the older denominations that had linked Christians throughout the nation, including the Presbyterians, Baptists and Methodists, split over the issue of slavery. The nation was tearing itself apart, and this was at a time when apocalyptic millennialist fervour about the imminent end of the world was reaching a crisis point. Both sides believed that the other needed to repent as a matter of the utmost urgency. Both believed that God was unambiguously on their side. As Mark Noll puts it, 'the civil war was a religious event because it consumed the energies of religious people'.[41]

At the conclusion of the war, the passing of the Thirteenth Amendment in December 1865 meant the prohibition of slavery, and the Fifteenth Amendment, in 1870, gave ex-slaves the right to vote. About 4 million slaves were emancipated, and for those who were Christians, the event was interpreted as God fulfilling his promise to lead his people to the Promised Land. The ending of slavery was not, unfortunately, the end of racial tension, which grew worse in the remaining decades of the nineteenth century, as slavery gave way to white supremacy and then to segregation. This particularly nasty boil might have been lanced, but the wound itself took a very long time to heal, and the scar remains all too visible. Relieved that the issue that had torn the nation apart was resolved, white Christians began to turn their attention in other directions. There was a renewed interest in revivalism which gave way to the holiness movement and the beginnings of Pentecostalism. There was also a sense of excitement that it was now possible to get on with settling the vast territories in the west without the issue of whether slavery should or should not be permitted getting in the way.

Noll suggests that 'the curious result of a war won (and lost) by people who felt that true religion was at stake produced a nation in which the power of religion declined'.[42] The denominations that had split over the issue found that reconciliation was not possible, and denominational concerns began to be increasingly expressed in term of north or south, but not both. The main branches of the northern and southern Methodists did not heal the breach until 1939, and among the Presbyterians divisions directly resulting from the Civil War were not reconciled until 1983. The Baptists never reunited.

In the immediate aftermath of the war, many black Christians in the south founded their own churches, both independent congregations and new denominations. Montgomery has argued that of all the ways in which former slaves displayed their newly acquired freedom, leaving the white-controlled churches and forming their own religious organizations was perhaps the easiest and most gratifying – a real source of happiness and security in an environment that was often hostile and frightening.[43] Some of the black Churches of the north, and the African Methodist Episcopal Church in particular, also took the opportunity to spread their work into the southern states, and large numbers of white missionaries also arrived. By the 1880s black Christians were establishing their own colleges, and by 1900 over 25 Church-connected colleges had been founded in the south. The alumni of these institutions rapidly became the 'talented tenth' that were seen as essential for racial progress, although as people became more educated, they became less tolerant of what they saw as the noisy emotionalism and theological limitations of the earlier generation of preachers.[44] This tended to result in the Church becoming a less well-esteemed institution, and was coupled with the unwelcome discovery that it was really the only institution over which blacks could have control. In these circumstances, religion could be seen as a sad compensation for lost opportunities in the 'real world'.[45]

The Roman Catholic Church also encountered a growth in its black membership in both the north and the south. It can be argued that of all the Christian Churches in late nineteenth-century America, the Catholic Church came closest to being racially non-discriminatory, presenting itself as a universal Church devoid of racism. This was a significant advance on the earlier period, for the Jesuits had owned slaves until 1838. In a sermon on the race problem in 1890, Cardinal John Ireland stressed the equality of all people and condemned social segregation, something which by this date most whites insisted on and most blacks regarded as inevitable. It was noted that the Catholic Church 'welcomed to its altars and communion men of all races and colours', and although they hardly rushed to seek out black candidates for the priesthood, in 1886 Augustus Tolton of Quincy,

Illinois, became the first American of pure African descent to be ordained. An unexpected testimony on the Catholic position on the race question came from an Arkansas Baptist, who observed, 'if those Catholics could get control there would be a good time all over the world'.[46] By the end of the century there were about 150,000 black Catholics in America.[47]

The uniqueness of Canada

Although Canada was clearly geographically part of North America, in cultural and theological terms it is more accurate to see it as located somewhere between the United States and Europe. Our discussion of Canada will focus first on the similarities between it and the United States, and then on the similarities between it and Europe, the argument being that it was the European influences rather than the American ones that were stronger in forging the particular ethos of nineteenth-century Canadian Christianity, until it began to place a greater distance between itself and France and the British Isles and take on a distinctively Canadian character.

Some similarities with the United States were real enough, however. The most obvious one was the pioneering spirit shared by a relatively small population in the face of a vast landmass. The population of Canada was very much smaller than the United States – about 600,000 at the beginning of the century and about 8 million at the end, compared with 8.5 million rising to 99 million in the United States – but many of the challenges were the same. For Christians, Canada represented a vast amount of space in which, if it contained an indigenous population or became settled by Europeans, the Gospel needed to be preached and the Church needed to be made present. Like the Americans, the Canadians were consciously building a new nation, and particularly so after modern Canada was formed with the federation of Quebec, Ontario, Nova Scotia and New Brunswick in 1867. The new nation was seen as requiring a clearly articulated Christian tone; indeed nineteenth-century Canadians, like Americans, naturally linked the progress of Christianity with the advance of civilization. A Methodist politician from New Brunswick declared that the text of Psalm 72.8 should be applied to the new country: 'He shall have dominion also from sea to sea.' In this way Her Majesty's Dominion of Canada was given a Christian baptism, although the political background to the decision was that the earlier preferred designation for the new country, the 'Kingdom of Canada', was dropped for fear of alienating the republican sensibilities of the United States. The self-conscious attempt to build a Christian nation led to high levels of churchgoing, with numbers increasing as the century progressed, as in America, rather than decreasing, as was more generally the case in Europe. By 1900 up to half of Toronto's population were in church every

Sunday, and the rural areas and smaller towns of Ontario often witnessed even higher levels of religious practice. In Canada's Catholic heartland of Quebec, weekly Mass attendance was often as high as 90 per cent.[48]

Like their American co-religionists, Canadian Protestants had been no strangers to revivalism, and they had had their own version of the Great Awakening, led by Henry Alline in the final quarter of the eighteenth century. Converted in 1775, Alline had preached what was known as New Light revivalism around Nova Scotia, and still had a significant following in the early nineteenth century, some 20 years after his death. By the 1790s, however, the movement had gone somewhat off course after some of his female followers had embraced full-blooded antinomianism (believing that having been saved they could commit no sin, and that therefore they might as well do whatever they pleased). They expressed their theological belief by advocating sexual freedom; the response from Alline's male followers was to try to pull the New Lights back in a direction which was more in accord with contemporary morality, and at the same time also more Calvinist. George Rawlyk has argued that at least up until the end of the first decade of the nineteenth century, the New Light influences meant that Canadian evangelicalism was more radical, more egalitarian and more democratic than its better-known variant in the south. It was certainly 'freer', because it was not packed up with the American baggage of civic humanism, republicanism and the special covenant relationship. Some evidently felt entirely uninhibited about doing whatever the Spirit seemed to suggest to them, without feeling that it might have an impact on the community outside the Church. Meanwhile, the seeming anarchy of much 'spirit-filled' Maritime New Light worship attracted strong disapproval from American evangelicals in neighbouring New England and New York. The American Methodist leader Francis Asbury was particularly disapproving, and eventually banned his preachers from itinerating in Nova Scotia. Drawing on the work of Elizabeth Mancke, Rawlyk explains these differences by suggesting that they stem from the fact that in New England, churches were much more part of the social fabric; they were supported by town governments, by legislative assemblies and at times by the courts. In Nova Scotia, however, churches were left to their own devices, and towns barely existed as political entities. It followed from this that there was nothing to contain extreme religious behaviour.[49] Naturally, not all early nineteenth-century Canadian evangelicals were prone to excessive behaviour – there were also plenty of Baptists, Presbyterians and British-orientated Methodists who lived and worshipped in ways which their American cousins would have approved.

The outbreak of war between America and Canada in 1812 had the important repercussion of steering Canadian church life away from American influences. Canadians ceased to look to American revivalism or to American preachers to supply them with what they needed. Revivalism continued to manifest itself at regular intervals, but it was usually in a distinctively British or Irish form. Indeed, Marguerite Van Die suggests that Canadian revivals were partly kindled by immigrants' desire for spiritual comfort in a way that approximated as closely as possible to what was remembered from home. In Ontario, in areas that had been settled by Scottish highlanders, annual long communions with their Gaelic services frequently erupted into periods of revival and awakening, as had been customary in Scotland. Elsewhere it was reported that Irishmen 'who would have borne any sorrow, any pain, any privation without a murmur, melted to tears under the sound of the preacher's voice, heard last in the pretty home chapel on that green isle far away'.[50] This may be a highly sentimentalized picture of what was actually taking place, but it may also suggest that after earlier Canadian revivalist excesses, there was a desire to re-direct the emotions of participants in ways that were seen as safer and more seemly.

The most obvious factor which placed Canada more in the European than in the American sphere of religious influence was the strength of Roman Catholicism. Indeed, Mark Noll has suggested that 'Canada was not so much *a* Christian nation as *two* Christian nations, Catholic and Protestant'.[51] Crucially different from the United States, in Canada, the first Christian presence had been Catholic; Protestants came later. It was the French who had colonized in Canada in the seventeenth century, and they brought with them Jesuit and Franciscan Recollet missionaries with the task of converting the native peoples to Catholic Christianity, as well as ministering to the ex-patriot French population. They operated in Nova Scotia and on the northern shore of the St Lawrence river, and Quebec was quickly chosen as the centre for the commercial, religious and political conquest of Canada. Thus Quebec became solidly Catholic – and French speaking – and never lost its cultural distinctiveness, despite the enormous linguistic pressures exerted by anglophone North America. Other early centres of Catholicism were Huronia (the area around Lake Huron), Ville Marie (Montreal) and Acadia (Nova Scotia and some adjacent areas). As early as 1620 the first Canadian seminary for French and Amerindian boys was being constructed, and in the years that followed, hundreds of members of French religious orders – male and female – poured in, devoting themselves to learning local languages, establishing schools and hospitals, and, as far as possible in so vast and lightly settled a territory, administering the sacraments.[52] The British, who had long been jealously coveting the French Canadian territories, launched a successful assault on Quebec in 1759, and thereafter French rule gave way to British. The Treaty of Paris (1763) gave

Britain unrivalled control over the northern part of North America (it became known as British North America) and raised interesting questions about how a constitutionally Protestant nation would deal with the large Catholic population in the St Lawrence river region. The answer came in the Quebec Act of 1774, which guaranteed to Quebec Catholics the religious freedoms that would not be extended to Catholics in the British Isles until 1829. Thus the *Québecois* became the most favoured Catholics in the British Empire. Although freedom for Catholics was seen as politically necessary and pragmatically tolerable, the British entertained the hope that Catholicism would wither away and that Catholics would in time submit to Anglicanism. To this end, the Jesuits and the Recollets were forbidden to take novices, thus ensuring that at that point in their history both orders died out in Canada. Meanwhile any Quebec clergy who wanted to marry were offered Anglican parishes. Five congregations of nuns, however, continued to be valued for their teaching and nursing skills and were permitted to keep working and taking novices.[53]

All this was enough to ensure that when the American Revolution broke out, Quebec remained firmly on the British side, and the loyalty of the *Québecois* was demonstrated again when they sided against American republicanism and in favour of British loyalism in the War of 1812. British officials began to feel reassured about the reality of managing a Catholic colony, whose conservatism had been further bolstered by the arrival of 45 émigré French priests, all of whom were deeply hostile to any form of revolutionary tendency. The fear that French revolutionary ideas might surface in Quebec did not materialize. Indeed, nineteenth-century Canadian Catholicism, centred on Quebec but by no means confined to it – there were majority Catholic populations in New Brunswick, Prince Edward Island, British Columbia, Saskatchewan and Alberta – developed as a strongly conservative, anti-revolutionary force, with an Ultramontanist character. The Church adopted an increasingly central role in society, to the extent that for more than a century after 1840, it had sole control over the education of all French-speaking citizens in the province of Quebec. Perhaps the high watermark of Catholic influence came during the episcopate of Bishop Ignace Bourget, who was bishop of Quebec for much of the second half of the mid-nineteenth century. He prohibited books on democracy and got into trouble with the Vatican for trying to exert excessive control over the way in which Catholics voted. Whilst Bourget's policies seem extreme, they produced a thoroughly cohesive Catholic society the like of which was found nowhere else in North America.

Whilst Quebec's Catholics looked to France, increasing numbers of Irish and Scottish Catholics began to arrive elsewhere in Canada from the early years of the nineteenth century, thus presenting the Church with the same problem of integrating different national groups that was being experienced elsewhere in the New World. But to a greater degree than in the United States, Irish and Scottish migrants to Canada, both Catholic and Protestant, seemed to want to retain the sharp edges of their national and religious identity and to play them out in their new homeland. Presbyterians re-enacted the Scottish Disruption, with the more evangelical group coming out to form the 'Free' Presbyterian Church of Canada. Irish Presbyterianism was strong in Toronto, which was sometimes called the 'Belfast of North America', and had been alone among North American cities in receiving more Irish Protestant immigrants than Irish Catholic ones. Orange Lodges were set up, which in addition to the Irish welcomed Protestant members of non-Irish background. In the 1850s and 1860s Irish Protestant Orangemen regularly clashed with Irish Catholics, and St Patrick's Day and the Protestant Twelfth of July became the flashpoints for bloody rioting. Canada's long history of Catholic–Protestant stand-offs is one of the features which most separates it religiously from the United States, although, as we have seen, Protestant–Catholic relations in the United States could be fuelled with bitterness too. Canadians knew that their nation had divided allegiances, and this fact had perhaps one positive spin-off – they were much less prone than the Americans to moral posturing about their nation standing in a unique covenant relationship with God.[54] Canadians also seem to have had little interest in home-grown forms of American religion. Denominations that emerged in America, such as the Mormons and the Disciples of Christ, have not thrived in Canada.

The establishment of British rule in 1759 had had significant implications for the Church of England, which assumed that it might be granted the same rights and privileges in Canada that it enjoyed at home. But as the Church of England was to find on other foreign shores, it was not a simple matter to export the paraphernalia of Anglicanism to somewhere that was under British rule and declare that the Church had been established. Although government officials might theoretically be favourably disposed to giving it special treatment, in reality they had to contend with trying to govern in a context where other denominations were usually in the majority. Later on, there would be successful legal challenges to the whole notion that the Church of England could exist as an established Church outside the British Isles. Perhaps partly because Anglicans in Canada had had such high expectations, they tended to feel beleaguered and insufficiently supported by the British missionary agency that was supposed to be assisting them, the Society for the Propagation of the Gospel. The SPG sent many of its missionaries to Canada – 1,597 ordained men between 1703 and 1900 – but its London-based secretaries usually failed to understand the reality of what they were dealing with. It was not until 1849 that an SPG secretary actually set foot on the continent, and not until 1901 that there was an SPG secretary who had actually served as a colonial missionary. Friction between SPG secretaries and colonial bishops was common, for it was the bishops who had the formal jurisdiction but the SPG secretaries who had the money. As a result of this, the Anglican Church in British North America developed a very strong dependence upon the finance of the SPG, some of which came from individual donations but the majority of which, after 1814, came from a British government grant. It came as a great shock to the colonial Churches when in 1832 the government decided that the grant should be reduced to zero over two years. The SPG had to adopt a policy of gradually making the dioceses which it had previously supported become self-funding.[55] But Anglicans simply could not get their heads around the idea that religion should be paid for by those that wanted it, basing their case in part upon the fact that they ran schools, hospitals and welfare facilities that were available to all, and were therefore entitled to state support and special treatment. Bishop Jacob Mountain of Quebec exhibited perfectly his very English model of what the Church was for when he commented that 'the less sincerely desirous people are of the benefits of religious instruction, the more they stand in need of them'.[56] He might still have got away with putting this view in an English parish, but he could not do so in the colonies, where by the middle of the nineteenth century almost all forms of Christianity operated in competition on a voluntary basis.

Between 1758 and 1803 the Anglican Church had been established in three provinces – Nova Scotia, New Brunswick and Prince Edward Island – a situation which lasted until the 1850s and which had initially raised Anglican expectations of government support. In Quebec, however, it was the Catholic Church that was established *de facto*. Bishop Mountain had been horrified to find that the British government, grateful to Quebec Catholics for their support in the 1812 war, had relaxed their efforts to control Catholicism, increased their grant to the Catholic bishop, Joseph-Octave Plessis, and, in 1817, given him a seat on the province's legislative council as an *ex officio* member. Plessis used the opportunity to press for political power for Catholics elsewhere and to organize and extend the work of the Catholic Church throughout Canada. In respect to its relationship with the British government, Anglicanism in Quebec was at a disadvantage to Catholicism. From Mountain's perspective, this seemed extraordinary in a British colony. Meanwhile the 1791 Canada Act had established a large grant of land known as the Clergy Reserves, which was intended to be 'for the support and maintenance of a Protestant clergy'. But Anglicans swiftly discovered that this did not just mean them. In addition to themselves, the money was distributed to Presbyterians, Catholics and to any Protestants who did not object on principle to taking government money.[57] This situation continued until the Reserves were secularized in 1854, and it illustrates how differently from the Americans the Canadians viewed the issue of government funding for religion.

It was not as if Anglicans in Canada were numerically insignificant, a further reason why they had hoped that more notice would be taken of them. From 1783 their numbers had been boosted considerably by the arrival of loyalists who were fleeing the 13 colonies after the American Revolution. It has been estimated that between one-third and one-fifth of the residents of the 13 colonies either remained loyal to Britain or harboured loyalist sentiments, and over 35,000 of them decided to escape from the United States and seek a new life in Britain's second American empire. Among those who were Anglican (which was by no means all) there was naturally variety in how much they knew about, and whether they preferred, the English or the American model of Church governance. Many Canadian Anglicans, however, began to see the episcopal system south of the border as malformed. They regarded its bishops as weak, its laity as overbearing and its theology as excessively flexible. They wanted a Church in British North America that was more authoritative, better ordered and more orthodox.

Anglicans in Canada kept a close eye on events in Britain and Ireland, either because they or their parents had come from there, or because they viewed Anglicanism in its British form as more closely approximating the ideal form of the Church than it did in its aberrant American manifestation.[58] They found their position of dependence on the British government and its colonial representatives increasingly frustrating and unsustainable; they wanted to submit to the church–state relationship, but found that their partner had limited interest and little to deliver. By the 1840s Canadian Anglicans were forced into greater independence; indeed, they became one of the earliest self-governing provinces of the Anglican Communion, providing a model for some of the others. In the second half of the nineteenth century, Canadian Anglicans began to lead the way in exploring the possibilities of cooperation with other Canadian Protestants, in the hope of producing a thoroughly Christianized Canadian nation. Together with the Presbyterians, Methodists and Congregationalists they moved towards the creation of a United Church, which ultimately they chose not to join, despite having pioneered the idea. The very bold vision was finally realized in 1925 with the creation of the United Church of Canada, a new denomination forged from a union of Methodists, Presbyterians and Congregationalists, together with a large number of federated congregations from the Canadian west. The path to the creation of the United Church had been trodden slowly and carefully over many decades. Once again, the Canadians had shown their preference for evolutionary rather than revolutionary change. By the end of the twentieth century, the United Church had become the largest Protestant body in Canada.

CHAPTER 5

Outcomes of World Mission

Catholic and Protestant responses to world mission

The nineteenth century was the great age of foreign missions programmes, as thousands of European and North American missionaries ventured forth into what were (for them) some of the remotest corners of the globe. In the twentieth century the emphasis shifted to the inculturation and indigeniza- tion of global Christianity, as foreign missionaries withdrew, were expelled or began to work in partnership with local Christians. As we shall see, there had been an early emphasis on developing a partnership approach to missions in the mid-nineteenth century, a model particularly favoured by Henry Venn, the secretary of the Church Missionary Society (CMS, founded 1799) and by Rufus Anderson, foreign secretary of the Ameri- can Board of Commissioners for Foreign Missions (ABCFM, founded 1810). Both men believed that the crucial activity was to plant the seed of a native church, pass responsibility for it quickly on to local leaders and then to withdraw from the scene, and this view was shared by almost all mission organizations at this period.[1] By the end of the century, however, the emphasis had shifted to one in which Europeans typically expected to move in and take control, a process which was sometimes linked with the European nations from which the missionaries came assuming politi- cal control of their newly acquired colonies. From the 1870s there was also far less inter-European Protestant missionary cooperation, as the combined Scandinavian, German, Swiss and British efforts, which had been a feature of the earlier period, began to be replaced by a more narrowly nationalist approach to missionary activity. The development of foreign missions had other consequences. It was during the nineteenth century that Christianity came into first-hand contact with all of the world's belief-systems and with most of its non-Christian cultures. Christians finally achieved the objec- tive which Jesus had set for his followers when he told them to 'go and make disciples of all nations' (Matt 28.19–20). This chapter considers some of the general issues that arose from the world missionary movement, and then looks in a little more detail at Africa, India, China, Australia, New Zealand and the Pacific Islands, all areas which received concerted attention from nineteenth-century missionaries.

Up until the beginnings of organized missionary activity by Protestants in the eighteenth century, it was the Jesuits who had done the most to promote the development of Christianity outside the Western world. Founded in 1540 with an explicit missionary imperative, the Jesuits proved spectacularly successful, both in attracting recruits (by 1600 there were 8,500 of them) and in fearlessly taking their faith to some of remotest corners of the world. Within a few years of the foundation of the order, Francis Xavier had taken it to India and Japan, and Manuel de Nóbrega had established it in Brazil. Other Roman Catholic orders were also active in mission in the early modern period; there were, for example, Dominicans and Franciscans in India, and Italian Capuchin friars in central West Africa (Congo). Sometimes these orders worked well together, but conflict, particularly with the Jesuits, was not uncommon. The Spanish and the Portuguese were the nations chiefly involved in attempting to extend the territorial advance of Christianity in the early modern world, an objective that was closely allied to their political ambitions. In the Spanish territories the task was seen as being to convey the faith to people who were given little choice but to receive it; Andrew Walls (among others) has argued that the brutality of the Spanish approach undermined its moral basis. On the other hand, the far more slender resources of the Portuguese, and the very extended nature of their interests – which stretched like a thread along the coasts of Africa, the Persian Gulf, across the Indian Ocean into South India and Sri Lanka, to Southeast Asia, offshore China and on to Japan, as well as Brazil – meant that they had to find a different way. To a far greater extent than the Spanish, the Portuguese missionaries had to adopt the methods of the modern missionary movement, with the emphasis on persuasion, demonstration and discussion of the merits of Christianity. At no time did Portugal have a standing army of more than 10,000 men, and so a policy of conversion by force was never a realistic objective.[2]

If, as Andrew Walls suggests, 'the missionary movement is a connecting terminal between Western Christianity and Christianity in the non-Western world',[3] in the nineteenth century it was to be the Protestant missionary societies that would have the greatest success in spreading Christianity in the non-Western world. Roman Catholic missionary activity had been at a low ebb after the suppression of the Jesuits in 1773, although they were re-established again in 1814. The Catholic Church was much weakened during the Napoleonic period, and had to re-group itself after the end of the Napoleonic Wars. It was thus a relatively late entrant into the nineteenth-century mission field. In 1820 it was estimated that there were only about 270 mission priests throughout the globe.[4] It was Pope Gregory XVI (1831–46) who saw it as an important task to promote missions, and during the course of his pontificate he created more than 70 new dioceses and vicariates, and appointed 195 missionary bishops.[5] When Catholicism did arrive (or return), large numbers of particularly Irish and French missionary priests and nuns threw themselves into the task of creating ambitious networks of churches and schools. These were intended to rival any being provided from Protestant sources and to establish Catholicism as the normative form of Christianity in those places that the Protestants had failed to reach. The newly resurgent Catholicism engendered a spirit of fierce competition with Protestantism, and from a Protestant perspective, Catholic missions increasingly became something to be feared. At the same time, British and American Protestants began to direct their attention towards attempting the conversion of Catholic Europe. In January 1850 the Evangelical Alliance's periodical *Evangelical Christendom* described missionary work that was taking place in France, Belgium, Switzerland, Bavaria, Schleswig, Austria and Hungary.[6]

The provision of schools, and in some cases medical facilities, was one of the most enduring features of nineteenth-century missionary activity. Throughout the non-Western world, the arrival of Christianity became associated, particularly in the minds of those who were on the receiving end, with education, books and writing, and gradually with an increase in material prosperity. The Protestant insistence upon receiving the Word made the acquisition of some level of literacy an absolute requirement, and often this went beyond simple Bible reading. Education was seen as imperative if an indigenous ministry was ever to develop, and facilities for ongoing learning were seen (at least in some quarters) as essential if missionaries were to remain effective. These principles were already established by the early eighteenth century, and it is significant that the first Anglican missionary society, the Society for the Propagation of the Gospel in Foreign Parts (SPG, founded 1701), worked very closely with the Society for Promoting Christian Knowledge (SPCK, founded 1689) and with the Royal Danish Mission (founded 1699) in order to ship out books and printing presses to remote parts of the world. In 1710 the SPCK sent a printing press to Tranquebar in India. En route the ship in which it was travelling was captured by a French privateer, and the SPCK had to contribute towards the ransom. Meanwhile the printer who had been dispatched with the press committed suicide off the Cape of Good Hope. But the press eventually reached its destination safely, and in 1714 the Gospels and the Acts of the Apostles were printed in Tamil.[7] In the nineteenth century, the ABCFM had mission presses in Izmir, Beirut and Urmia, where printing in a variety of local languages was undertaken, and the CMS had much of its printing done in Malta.[8] In stressing the importance of books and learning, some of the early missionaries had been influenced by the great German Pietist August Hermann Francke of Halle, who believed that proper belief was biblical belief, and that biblical belief without literacy was impossible, and therefore universal literacy and education were intrinsic to Jesus's Great Commission. Francke believed that every person should be able to read the Bible in his or her mother tongue, and also that they should be taught a useful skill, thereby making the provision of some form of technological education also necessary.[9] Meanwhile Thomas Bray, one of SPCK's founders, was a powerful advocate of missionary education. He believed that missionaries should be able to keep up their reading, even in the sometimes trying circumstances of the mission field. It was one of the particular features of the eighteenth-century missionary clergy who were sent out under the auspices of SPG that they were provided with a generous box of books, with further supplies being sent out on request at intervals. Fifty-two volumes were listed in 1702 for the equipping of clergy abroad, including biblical commentaries, the Fathers, Aquinas, George Herbert and Richard Hooker.[10] The SPCK continued with its mission of supplying theological books for the developing world for the next three centuries.

Throughout the non-Western world, many different sorts of Christian educational institutions were established in the period after 1800. In places where there was ambivalence towards the religion, the schools remained the missionaries' most important legacy. In India today, Christians are reckoned to possess some of the finest educational institutions in the country, with members of the ruling elites preferring to send their children to them.[11] Indeed, it has been argued recently that the greatest achievement of Church of England and Church of Scotland missionaries in India was in establishing institutions of higher learning for the Hindu elites of Calcutta, Madras, Bombay and other cities.[12] Roman Catholics have also been assiduous providers of schools and colleges, particularly since the middle of the nineteenth century. In Australia there was a large Catholic population of mainly Irish descent. In 1879 the bishops of New South Wales declared in a joint pastoral letter that the secular schools were 'seedplots of future immorality, infidelity and lawlessness'.[13] In response to this the Church set about creating a complete system of schooling for Catholic children under its sole control. By the end of the century, almost every Catholic parish in Australia had at least a primary school, with a convent next door for the teaching nuns.[14]

Colonialism and evangelicalism

If the initial impulse behind missionary activity in the nineteenth century was from Protestant evangelicalism, and only later in the century from Roman Catholicism, the major context for that activity was the growth of colonial power. Britain developed the largest colonial empire, which at its height incorporated one in four of all the people on earth. Other European powers were anxious to secure their own share, and by the late nineteenth century an immense part of the earth's surface was under European control. In Africa, the entire continent, with the exception of Ethiopia and Liberia, had by 1910 been divided between Britain, France, Belgium, Germany, Portugal, Italy and Spain.[15] France, in addition to its very significant holdings in West Africa, controlled Madagascar, Indo-China, a few Caribbean islands and French Guiana, which was located to the east of British Guiana and Dutch Guiana in South America. The Dutch controlled Sumatra, Java, Borneo and New Guinea. Germany, the only other European nation to have significant colonial interests outside Africa, controlled some smaller Pacific Island territories.

In a British context, it is sometimes assumed that the development of empire and the growth of missionary activity were inextricably linked. Certainly many British missionaries were clearly inspired by a sense of responsibility for people in parts of the world that were being newly brought under British rule. Some also had a sense of Britain as being God's chosen nation, with power over the 'subject peoples' conveyed to the British as a sacred trust. This was one British variant on the prevalent American idea of America being the chosen nation in a covenant relationship. It needs to be remembered, however, that worldwide the majority of missionaries were not necessarily predisposed to favour the development of the British Empire, or indeed of colonial power more generally. Writing about India, R.E. Frykenberg, who believes that Christian movements were most successful when least connected to empire, notes that:

> At no time were the majority of missionaries – from some sixty Catholic and some fifty non-Catholic missionary societies, whether British or not – predisposed in favour of colonialism. Indeed, pre-colonial, non-colonial and anti-colonial missionaries, taken together, outnumbered those British missionaries of the Anglican establishment who might have wanted to make India into another fiefdom of their own Christendom. The fact that so many Catholic missionaries were not British (being French, Italian, Irish and so on), and that so many non-Catholic (Evangelical or Protestant) missionaries were from North America or Northern Europe, was bound to make this so. Opposition to the Raj, moreover, tended to increase as voluntarism drew more and more recruits from lower and lower classes (or cultural levels) of

the Western world and as these recruits came from 'faith' societies beyond the control of mainline denominations, with their established systems of ecclesiastical control.[16]

It is important, then, to avoid falling into simplistic assumptions about missionaries as the agents of foreign powers, intent on pursing the imperialist agenda, or, worse still, arriving with 'the Bible in one hand and a gun in another'.[17] There was enormous variation, depending on the inclinations of the individuals, the policies of the particular mission agency, the local circumstance and the decade under discussion (there was much less interest in imperial expansion in the earlier period). Kevin Ward has argued that in the feverish atmosphere of the late nineteenth-century scramble for Africa, some missions did take an overtly political stance, urging the British government to defend national interests against other European predators, whilst others were highly critical of aspects of British imperial policy. Thus the CMS campaigned vigorously for the British government to take over Uganda, in the face of internal disorder and German expansionist desires. On the other hand, missionaries were outspoken against the use of forced labour in various East African British colonies.[18]

The incentive for most Protestant missionary endeavour, was, as Brian Stanley has persuasively argued, the evangelical revival, not the desire for colonial aggrandizement. Several British Methodists and Baptists began taking the evangelical Gospel overseas in the late eighteenth century. Thomas Coke, a close associate of John Wesley, produced a *Plan of the Society for the Establishment of Missions among the Heathen* in 1783, and he planted the first Methodist missionaries in the West Indies in 1787. By 1793 Methodist membership in the islands had grown to 6,570.[19] Meanwhile William Carey established in 1792 what was to become known as the Baptist Missionary Society, and he went to India. Carey's initiative was the first evangelical missionary society to be formed in Britain, and it was followed over the next couple of decades by several more, each representing a different denomination or denominational coalition. By the 1830s even the traditional high-church Anglican SPG had entirely reconceived its approach, adopting more of the methods, though not of course the theology, of the evangelical societies.[20] But, as has been said, in the first half of the nineteenth century most missionary enterprise was solidly Protestant evangelical, and much of it was German Lutheran or British in origin. American efforts were initially channelled through the ABCFM. It was founded by New England Congregationalists, although early on it elected Presbyterian representatives. Although officially devoid of creedal affirmations, it has been argued that ABCFM was very clearly the product of Congregationalism's 'New Divinity', which decisively moved away from hyper-Calvinism, with its view that the atonement was only designed to save God's elect, and towards the belief that Christ's atonement was unlimited, and 'sufficient for all'. As one proponent of this view put it, 'This great atonement is as sufficient for Asiatics and Africans, as for us … The mercy of God is an ocean absolutely exhaustless.'[21]

Missionary activity was motivated by a number of theological beliefs, of which the waning of hyper-Calvinism was a crucial one. Members of those denominations which had Calvinist roots (Presbyterians, Congregationalists and Baptists) began to think that it was within the scope of human agency to encourage other human beings to believe. Baptists like Andrew Fuller had argued on the basis of his reading of the American Calvinist Jonathan Edwards that divine sovereignty in the spread of the Gospel operated through the channel of human responsibility.[22] Equally the strongly Arminian ethos of the evangelical revival had undermined much of the strict Calvinist theology. Whatever their level of theological sophistication, Christians increasingly believed that everyone who had the chance to hear it could respond to the Gospel and be saved. For evangelicals, preaching the Gospel in non-Christian countries was a particular imperative, not only because they generally believed that without acceptance of the Gospel souls were eternally lost, but also because they believed that the existing lifestyles of the 'heathen' made them already guilty of the sin of idolatry. Idolatry was in breach of the second of the Ten Commandments (Exodus 20.4–5) and involved the creation and worship of 'graven', that is to say man-made, images. To the nineteenth-century Protestant mind, any religion that was not Protestantism, whether Roman Catholicism, Hinduism or African Traditional Religion, was likely to contain strongly idolatrous elements. It therefore seemed imperative that those who were labouring under such dangerous beliefs should be confronted with the error of their ways and given the opportunity to hear that the true religion involved the worship of Jesus Christ. Many evangelicals also believed that preaching the Gospel to all nations would usher in the last age in human history and hasten the return of Jesus Christ to earth. This view was expressed in the early reports of the ABCFM, which predicted the beginning of the millennial reign of Christ as the 'great pillars of the Papal and Mahommedan impostures are now tottering to their fall'.[23] Such notions could hardly be further removed from the idea that world mission was simply part of a larger attempt to promote national political and economic interests.

Africa

In 1800 well over 90 per cent of the world's Christians lived in Europe or North America. Today, 60 per cent live in Africa, Asia, Latin America or the Pacific, and the balance of power has shifted decisively to the southern hemisphere. By the end of the nineteenth century, there were 10 million Christians in Africa. The activities of the missionaries who had devoted themselves to that continent in that century were clearly important in bringing this about, but it is worth noting that most Africans were converted by other Africans, and that the first Christian church in tropical Africa in modern times was established by Africans in 1792. That year saw the arrival in Sierra Leone of some 1,100 people of African birth or descent from Nova Scotia, and they brought with them their own churches (Baptist, Methodist and the Countess of Huntingdon's Connexion) and preachers.[24] These people had supported Britain during the American Revolution. As a reward for their loyalty, they had been promised land in Nova Scotia, but the land had not materialized. In 1808, after the slave trade became illegal for the British, Sierra Leone became a British crown colony, and the landing place for intercepted slave cargoes from all over West Africa. These were people who had been bound for the United States, but who had never arrived there. It also became the dropping-off point for newly freed slaves who had been in places like London. From this melting pot of diverse and uprooted peoples emerged a significant Christian society, one in which both the Anglican CMS and the Methodist Wesleyan Missionary Society invested considerably, and one which has been described as 'a sort of stepchild of the Evangelical Revival'.[25] Once again, Christianity and education were seen to be intimately linked, with the establishment by CMS in 1827 of Fourah Bay College, which became West Africa's premier educational institution, affiliated to the University of Durham in 1876.[26] From an early date, African missionaries from the emerging Protestant, literate, English-speaking Krio community set about evangelizing extensively in West Africa. One of these, Samuel Ajayi Crowther, became the most famous Christian in nineteenth-century Africa, the first and for many years the only African to become an Anglican bishop.

The remarkable circumstances of Crowther's life are worth retelling, illustrating as they do the changing emphases within the missionary movement under colonial rule.[27] He was born in Oṣogun in Yorubaland, in what is now Western Nigeria, around 1807, and given the name of Ajayi. When he was 13, Oṣogun was raided by slave traders, who were still operating the by now illegal traffic in human beings. Ajayi changed hands six times before being sold to Portuguese traders for the transatlantic market. The Portuguese ship on which he was placed was intercepted by a British naval squadron in April 1822 and Ajayi was put ashore in Sierra Leone. Here he came into contact with the Church Missionary Society, and about three years later he was baptized by a missionary of the CMS, taking the name Samuel

Crowther, after a member of the CMS's home committee. He was given an English education and, as a promising pupil, was entered at Fourah Bay College. The clergyman who had baptized him was strongly committed to the study of African languages and had therefore encouraged Crowther to retain and develop his linguistic skills. Crowther was thus able to publish a number of grammatical works about the Yoruba language, which not only proved invaluable to European missionaries but also assisted the development of the written form of Yoruba. His skills were invaluable as speakers of many diverse tongues poured into Sierra Leone from confiscated slave ships. When the English Evangelical Thomas Fowell Buxton sponsored the Niger Expedition of 1841, which was designed (unsuccessfully) to destroy the slave trade by bringing Christianity and legitimate commerce to the Niger delta, Crowther was invited to take part.[28] He was sufficiently impressive to be deemed worthy of further training at the CMS College in Islington, leading to ordination by the bishop of London in 1843.

Crowther's ordination marked the beginning of the indigenous ministry in Sierra Leone. He engaged in further missions to the Yoruba and again up the Niger. He returned to London in 1851, and met Queen Victoria and Prince Albert. The British public were captivated by 'this grave, eloquent, well-informed black clergyman [who] was the most impressive tribute to the effect of the missionary movement that most British people had seen'.[29] The evangelical press took him to heart, and it is significant that in 1861 the popular weekly Sunday at Home chose as its lead story for several weeks 'The Gospel on the Banks of the Niger', told from the perspective of Crowther and his colleague, another black missionary, J.C. Taylor. What is interesting in this account is the highly respectful tone of the paper towards the black missionaries and the extent to which the racial background of converted and baptized Africans was at this point not regarded as an issue.[30] It was only the engravings which accompanied the articles, which depicted Crowther, Taylor and the others in European attire but with clearly dark skins, that would have reminded readers that they were not reading about the exploits of some British missionaries. In 1864 Henry Venn, the secretary of CMS, successfully campaigned for Crowther to be consecrated as a bishop. He was given the somewhat vague title of 'bishop of the countries of Western Africa beyond the limits of the Queen's dominions'. Special trains were run from London and elsewhere to bring people to Canterbury Cathedral for Crowther's consecration.[31]

Crowther's episcopal ministry became overtaken by a rising tide of more hostile forces as the imperial era gathered pace, with the so-called native pastorate controversy of 1871–74. He was not given authority over white clergy. His enormous and unresourced diocese was organized more as a mission than as a diocese.[32] When the behaviour of some of his colleagues was called into question, very youthful British missionaries who had just finished at Cambridge and who were influenced by the new Keswick holiness movement, swiftly moved in and sidelined the bishop, firing his staff and interpreting his genial methods with difficult personalities as a lack of leadership. When the embittered Crowther died in 1891 it was declared that 'the African race' lacked the capacity to rule, and a white man was appointed. European thinking about Africa had changed dramatically since the time of Venn and Buxton, and the Europeans now made it quite clear that they were in Africa to rule. The notion of a self-governing, indigenous Anglican Church was to be abandoned, and no other African bishop was to be appointed to an African diocese until 1951.

African reaction to the poor treatment of Crowther also marked a significant moment of growth for the African independent, or 'Ethiopian' churches. For the Ethiopian churches, who took their biblical root from Psalm 68.31: 'let Ethiopia hasten to stretch out its hands to God', 'Ethiopia' became a synonym for all of black Africa that was free of missionary control. Church members had often seceded from missionary churches, sometimes because of their antipathy towards the increasingly intense holiness and piety exhibited by many late nineteenth-century evangelical missionaries, who were becoming less and less tolerant of the African status quo. Ethiopian Christians emphasized the acceptability of polygamists in church membership, the rejection of European baptismal names, the use of African clothes and praying for chiefs instead of for the British monarch. The movement was particularly strong from 1860 until about 1915.[33]

In South Africa, the origins of Christianity were quite different as a result of the presence of Boer farmers. These were people of Dutch, German and Huguenot origins, who by 1800 were clearly identifying themselves as white Africans. Their religion, focused on the Dutch Reformed Church, was to become strongly influenced by Scottish evangelicalism as the nineteenth century progressed. There was also a stronger European missionary presence on the Cape at an earlier date than elsewhere in Africa. In some cases the Boer families and the missionary families intermixed within a generation of two. In such circumstances, Protestant communities developed, but with little sense of mission to the Africans in the immediate vicinity. Rather oddly, the evangelization of black Africans was seen as something which should take place further north, even as far afield as Nigeria. It was not until the end of the century that mission was also interpreted in terms of evangelizing the black South Africans among whom they lived.[34]

The first English-speaking missionaries, sponsored by the largely Congregational London Missionary Society, arrived on the Cape in 1799.

Being highly critical of the effects of Cape society on the indigenous South Africans, the imported slaves and the growing Cape coloured community, they sought to improve their dignity by advocating the establishment of separate and economically dependent communities, both at the Cape and in the hinterland. Afrikaners saw this as unwarranted missionary interference; some African rulers, on the other hand, perceived the potential which the missionaries seemed to offer for the consolidation and preservation of their own societies, and were more welcoming. Closer contact between the missionaries and the Africans placed relations under strain, as it became clear that missionaries disapproved of many aspects of African traditional society. Particularly after the discovery of rich deposits of gold and diamonds, the arrival of international capitalism brought a whole new raft of issues into play.[35] By the middle of the nineteenth century, education became a crucial commodity, with the Methodists, Presbyterians and Anglicans establishing high schools for the Xhosa people, which provided a high standard of Western education. Xhosa society began to divide between the 'traditionalists', who shunned such innovations, and the 'school people', who took advantage of what was being offered. By the end of the century, an impressive group of educated Christian Xhosa had emerged. It was from among this group that some of the first leaders of the African National Congress were to be appointed, in the early years of the twentieth century.[36]

Kevin Ward makes the point that whereas in West Africa and South Africa, Africans responded to the Christian faith from an early date and made it their own, in East Africa, the role of the missionary had a greater importance.[37] The image of the missionary as independent explorer, strategist and medical man was encapsulated in David Livingstone. A Scot, born in 1813 and employed at the age of ten in a cotton mill, he overcame adversity in order to study medicine in Glasgow, going first to the Cape of Good Hope under the auspices of the London Missionary Society (LMS, 1795).[38] He was entranced by Africa, where he was to spend the remainder of his life, 'discovering' various lakes, exploring the basin of the upper Nile and encouraging other more conventional missionaries to set up mission stations in his wake. His reports, like Crowther's, were eagerly received in London, and he was much feted when he made visits to Britain, particularly in 1857, when he made a speech which resulted in the setting up of the Universities' Mission to Central Africa (UMCA, 1857). Unlike Crowther, however, he remained such a celebrated national figure that (although he died thousands of miles from home) he was deemed worthy of burial in Westminster Abbey. Public interest in him had been so great that the *New York Herald* had sent its journalist, Henry Morton Stanley, in search of him in 1871, thus providing perhaps the most iconic meeting that took place between two men in the whole of the nineteenth century. After his death, his legacy was regularly reinvented, both by later advocates of missionary imperialism and by schoolbook historians.

East Africa was the part of the African continent in which Roman Catholic missionary activity met with the greatest success. A number of missionary orders were established, among them the White Fathers, a title which referred to the colour of their cassocks, not their skin, for from an early date they encouraged black recruits. The White Fathers were set up in 1868 by Charles Lavigerie, Archbishop of Algiers, who established them along Jesuit lines. There was a strong emphasis on the development of self-supporting principles and relevant linguistic skills for members, and on a lengthy catechumenate for new Christians.[39] Lavigerie founded the White Sisters in the following year. It was from among the White Fathers that emerged the first Catholic African bishop in modern times. He was Joseph Kiwanuka, who led the Church in Masaka (Uganda) from 1939, becoming Archbishop of Rubaga from 1961, until his death in 1966. The adoption of indigenous church leadership in Catholicism on a completely different timescale from that attempted by the Anglicans, with the seemingly premature appointment of Crowther, was significant. By the time Kiwanuka emerged, there was a very large indigenous clergy and Catholic infrastructure in the great lakes area of East Africa, and Kiwanuka's episcopate was judged an unqualified success.[40] But even in the 1960s, this White Father remained a rare black leader among the Western forms of African Christianity.

India

Largely for commercial reasons, India had long been the object of interest of the Western powers. Indeed, the Cape of Good Hope, on the southern tip of Africa, had developed largely as a stop-off point on the trade route to India. In addition to the indigenous 'Thomas' Christians who regarded Thomas the Apostle as having been their founder, Catholicism had been introduced from the end of the fifteenth century, and the Jesuits had had a very significant influence after 1622. Dutch, German, Danish and British Protestants were active throughout the eighteenth century and some were very successful at gaining converts. Most notable was the Moravian Pietist Christian Frederick Schwartz, who recruited a band of Indian disciples who spread Christianity over large swathes of Southern India, despite the strong opposition of the East India Company, which disapproved of missionaries unless they could make them politically useful. As a result of their efforts, the numbers of Tamil Christians doubled or tripled in each decade.[41]

Whilst all the forms of Christianity already present continued to be influential, the beginnings of nineteenth-century missionary activity may be traced to the arrival in Bengal of the Baptist William Carey in 1793. Carey had been partly inspired to come to India by reading about the exploits of the German Pietists. Like them he had to contend with the policies of the East India Company, which was in the process of extending British rule over much of the Indian sub-continent, and was behaving more like a department of the British state, albeit a somewhat detached one, than a commercial trading company. It was only after 1813, when, under strong evangelical pressure in London, the so-called 'Pious Clause' was inserted into the Company's charter renewal, that it became possible for missionaries to operate in British India under fewer restrictions, and under no restrictions after 1833.[42] Even then the East India Company remained a distinctly ambivalent force. Under pressure, it was prepared to go as far as was needed to satisfy evangelical outrage, but it refused to condone anything which might inflame Hindu opinion. Eventually the Company did respond to protests from both Hindu reformers and Christian missionaries by outlawing in 1829 the practice of throwing widows on to the funeral pyres of their husbands, but they were unmoved by Christian requests to tackle other abuses, such as temple prostitution and the forcing of Christian soldiers to pull temple cars in procession, occasions on which some would inevitably be crushed to death.[43] In the 1840s, Lord Tweeddale, the Governor of Madras, was censured and recalled by Company officials for using the term 'heathen' in official communications and for favouring missionary schools.[44]

The highly developed nature of Hindu religion tended to result in evangelicals regarding India as the chief stronghold of idolatry – more deleterious in this respect than Africa. It shocked evangelical sensibilities greatly to discover that the British government in India was actually making money out of 'idolatry' by levying a tax on pilgrims attending sacred sites. It was estimated that the East India Company had made a net profit of nearly £100,000 out of Hindu festivals in the 17 years up to 1831. Pilgrim tax was not discontinued until 1841, and annual government grants to numerous Hindu temples continued into the next decade. The widespread Christian belief that the East India Company had been unforgivably lax in failing to give adequate support to the development of Christianity in India, and that it had fatally compromised with 'idolaters', formed the background to Christian responses to the so-called Indian Mutiny of 1857–58.[45] The mutiny began as an uprising in the Bengal army against the attempt to enforce British-style military practices, and developed into a widespread revolt against British rule. It was interpreted by evangelicals as divine judgement upon the British, signalling as it did the end of the rule of the East India

Company, and its replacement with powers vested in a secretary of state for India.

In India the caste system created particular difficulties which Christianity did not experience in the same way elsewhere in the world. It produced a mindset in which it became seen as impossible for Christians of different birth to participate in religion together, which meant that different groups had to be catered for separately, thus producing a bewildering array of mutually isolated bodies with different needs and expectations. Western missionaries were often at a loss to know how to respond to the implications of the Indian caste system. Should they oppose it as inimical to the Gospel, or should they condone it as being intrinsic to the culture in which they were operating? Was it acceptable for them to devote their energies to preparing Hindus for lucrative careers or should they be identifying explicitly with the downtrodden? Even within the same denomination, missionary attitudes could be polarized. During the 1850s an SPG missionary in Thanjāvur insisted on having Christians publicly flogged for refusing to abandon caste rules. At the same moment, a CMS missionary was being criticized by his fellow missionaries for focusing his attention exclusively on the Brahmans, to the detriment of people lower down the social scale. Among the Roman Catholics, it appeared that French missionaries were more willing to respect existing caste and cultural norms, Irish missionaries opposed them and the Italians were more evenly divided.[46] In 1744 Pope Benedict XIV had decreed that Catholics of high and low birth alike should attend the same Mass, and meet in the same building at the same time. In South India the Jesuits had got around this by erecting little walls and opening different doors for those of high and low caste. Thanjāvur Christians arranged for segregated seating within the church. Missionaries who favoured such arrangements could argue that in America, black Christians often worshipped separately, and in Europe, servants sat at the back, or in galleries.[47] For many lower-caste Indians, Christianity, with its promise of equality, had a strongly attractive message. It was hardly surprising that mass conversions should occur among those who, being regarded as outcasts, had been ignored by India for centuries. But whilst conversions proved relatively easy to secure, it proved much more of a challenge to develop an indigenous ministry among such peoples.

China

In China, Syriac Christianity had existed between the seventh and the fourteenth centuries, and it was, once again, the Jesuits who were responsible for its modern introduction from 1582. In the seventeenth century they were joined by Franciscans, Dominicans and other Roman Catholic missionaries. Conflict between the various orders, together with Chinese imperial anger at the decision of Rome to assert papal authority in China, led to Christianity being banned. The ban officially lasted from 1724 to the 1890s, although greater tolerance towards Christianity was shown from the 1840s. There had been significant persecution of Catholics during the eighteenth century, with the numbers of Catholics in China dropping from 300,000 to 200,000 during the period, most of them concentrated in the provinces of Sichuaun, Jiangsu and Chihli (Hebei). Catholics tended to be persecuted, or to apostatize, when the authorities assumed them to be similar to groups like the White Lotus, a folk Buddhist sect that was seen as both heterodox and dangerous, with theological views that were superficially similar to Catholicism.[48] When Catholics were tolerated, it was because they were seen as passive and non-threatening. Whenever they drew attention to themselves, for example by holding conspicuous religious festivals, by fasting, or by adopting female religious leadership, trouble was likely to result.[49]

Eighteenth-century Chinese Catholicism was rooted within certain large families; it had no structures outside the domestic. The members of the influential Institute of Christian Virgins were women who affronted the conventions of Chinese society by their independence, leading prayers loudly, teaching and on occasion 'preaching like missionaries', but they had to rely on living in the homes of their parents and on the protection of male relatives when they attracted hostile attention. It was hard for the authorities to take action against a father who promised that he would make his wayward daughter marry. In the event, once the moment of official scrutiny had passed, she was likely to carry on just as before.[50] In the almost total absence of clergy, it was these women, together with a small army of male lay catechists, who prevented Catholicism in China from dying out.[51] When European missionaries arrived from the late 1840s they found the virgins' autonomy scandalous and sought to reduce their liturgical and religious role. The Jesuits attempted to 'regularize' them, and various groups of European nuns tried to phase them out by founding native Chinese congregations.[52] Nevertheless the virgins proved to be tenacious; in some places, for example Sichuan, their Institute was still in place when the People's Liberation Army arrived in 1950.[53]

In the nineteenth century, China became the missionary movement's major focus in East Asia. The first Protestant missionary to reach China was Robert Morrison, a Northumbrian who arrived at Canton in 1807 under the auspices of the LMS. Having improved his Chinese from the level that he had managed to attain in England, after two years he was employed as a translator by the East India Company (who operated in China as well as in

India). In his free time he translated the Bible and produced a six-volume dictionary, which remained the standard work for many years. Despite having to operate throughout his ministry under very severe restrictions, he also founded the Anglo-Chinese College at Malacca. Life only began to become easier for missionaries once the ban on Christianity of 1724 began to be lifted in the period from 1842. A succession of treaties permitted the propagation of the faith, missionary travel, the purchase of land and the erection of buildings. The French government declared a religious protectorate over Catholic missions, and the numbers of Catholic missionaries began to increase; almost 60 Jesuits arrived in the space of a few years. In 1890 there were over 700 Catholic missionaries and more than 1,300 Protestants in China.[54]

A particular feature of the missionary enterprise in China was its entanglement with the opium trade. The British had developed a taste for China tea, and in order to satisfy the demand the East India Company paid China for its tea first with cotton from Gujarat and then with opium from Bengal. In the early nineteenth century, missionaries who wanted to travel had little choice but to make use of the transport provided by opium traders and smugglers. The Prussian Lutheran independent Karl Gützlaff, who was the first non-British Protestant missionary to enter China, sailed the China coast on a variety of opium boats, distributing Chinese tracts and Scriptures whilst working as an interpreter for opium traders.[55] Whilst the recklessness of his activities has been especially criticized, it remains the case that all missionaries had to rely on the opium trade, if not for transport, then for donations from Western companies associated with it.[56] By the early 1830s the opium trade had become essential for financing the tea trade. Until 1834 the East India Company had a monopoly on opium, but this was broken by the pressure of British free-trading interests. This resulted in a massive increase in the amount of opium being poured into China, much to the alarm of the emperor who wanted to control all imports, and particularly that of hard drugs.[57] As a result of these conflicts the first Chinese Opium War broke out between Britain and China from 1839 to 1842, with a second flare-up between 1856 and 1860. These were unequal conflicts, as the Chinese came under fire from the gunboats of the East India Company, and they resulted in the Chinese capitulation spelled out by the Treaty of Nanking (1842). The treaty forced the emperor to pay compensation for the drugs that he had had destroyed, and gave Britain access to six crucial Chinese trading ports, including Hong Kong island, which was to remain a British colony until 1997. It also paved the way for a great increase in missionary activity, first at the treaty ports, and then gradually into inland China. European missionary activity in China was, then, founded on a somewhat dubious moral basis, something which undoubtedly troubled the evangelical conscience. Evangelicals set about trying to demonstrate that the sequence of events which had led to the opening up of China for Christian missions, and the development of the opium trade and the further military skirmishes which resulted, were all part of God's providential plan.[58]

The spread of Christianity in China in the second half of the nineteenth century was slow and difficult. Many missionaries spent years of preparation attempting to master difficult languages and dialects, only to fall sick or die or to become disillusioned and resign within a short period of arrival. Converts risked ostracism and being linked with 'foreign devils'. Christian prohibition of many of the staple elements in Chinese society led to the exclusion or persecution of many. Opium addicts, often converting in the hope of being able to overcome their addiction, tended to find the adoption of a new way of life a particular struggle.

Missionaries differed in their approaches to this most difficult of mission fields. Among the most influential were Karl Gützlaff, James Hudson Taylor and Timothy Richard. As a German Pietist heavily influenced by Moravianism, Gützlaff's objective was seeking evidence of conversion; a sense of sin, repentance and rebirth were fundamental, and he had little interest in creating denominational structures or setting up schools.[59] He became convinced that only the Chinese could convert the Chinese, founding the Chinese Union in 1844 in order to effect this purpose. He also advocated that where Europeans were involved, they should adopt Chinese styles of cooking and appearance. Gützlaff's approach was indeed the one that would be identified as the most effective in the long term, but in the mid-nineteenth century it was decades ahead of its time. The Chinese Union collapsed shortly after Gützlaff's death in 1851, and despite years of unremitting endeavour, he himself converted only a handful of people. The lack of tangible results led to great disappointment from among his European supporters, for it appeared that Gützlaff had somewhat over-egged the pudding of Chinese missions, with his promises of hundreds of converts and the wide-scale abandonment of idols.

As an independent missionary of very strong character, Gützlaff was a major influence on others, including the German and Swiss mission agencies. David Livingstone was inspired to missionary service after reading one of his pamphlets.[60] Meanwhile, Hudson Taylor, a Yorkshireman of Wesleyan origins, was influenced by the legacy of Gützlaff to found the non-denominational China Inland Mission in 1865. The CIM was distinctive in being a 'faith mission', meaning that it never appealed to the public for funds but waited for God to provide what was needed. It was a form of missionary activity that was seen as returning to the immediacy and spontaneity of total dependence on God, cutting out the bureaucracy of committees and formal fundraising, which were believed to stultify the work of the Holy Spirit. It was an approach that would become characteristic of much missionary activity in the final decades of the nineteenth century, and particularly of that which was influenced by the holiness movement. The theological rationale dovetailed neatly with the practical rationale that missions needed to become cheaper and more sustainable, and less focused on replicating hugely expensive Western-style 'plant' in the form of churches, missionary housing, printing presses, hospitals and schools.[61] Like Gützlaff, Hudson Taylor insisted that his missionaries adopt Chinese dress and hairstyles, and he believed that indigenous Church leadership was the goal towards which he should be working. Despite formidable difficulties, the missionaries of the CIM succeeded in making headway in all 12 of China's provinces. Growth was so rapid that by 1895 Taylor was directing almost half of the Protestant missionaries in China. By 1890 the CIM had become the second largest of all British missions.[62]

In the Chinese context, Timothy Richard represented a new type of missionary. A Baptist from deeply rural Carmarthenshire, he was a Welshman for whom English was a second language and Chinese a third. As a youth, he had been deeply affected by the revival movement of 1859–60. After farm work and school teaching, he entered the Baptist College in Haverfordwest for training, and arrived in China in 1870. He was critical of the conventional (and frequently unsuccessful) missionary methods that he found there, which involved daily preaching or the distribution of tracts or Scriptures – bombarding people with words and concepts that they found largely meaningless. Instead he favoured the Chinese method of the wall poster – a short, perhaps elliptical, utterance replaced the dense tract. People responded positively. Between 1876 and 1879 the largest famine then known in history hit the province of Shandong. As well as putting up wall posters, Timothy Richard devoted himself to getting food supplies into some of the stricken areas. In doing so he became the first modern missionary to engage directly in disaster relief. Andrew Walls makes the point that not since the days of the anti-slavery campaigns had the consciousness of so many been raised about the extent of human suffering. Timothy Richard showed that 'mission was not only about speaking, but about being and doing'.[63] Thereafter it became part of the normal expectation of a missionary that he or she would, if necessary, become involved in humanitarian relief. Richard's next strategy was to develop a greater understanding of science, so that people could understand, and if possible prevent, the factors that made famine likely. He believed that what was needed was the re-education of China's governing officials and intelligentsia, which would bring about a transformation of Chinese institutions. The ambition of his schemes led to his estrangement from the Baptist Missionary Society, and he became secretary of the Society for the Diffusion of Christian and General Knowledge, where he was to remain for 25 years. He embarked on a publishing programme that encompassed works that would be 'useful' on science, history, geography and the constitution, as well as Christian theology and practice. In all his publications, Richard was seeking to express his belief that the best philosophy for China to adopt would be the Christian one. It was the perfect fusion of educational and missionary ideals. His efforts earned him the status of an international statesman, credited with ideals that would ultimately be embodied in the League of Nations.

Both Timothy Richard and Hudson Taylor accepted the persecution of Christians as something usual, but whereas Richard saw it as neither inevitable nor desirable, Taylor actively embraced it as something that might further the Gospel. In developing a psychology of martyrdom, he was drawing on theological roots from the early Church. Taylor argued in 1886 that bearing persecution patiently allowed Christians to conquer by example. Were not victories won through persecution 'ten thousand times better than writing to the Consul, and getting him to appeal to the Viceroy?'[64] As an advocate of the faith mission principle, Taylor naturally disapproved of the political protection that had been given to missionaries under the Treaty of Nanking. He saw all such state interference as a hindrance to the Gospel.

The story of Christianity in nineteenth-century China ends with the Boxer uprising of 1899–1900. The Boxer uprising, so named because some of its supporters practised a form of martial arts that used moves similar to those of boxers, was a violent protest against foreign influences in China, in which Christians were natural targets. Taylor's missionaries, along with many other missionaries and converts, both Catholic and Protestant, experienced bitter persecution; the theories of Hudson Taylor were fully put to the test. The Catholics lost nearly 50 missionaries and perhaps 30,000 Chinese Christians. The Protestants lost far fewer converts, about 2,000, but a higher number of missionaries, 135 adults and 53 missionaries' children. Eight Western powers sought to protect their nationals by unleashing an equally violent onslaught against the Chinese and then imposing a humiliating settlement which required the Chinese to pay compensation to foreigners for loss of life and damage to property.[65] This produced a dilemma for the mission agencies. Would they accept government compensation and indicate to the Chinese that they were prepared to gain substantial financial benefit from Western military conquests? It was only Taylor's China Inland Mission, which had suffered more than any of the other agencies, with the loss of 79 of its missionaries and children, that refused to have anything to do with compensation, in order to emphasize their dependence on Christ only, not on the temporal power.

Australasia and Oceania

Australasia and Oceania, encompassing Australia, New Zealand and the Pacific Islands, were a success story from the point of view of nineteenth-century missions. Missionaries tended to find that the pre-existing belief-systems that they encountered were less tenaciously maintained once the Gospel began to be preached, and therefore they posed less of a challenge than Hinduism in India and Confucianism in China. The population was very much smaller, and concentrated in certain areas. Furthermore, most of the early colonial arrivals were English speaking, and ministry to them was balanced by attempts at converting Maoris, Aborigines and the peoples of the South Pacific Ocean.

In 1788 the British government founded a penal settlement for convicts in Sydney, New South Wales, which was intended to relieve the pressure on British gaols and to act as a deterrent – transportation being seen as worse than imprisonment in Britain, but more humane (not surprisingly!) than execution. Soon, the penal settlement overspilled to Norfolk Island and Van Diemen's Land (Tasmania). For the first 30 years, Anglicanism was the only officially sanctioned religion in the convict colonies. Its clergy were paid as government chaplains, and their emphasis was on the moral reformation of the inmates; indeed, their compulsory exposure to lengthy sermons and Prayer Book services may perhaps have been seen as part of the punishment.[66] Although one-third of the convicts transported to Australia were Irish, and 90 per cent of them were Catholics, no Catholic priests were permitted to minister to them until after the Napoleonic Wars, such was the fear that the clergy might incite them to sedition and rebellion. From the 1820s the Catholic Church began to adjust to its new position as a legally free religious minority in a predominantly Protestant society. It continued to be a Church heavily dominated by the Irish. Convict trans-portation to New South Wales ceased in 1840, and to Van Diemen's Land in 1853. This began to make migration to the Australian colonies a very much more attractive proposition for British and Irish emigrants. Further British colonies began to develop in south and western Australia, and as they did so, the construction of churches (together with banks, railways and a regu-lar postal service) were seen as the essential prerequisites of civilized life. By the late 1840s, the number of regular churchgoers in Sydney had risen to one in five. The Christianization of Australia from its inauspicious convict beginnings was an extraordinary achievement. Indeed, Stuart Piggin and

Allan Davidson suggest that 'the transformation of a convict society into a nation of the healthy and law-abiding may be understood as one of Christianity's major achievements in the nineteenth century. Australians may have had difficulty in resisting materialism and secularism, but there was no doubt in anybody's mind that, in the nineteenth century, Australia was a Christian country.'[67]

In 1814 the first group of CMS missionaries had sailed from Sydney to New Zealand. In this part of the world, the most famous CMS missionary was George Augustus Selwyn, who was almost the Anglican answer to David Livingstone. Selwyn, who was famed both for his intellectual prowess and for his physical strength, was missionary bishop of New Zealand from 1841 to 1867, whereupon he returned to England to become bishop of Lichfield. Selwyn was one of the earliest and most decisive world leaders of the newly emerging Anglican Communion. He pioneered the idea of synodical government, which meant that each province of the Anglican Communion made its own decisions on key issues, rather than turning for decisive rulings to the Archbishop of Canterbury. Selwyn is supposed to have preached in the Maori language on his first Sunday in New Zealand, and the CMS missionaries were extremely optimistic about the potential of the Maori people to receive Christianity. Their optimism was justified, for by about 1850 three-quarters of them were attending Christian worship, reading the Bible in their own language, and an indigenous Maori-Christian leadership was developing. More than anywhere else in the Pacific, New Zealand had to contend with the developing indigenous Church, as well as the impact of European migration. Selwyn had to give Anglican episcopal oversight both to the Maori and to the colonial Churches. As the settlers became more dominant, hopes for an indigenous Maori Church began to be eclipsed.[68]

The missionaries were much less optimistic about the Aboriginal people of Australia, who were being dispossessed from their lands and ravaged by European diseases to which they had little immunity. After various assimilationist approaches were seen to have failed, the government moved towards a policy of protection and segregation, as the Aborigines were removed from their nomadic lifestyle and encouraged to settle in agricultural communities. Some of these were set up as Christian missions, with an emphasis on conversion, the English language and farming. These missions were not conspicuously successful, and an indigenous Aboriginal Church did not emerge until the middle of the twentieth century.[69]

The Pacific Islands produced particular challenges and particular successes. The LMS sent missionaries to Tahiti in 1797, a bold move as the Society had been in existence for just two years, and Tahiti had only been 'discovered' in the late 1760s. At first the mission did not flourish, but a critical moment came in 1815 when the principal chief changed his allegiance from the god Oro. After this, it being the custom for the people to follow their ruler, hundreds of Tahitians sought baptism, began to observe Sunday as a holy day and formed themselves into congregations. The Church which evolved was one in which pastors were men of high social standing, and other men of rank were given prominent positions in the local congregation. In a region of hundreds of remote islands, the Protestant missions did not normally compete with each other, but adopted the 'comity' principle – deciding by mutual agreement which agency would work in each island group. The LMS had an early monopoly on eastern Polynesia, extending westwards to the Cook Islands and Samoa. As we have seen, the CMS introduced Christianity to New Zealand, but New Zealand was too large to be left to any single denomination, and the Methodists arrived shortly afterwards. The Methodists had Tonga and Fiji, but departed from the comity principle in also working in Samoa. The ABCFM founded a mission in Hawaii, and extended out to the Gilbert Islands (now Kiribati). In Polynesian societies, the spread of Christianity was often very rapid. It was very much slower in the Melanesian islands of the south west Pacific, where there were many more languages, tropical diseases and geographical challenges. In 1848 Presbyterians from Nova Scotia and Scotland sent missionaries to the New Hebrides (now Vanuatu) and in the following year, Bishop Selwyn launched the Melanesian mission, an ambitious but unworkable scheme to claim the remainder of the south west Pacific for the Church of England.[70] In 1861, J.C. Patteson was consecrated missionary bishop of Melanesia and was subsequently martyred, as were a number of other missionaries of various denominations.

One factor in the successful spread of Christianity in the Pacific Islands was the extent to which the efforts of European and American missionaries were enhanced by the efforts of Pacific Islanders themselves. From the 1820s hundreds of men and women volunteered to leave their own islands in order to evangelize elsewhere. Tahitians went to the Cook Islands, Hawaii, Fiji and Samoa; Cook Islanders and Samoans worked in New Caledonia and the New Hebrides; Tongans evangelized Fiji. The advantages these indigenous missionaries had were legion, particularly in their ability to participate fully in island life and to explain the new religion in a familiar idiom.

Roman Catholic missions were also active in the Pacific Islands. Two French religious orders undertook work in the Pacific, the Congregation of the Sacred Hearts of Jesus and Mary (Picpus Fathers) and the Society of Mary (Marists), of whom the latter became the most widespread religious order in the South Pacific and New Zealand. The English and the Irish did not arrive until later. The Marists began on the remote islands of Wallis and Fortuna, west of Samoa, in 1837, and from there extended to places where the Protestant 'heresy' had already embedded itself, arriving in New Zealand in 1838 and Tonga in 1842. In 1843 they began a mission to New Caledonia, which was later annexed by the French and became a colony. By the end of the period most of the Pacific Islands with the exception of Methodist Tonga had been absorbed into the colonial empires of Britain, France and Germany. British missionaries were reluctant imperialists, however. They usually wanted to support the local government, and it was only after it became known that French warships had assisted Catholic missionaries in Tahiti that they began to turn to the British forces for similar protection and aid. Competition between French Catholics and British Protestants was inevitably intense. David Hilliard suggests that although Catholicism had less impact than Protestantism, the worship, feast days and devotional practices of nineteenth-century French Catholicism coalesced more readily with South Pacific traditional religion. The alternative which it offered to Protestant Christianity provided a way for the islanders to express long-standing rivalries and feuds between neighbouring chiefs and villages.[71] It was not an attractive proposition to adopt the new religion which your sworn enemy had just adopted. But adopting it in another form which your sworn enemy was known to revile could prove quite satisfying. Even when translated to the South Pacific, the enmity between Protestantism and Catholicism had its uses.

The World Missionary Conference

In 1910 the World Missionary Conference was held in Edinburgh. Its aim was to bring together the whole of the Christian world, with the exception of the Roman Catholic and the Greek Orthodox, who were still seen as representing a deviant form of the religion. In doing so, the Conference is commonly said to have been the first event of the ecumenical movement, which was to be the most significant feature of Christianity in the twentieth century. It is also said to have been the starting point of (Protestant) mission theology. But although it sowed the seeds for these important twentieth-century developments, the Edinburgh Conference was very much a nineteenth-century event, marked by the preconceptions and priorities of that century. What it brought together were 500 Britons and 500 North Americans, 170 from continental Europe and 26 from the white populations of Australia, New Zealand and South Africa. These delegations were a fair reflection of the proportional size of the national groupings who engaged in Christian mission, although the descendants of continental Pietism seemed rather sparsely represented in view of the major contribution that their forefathers had made at the beginning of the nineteenth century.

Those on the receiving end of missions were much more sparsely repre-sented. The invitations were all sent to Asia, inviting representatives from China, India, Japan, Korea, Burma and Ceylon (Sri Lanka). These Asians were seen as the representatives of 'the infant churches', belonging to eccle-siastical bodies which were simply extensions of the missionary movement.[72] No Africans were invited, a fact which can be interpreted at best as reveal-ing the extent to which the Anglo-American-led missionary movement had completely failed to grasp the significance of the spread of Christianity in Africa, and at worst as undisguised racism. The Conference organizers divided the world into 'missionized' and 'not yet fully missionized' areas. In the former category it placed Europe, North America, Australia and New Zealand. The rest of the world, with the small exception of South Africa, was deemed to be in need of further attention from Western missionaries. They set themselves the target of 'the evangelization of the world in this generation', and they were of course ignorant about the extent to which 'this generation' was on the brink of widespread destruction as a result of the First World War. Much of the world had been evangelized in the previous two generations. The Edinburgh Missionary Conference was in fact the high watermark of world mission.

PART II
THEMES

CHAPTER 6

Revival and Renewal

Evangelical revivalism in America

In October 1834 Rachel Stearns, a 22-year-old Congregationalist from Greenfield, Massachusetts, attended a Methodist camp meeting. At first she felt uncomfortable about the activities taking place around her. Soon, however, she 'became interested in the plain & simple truths of the Gospel, there preached in such a fervent and earnest strain as I never before heard'. By the end of the meeting, Rachel Stearns had experienced what would turn out to be a life-changing conversion. She confided in her diary, 'every thing is changed. I am to live in a new world. I almost doubt my identity sometimes. Indeed, I am not the same, I have been born again.'[1] The following year, Rachel took the momentous decision to forsake her family's Congregationalist place of worship for the very different environment of the Methodist meeting house. The meeting house was attended by those whom she regarded as her social inferiors, but she enjoyed the much freer worship and being able to participate by leading prayers. Rachel, who in the outside world regarded herself as timid and self-controlled, particularly relished the opportunity which Methodist worship gave her for shouting. Theologically she believed that the Methodist emphasis on the universality of the atonement made Methodists much happier than those known to her of other denominations, particularly the Congregationalists and Unitarians. Her decision to become a Methodist resulted in her being shunned by some family members and many friends, and ultimately in her leaving her home town in order to 'follow Christ' by taking up a position as a school teacher in the completely alien environment of Mississippi. The key elements in the experience of Rachel Stearns – religious crisis, conversion and a new focus on a more spiritual way of living – were to be replicated in different ways by hundreds of thousands of men and women all over the Protestant world. Many more would be slightly warmed by the fires of revival, which burned long and brightly throughout the English-speaking world, but in less powerful or enduring ways than Rachel Stearns.

This chapter explores the themes of revival and renewal within the Churches and for individual Christians. It was, of course, a very varied process, manifesting itself in markedly different ways according to the theological and cultural sensibilities of the individuals and groups involved, but it was a feature of the nineteenth century that the majority of Christian denominations emphasized the importance of revival as either a personal or corporate necessity, and sometimes as both. The term 'revival' is sometimes seen as belonging firmly within the vocabulary of Protestant evangelicalism, although, as we shall see, the language was used by contemporaries to describe the renewing of both Catholicism and the 'high' wing of the Church of England. For Protestant evangelicals, revival meant a usually relatively short and intense period of religious enthusiasm, in which the focus was on individual response and personal commitment. It is a different meaning from the protracted and more general period of 'evangelical revival' that began in the 1730s. For Presbyterians it meant a focus on spiritual events surrounding the infrequent communion season, and we have seen how this continued for Scottish Presbyterians who moved to Canada. For Anglicans it meant the longer-term renewal of the theological and sometimes also the liturgical and ecclesiological life of the institution, and it was sometimes linked with specific missionary attempts to capture the support of the urban working class. For European Catholics the emphasis was on renewing the faith of the parish and also on deepening the commitment of those who, shaken and often dislocated, were at risk of becoming alienated from their religious roots. For American Catholics, the context was far more similar to that of evangelicalism; it entailed an intense period of religious teaching aimed at building up a New World Catholic identity more or less from scratch, and in the expectation that those affected might have only very limited contact with a priest thereafter. In whatever denominational context it took place, the renewing process demanded large amounts of time and energy. It required leaders with a message which convinced and compelled, and it required congregations who were capable of being moved by the message, and of taking some action on it in the aftermath. Wherever it occurred, it provides a useful window through which to observe nineteenth-century Christianity's inner dynamics, as well as some of the pressure points and fault-lines which occurred between Christians of similar theological outlook in different parts of the world. It also serves to demonstrate the international character and rapidly transmittable nature of both evangelical Protestantism and Roman Catholicism, as individuals and groups became influenced by ideas and people from other parts of the globe.

The USA provides the largest Protestant revivalist case study. By the beginning of the nineteenth century, the Great Awakening was beginning its second phase.[2] After the extraordinary success of the first Great Awakening, the unsettlement of the revolutionary era had witnessed a period of religious decline, with well under 10 per cent of the population belonging formally to local congregations.[3] The second Great Awakening signalled the rekindling of interest in Christianity, and its spread into parts of the nation which had hitherto been little touched by it. It differed from the earlier revival in being more explicitly Arminian in theology, with a more optimistic view of the human potential to respond to God's offer of salvation. The leaders of the first Awakening, George Whitefield and Jonathan Edwards, had, as Calvinists, emphasized the inability of sinful people to save themselves. Many of the revivalists prominent in the second Great Awakening were either Methodists and therefore explicitly committed to the Arminian doctrine that all could be saved, or Baptists for whom the traditional Calvinist heritage was being smoothed away, as it came to be believed that the atonement was 'sufficient' for all. The second Great Awakening also prompted the beginnings of a more organized and systematized approach to American religion. In the early years of the nineteenth century, societies were founded to promote foreign missions, Bible and tract distribution, education and temperance, and support for liberated slaves. These developments provided the American Churches with the beginnings of a national infrastructure.

Early American revivalism had taken a different form from its European cousins, continental Pietism and British evangelicalism. Rather than being culturally and theologically subversive, as had often been the case in Europe, in America revivals became, as Mark Noll has argued, the standard American way of drawing a crowd and then building up the churches. Early American revivals had been essentially spontaneous and self-generating. They did not require elaborate planning. All that was needed was a vigorous, dedicated and persuasive revivalist, who was not usually a full-time minister.[4] But not all revivalists were frontier farmer-preachers, important though such people were. By the early decades of the nineteenth century, a few had become figures of national, and in the case of Charles Finney, international importance. As this happened, the revivalist became part of the national establishment, in a way which did not occur outside America. Indeed, Finney, who had refused formal theological training, gave up full-time revivalism in order to become a theological professor at Oberlin College, Ohio. It was a remarkable manoeuvre, and it would have been unthinkable for a British revivalist to have been credited with sufficient respectability to have been given a similar position in a British higher education institution. In keeping with his belief that revival was something which could be manufactured (because God had commanded repentance) rather than being a mysterious gift (which God might – or might not – bestow), Finney pioneered a much more orchestrated approach, known as 'new measure' revivalism. He believed in careful planning and in holding nightly gatherings over several weeks. The climax was the invitation to those wishing to respond to come forward to an 'anxious bench'. The practice of the anxious bench was controversial and died out in America after the Civil War because it was seen as putting undue psychological pressure on the emotionally vulnerable. Other American evangelists preferred the adoption of the 'altar call'. This retained the invitation to potential converts to identify themselves by coming to the front, but was designed to protect them from the interference of over-excited members of the congregation, and permit the possibility of individual pastoral counselling.[5]

Wherever it occurred, evangelical revivalism exhibited a pattern that was characterized by a repeated cycle of expansion and decline. When the underlying conditions were favourable, a wave of conversions could sweep through a community like a forest fire. 'Fire' imagery was very frequently used – a reference to the 'tongues of fire' which rested on the participants at the day of Pentecost (Acts 2.3). Indeed, the region in New York State where revivals happened with particular frequency and intensity was known as the 'burnt-over district'. As the conversions multiplied, emotional intensity heightened until it reached a pitch which was unsustainable. Eventually religious interest would collapse and the revival would burn itself out. New converts would be hard to find, recent converts would prove uncommitted and existing converts would have their energies dissipated by other activities. Life in the community would return to the normality of the pre-revival state. Church attendances would fall, although only exceptionally to a figure significantly below the pre-revival figure. Then gradually the sense of religious exhaustion would be replaced by a new sense of expectation, and the cycle would begin again. Thus although intense revivalist activity occurred in relatively short bursts, the overall tendency was a steady increase in church attendances.

Using detailed analyses of Methodist growth patterns, Richard Carwardine identified the periods which witnessed the most dramatic peaks and troughs, which occurred more or less simultaneously in both America and Britain. The years of growth were 1799–1813, 1819–34 (with a slight lull in 1825), 1838–44 and 1857–58. The years of decline were 1793–96, 1813–16, 1834–37, 1844–47 and 1860–65.[6] It has been suggested that poverty, epidemics, industrial disasters and, in America, environmental factors such as earthquakes had a role to play in shaping these cycles. Interest in religion was always most intense during periods of economic depression or disaster, particularly if the disaster was likely to result in sudden death. When the economy picked up or the epidemic ended, people's interest in spiritual matters became less urgent, although it was not usually totally obscured. Other factors might bring a revival to an end, such as the need for a community to re-engage with the activities which contributed to its livelihood, such as planting or harvesting or fishing. For these practical reasons, revival was often seen as a winter rather than a summer activity.

Revivalism and overseas mission

Revival coincided with the growth of overseas missionary activity among British and American Protestants, which, as we saw in the previous chapter, developed rapidly from the 1790s. For evangelicals, there was an obvious link between revival at home and missionary activity abroad. From an early date, even quite remote and impoverished Christian communities in Britain and America proved capable of nurturing and sending out 'their missionary' under the auspices of organizations like the Wesleyan Missionary Society. A link was then established with a previously little-known part of the world, and reports of the missionary's evangelistic successes were eagerly awaited. It was reasoned that if 'the heathen' could be brought successfully to conversion, then how much more should be expected in the Protestant nation at home? Such feelings of longing and anticipation, combined with a very positive outlook about humanity's potential to embrace Christianity which was enshrined particularly in the Methodist denominations, seem to have been partly self-fulfilling. People began to believe that if there was enough effort on the part of the Christian nations, the whole world would turn Christian within a few decades. These ideas also began to be linked to the belief that the Gospel had to be preached to all nations in preparation for the imminent return of Christ. Mission and revival were therefore given an eschatological significance; they were needed for the beginning of the end of time.

As a result of the missions, Christianity with an evangelical hue spread to other parts of the English-speaking world, such as Australia, New Zealand and Canada, but not always with the emphasis on revivalism which was such a notable feature of the British–American experience. In Australia, Methodism undoubtedly did grow as a result of revivalist activity in the Sydney district in the 1840s,[7] but more generally, Stuart Piggin has argued that because Australian evangelicalism was so solidly Anglican, it tended to be put off revivalism. Anglican Evangelicals were more interested in promoting individualistic morality than religious experience; it was a feature which may reflect the early origins of Christianity in Australia, where it was initially part of the mechanism for enforcing law and order in the penal colonies. Piggin suggests that revivalism made no large impact on Australia until the American evangelist Billy Graham visited in 1959.[8] A broadly similar trend seems to be discernible in Canada, where, as we have seen, revivalism was regarded as dubious both because of earlier New Light excesses and because of the desire to distance the nation from the influences of the United States. Much evangelicalism was Scottish Presbyterian in origin, where the focus was on the different style of revivalism associated with the communion season. Meanwhile, Methodism was more influenced by British than by American models, and had a tendency to emphasize discipline and decorum.[9] In New Zealand, the Evangelical missionaries sponsored by the Church Missionary Society were anxious to promote religious experience, but they frequently failed to do so. On the face of it, they were successful at winning new converts, and by 1845 nearly two-thirds of the population were attached to the Anglican, Methodist or Roman Catholic missions, and there was a copy of the New Testament in Maori circulating for every two of the population. The Evangelicals were, however, disappointed by the formalism of conversions among the Maori; they themselves had known the full emotional intensity of evangelical conversion, and they were saddened by the seeming inability of their converts to have 'real' Christian experiences.[10] The Maori, it seemed, were often more interested in the commercial, trading and educational possibilities which Christianity opened up for them.

The Swiss *reveil*

Within Europe, there was significant mutual influence and interchange between early nineteenth-century Swiss and British evangelicals. This was a result of the Swiss *reveil*, a movement which began among Genevan theological students in the second decade of the nineteenth century and which spread quickly to the Swiss Cantons of Vaud and Berne, and within a few decades to some other French-speaking areas. The *reveil* was a movement that had its roots deep within Moravian Pietism, and it cannot therefore be attributed entirely to the interventions of the various British evangelicals who travelled in Switzerland in the immediate post-Napoleonic period. In Geneva it was, however, given a more biblical basis as a result of the Scottish Evangelical Robert Haldane, who visited from 1816 to 1817. Haldane, much to the annoyance of the Genevan professors, gave an informal series of lectures to the theological students, and was described by one admirer as 'a living concordance'. The depth of his biblical knowledge, ability to apply it to the lives of his hearers, and the clarity of his answers to the students' questions were seen as remarkable. Shortly after Haldane's departure, another zealous British evangelical, the newly converted banker Henry Drummond, arrived in Geneva. Drummond would later throw in his lot with the strongly pre-millenialist Catholic Apostolic Church (the Irvingites), for whom he became the second Apostle.[11] As a member of the Catholic Apostolic Church, Drummond retained his links with the *reveil*, as he was given responsibility for French Switzerland and France.

The Swiss *dissidents*, some but not all of whom eventually seceded from the state Church, attracted extreme hostility from the Genevan Church authorities. This was not least because they were seen as undermining traditional Calvinism on its home turf. Timothy Stunt has traced the complex network of relationships between the Swiss evangelicals of the *reveil* and their British counterparts, many of whom, like Drummond, were on the radical wing of evangelicalism at the point where it shaded into enthusiastic millennialism. Whereas the Swiss students had admired the way in which their British visitors had managed to combine biblical learning with vital religion, the nineteenth-century cult of the celebrity preacher meant that the British evangelicals welcomed the Swiss visitors very warmly, even when they struggled to preach in English. Stunt identifies the shared influence of the Romantic movement as one important factor that shaped the thought and behaviour of both Swiss and British radical evangelicals, and gave them a sense of common purpose.[12]

Transatlantic developments

There was also a particularly close cross-fertilization between revivalist preachers (and their publications) from the British Isles and the United States.[13] In the earlier part of the Great Awakening, many of the revivalists who operated in America had come from Britain or Ireland, which was hardly surprising in view of the fact that Methodism, the biggest revivalist denomination in America, was really a British import. In the 1800s some 9.4 per cent of the men entering the itinerant ministry of the American Methodist Episcopal Church were British born, and the figure was still 10.3 per cent in the 1850s.[14] In what was to be the earliest example of American popular culture having a major impact on that of the British Isles, American revivalist techniques and theology – and holiness teaching in particular – proved to be hugely influential, with publications, and also personal visits, proving decisive in shaping the path of popular Protestantism in Britain and Ireland.

The American Methodist Lorenzo Dow first visited Ireland in 1800, convinced that he would be God's instrument in the overthrow of Catholicism. Instead he found himself attracting hostility not just from Catholics and local magistrates but from the Methodists themselves, who were worried that the hostility Dow stirred up might be transferred to their officially sponsored Wesleyan outdoor itinerants. Dow's second visit, to England and Ireland between 1805 and 1807, attracted similar hostility. Despite this, and his eccentricities in manner and appearance, his importance turned out to be considerable. First, he succeeded in increasing cohesion between a number of disparate and fragmented revivalist groups, particularly in Lancashire and Cheshire. Secondly, he encouraged Hugh Bourne, who was one of the earliest leaders of Primitive Methodism, to experiment with the American method of the camp meeting, and to hold such an event at Mow Cop in Staffordshire in 1807. The Mow Cop Meeting, attracting as it did between 2,000 and 4,000 participants, proved decisive in giving momentum to what would become the largest of the Methodist breakaway denominations, although it differed from the American model in being a one-day event rather than a true 'camping' experience lasting for several.[15] By the time of Dow's third and final visit to Britain, in 1818 and 1819, Primitive Methodism was sufficiently well rooted to be able to offer him its pulpits for his indoor meetings. In turn, in the late 1820s, the Primitives sent some of their own missionaries to America.[16]

James Caughey was a northern Irishman whose family had emigrated to America when he was a child, and so he was perceived as an American when he returned to the British Isles. He was converted in a Methodist revival in 1830 at Troy, New York State, in the 'burnt-over district', and was ordained as a Methodist elder in 1836. After receiving a 'special message', he decided to journey to Canada and Britain, after which he achieved his first evangelistic success in Dublin. Back in Britain, Caughey became a specialist in urban evangelism, taking revival indoors and leading big campaigns in Liverpool, Birmingham and the Yorkshire towns, as well as shorter events in various other northern centres. After nearly six gruelling years of preaching revival on a nightly basis, Caughey could claim to have been instrumental in over 20,000 conversions and to have brought 9,000 people to experience 'entire sanctification'. Caughey argued that it was not enough for a convert to be justified by faith. What was needed was entire sanctification, which he also termed 'purification', 'holiness of heart' or 'perfect love'. The argument, which was shared by Finney, was that because sin was voluntary and therefore avoidable, entire sanctification was a human possibility. Someone who felt themselves to be justified but not purified was, according to Caughey, only half a believer; this was disconcerting for those who were thus defined.

Caughey argued that the marks of sanctification were a greater mental equilibrium and a triumphant acceptance of death. Essentially this was orthodox Wesleyanism, but the fearsome manner in which Caughey advocated the doctrine clearly had the effect of unsettling some of his hearers, making them strive ever harder for this second stage of Christian experience. It was also significantly different from what Wesley had taught, which had been that the religious life was like a moving vortex, which should be fuelled by Scripture and divine love, and shaped by experience, reason and tradition, and should be moving the individual dynamically towards holiness and Christian perfection.[17] For Wesley, this state of total death to sin had to be striven for, and a believer should only expect to experience it after a long quest. Furthermore it was a state which, once gained could be lost through wrongdoing, although Wesley taught that it could be regained if the process was entered upon again. Wesley's holiness teaching remained official Methodist doctrine until the middle of the nineteenth century. What Caughey was teaching was something quite different, a quick fix which could be rapidly offered to the thousands that he encountered as he travelled round the British Isles and North America. According to Caughey, entire sanctification could be obtained through a deliberate act of will and without the need for a long search. It was a much more shallow version of the holiness experience which Wesley had advocated, but it allowed thousands to claim that they had experienced the full salvation of entire sanctification.[18] Untainted by the political radicalism and republican sentiments that had marked Lorenzo Dow, Caughey was, initially at least, regarded as far more acceptable by the hierarchy of British Wesleyanism. His sermons explored the popular mid-nineteenth century themes of the urgency of repentance, the stern severity of God's law, the often unexpected timing of death, and the terrors of eternal damnation that awaited those who had failed to choose Christ. The tone agitated hearers into a frenzy of unsettlement, driving them forward to the front of the building in ever greater numbers. Caughey did not elaborate on the theme of God's love, which would figure much more prominently a decade later in the sermons of the most famous of nineteenth-century evangelists, Dwight L. Moody.

Eventually the feeling of unsettlement about Caughey's freelance evangelism extended to the governing body of Wesleyan Methodism, and in 1846 the Conference asked that the American bishops should recall him, on the grounds that he had been in their country for several years, acting without any of the ecclesiastical supervision or responsibility that was normally required of Methodist ministers. Caughey assented and went home with reluctance, but without formal protest. His notions of how a Methodist minister should behave had been formed in the much freer atmosphere of American revivalism, and they were not well suited to the more restrained and disciplined environment of British Wesleyanism.[19] Whereas in America revivalism might be the standard way of building up the Church, the experience of both Dow and Caughey had shown that in Britain it tended to lead to conflict with, or even schism from, existing Church authorities.

Charles Finney's *Lectures on Revivals of Religion* (available in Britain from 1837 and translated into Welsh shortly thereafter) developed its author's belief that revival could be manufactured through human instrumentality, and gave detailed practical advice on how to achieve a revival. The book was credited with promoting powerful revivals in different parts of Wales between 1839 and 1843. In 1849 the man himself arrived; it was the first time that an already well-established transatlantic revivalist had appeared in Britain with the explicit intention of conducting large-scale evangelism. During the course of the next two years, Finney employed his distinctive 'new measures' in Huntingdon, Birmingham, Worcester and London, mainly at the invitation of Baptists and Congregationalists. Although generally welcoming of Finney's efforts, these denominations of the 'old Dissent' were less attuned to the revivalist wavelength than were the Methodists, and the pressure points which emerged during his campaign reveal some more of the fault-lines between English and American evangelicalism. English Nonconformity was a sophisticated, multi-layered theological tradition that had evolved over more than two centuries. Many of its advocates possessed high-level theological literacy; they were not impressed by excessive emotionalism, demands for instant conversion and seemingly novel doctrines such as Oberlin Perfectionism, which contended that a state of entire consecration to God in this life was a form of moral perfection attainable by individuals, a belief that was largely anathema outside Methodist circles.

Richard Carwardine has argued that the part of Britain where church life most closely resembled American frontier Christianity was Wales, where emotional preaching had developed into an art form, where able preachers emerged from among the people as folk heroes and where camp meetings were put to use to bring scattered communities together. Furthermore the isolation of a linguistically and geographically separated population, the absence of an educated middle class and the dislocation experienced by those forced to move in search of work underlined the comparison with the American West. Had Finney chosen to go to Wales, his methods would have been better received, but the barrier of language meant that he chose to stay in England. Nevertheless Finney's writings, together with widespread migration from Wales to America, helped to cement a special revivalistic bond between the two nations. When revival broke out again in Wales between 1858 and 1860, it was seen as owing its origin to Humphrey Rowland Jones and his associates (who had either recently returned to Wales from the United States, or who had been heavily influenced by Finney-ism) and as being heavily American in origin and style. The revival resulted in the four major Welsh evangelical denominations estimating that their total gains had been in the order of 80,000 worshippers, a massive increase within a population of only just over 1 million.[20] Converts included Timothy Richard, the missionary to China.

The Welsh revival of the late 1850s was part of what was to be the biggest expression of pan-evangelicalism as a global phenomenon during the period under discussion. It had begun in America in 1857 and 1858, and was more urban and more focused on Sunday school children, businessmen, and on men generally, than had been the case with earlier American revivals. Once again, it was linked to a period of economic recession. As the American revival burned out, a series of linked revivals spread to Ulster, Wales, much of Scotland and parts of England. Finally it reached even to Madras in India and Monrovia in Liberia.[21] Hundreds of thousands were said to have been converted, and for evangelicals on both sides of the Atlantic it seemed as though they stood at the dawn of a glorious new age of truly global evangelical Christianity. At its height the revival was even seen as making an impact on the secular world, and it was alleged that crime levels plummeted. In Atlanta, Georgia, it was claimed that half the police force was disbanded, and in Sunderland and North Shields that no criminal cases were brought before the assizes. It was claimed that in Sunderland, North Shields, Macclesfield and Cardiff, taverns and theatres had to close for lack of business.

Holiness teaching was brought once again to the attention of the British public. Both Caughey and Finney returned to Britain, and the legendary American holiness teachers Walter and Phoebe Palmer arrived for an extended visit. For some decades Phoebe Palmer had been teaching a form of holiness in New York that approximated to Caughey's. In particular she urged believers to 'lay all on the altar of Christ' in order to achieve immediate sanctification. Some British revivalist preachers rose to prominence, among the best known of whom were the Baptist Charles Haddon Spurgeon and the (at this point) Methodists William Booth, who was a conscious imitator of Caughey, and Catherine Booth, who was a conscious imitator of Phoebe Palmer. In the longer term some new holiness denominations began to emerge, of which the best known were to be the Church of the Nazarene and the Salvation Army. In Britain and America, the revival also saw a broadening of the influence of perfectionism and a widening of the belief that sanctified Christians should work for the perfection of society. In America, this led to the adoption of the rhetoric of cleansing and purification in party politics, a further indication of the extent to which American revivalism had become wedded to the national mainstream. But, as was to be expected from earlier revival patterns, none of this would last. By the early 1860s all the denominations which had experienced recent rapid growth were back into the decline part of the cycle.[22] Such intense, simultaneous transatlantic revivalism would not come again. Britain would experience only one further large-scale revival, and that affected Wales only, in 1904.

The final late nineteenth-century fusion of revivalism, pre-millennialism and holiness teaching produced the movement known as Pentecostalism. For Pentecostalists the Welsh revival was interpreted not as the end of mass revivalism but as the immediate forerunner of their own movement, which they considered to have begun in a revival at Azusa Street in Los Angeles between 1906 and 1909. They saw the Welsh revival as the 'early rain' which had been prophetically foretold as preceding the 'later rain' of Azusa Street (Joel 3.23). Joe Creech has argued that the prominence of the Asuza Street revival was played up by early Pentecostalists who were anxious to fashion their own origins myth, in which Asuza Street was at the epicentre of a worldwide revival that was signalling the end of the age. [23] In fact Pentecostalism emerged from 'multiple pockets of revival that retained their preexisting [sic] institutional structures, theological tendencies and social dynamics'.[24] He argues that it was the smaller revivals, which occurred in Kansas, Chicago and North Carolina around the turn of the century and which featured speaking in tongues (seen as a fulfilment of Acts 2.4), that actually contributed to Pentecostalism's multiple points of origin.[25]

Renewal, revival and Roman Catholicism

Some of the revivalist techniques that became a prominent feature of nineteenth-century Protestantism began also to surface in Roman Catholicism. The theology, of course, remained very different. In terms of technique, mid-nineteenth-century Catholic revivals, often known as missions, were more similar to than different from their Protestant equivalents. If we consider the British experience, five areas of similarity may be noted. First, the locations were often similar: rapidly developing urban or suburban areas in which poverty was endemic, many had recently arrived, and people were judged to be at serious risk of alienation from their religious roots, and being lost in an impersonal and vice-filled urban world. Secondly, Catholic missions, like mid-nineteenth-century Protestant revivals, relied on organization, advanced publicity, and the creation of a sense of occasion. It was important that a sense of excitement about the impending event was generated beforehand, and that large numbers would be keen to participate, otherwise the event would fail before it had started. Thirdly, Catholics relied heavily on foreign assistance, often Italian members of missionary orders, to be the bringers of revival. It was understood that the missioners would move on after a specified period of usually a few weeks, and so the mission would be brief and intense. Like the American revivalists, the Italian missioners were exotic, international figures, who were famous within their denomination. Having the opportunity to hear them preach and to witness their legendary piety might be a once-in-a-lifetime opportunity that should not be missed; there was no likelihood that over familiarity would dull the congregation's responses. Fourth, the basic technique of gathering a crowd and then preaching to them intensively for a specified period was a further shared characteristic, as was the use of prayer and singing. Fifth, although the theological world evoked by the missioners contrasted strongly with that of the revivalists, some of the elements of the message were the same, in particular the urgency of making or renewing serious religious commitment, and the power of the saving grace that would be bestowed upon those making such a commitment. The uncertainty of the time of death, the awfulness of dying unprepared and the torments of hell that awaited the lost was another common theme. This was usually balanced by an emphasis on the joys and delights that awaited those who were prepared to make the preacher's message their own. As in later Protestant revivalism, for example that of Moody and Sankey, there was progressively less emphasis on hell and damnation in Catholic mission preaching as the century wore on.

The main areas of difference obviously related to the theological content of the message. For Catholic missioners it was commitment to the Catholic Church that they were trying to impart to those who were seen as at least nominally Catholic. They had relatively little interest in converting Protestants, although it is evident that Protestants sometimes attended their missions and were sometimes converted. Indeed, amongst those Anglo-Catholics who were teetering on the brink of conversion in the 1840s and 1850s, attending a mission may have seemed the best preparation before taking the momentous step. It is difficult to know from the sources whether the 'Protestants' who attended were in fact Anglo-Catholics on the point of conversion or those who would have seen themselves as Protestants, such as Methodists. At Newcastle-under-Lyme, a Passionist missioner, Gaudentius Rossi, received a Methodist preacher into the Church in the mid-1840s, and Protestant families who attended Rossi's mission in Cheadle were 'very much pleased to see that the Revd Father never said a word against their religion'.[26] The Oratorian Frederick William Faber claimed to prefer 'the pattern of the Wesleyans and the Whitefieldians to the calm sobriety and subdued enthusiasm of the Protestant establishment',[27] but he was a convert (and an ex-Evangelical) with somewhat jaundiced views about his Anglican past. Such attitudes were exceptional. Most Catholic missioners were only targeting Catholics, and wanted to teach them more about their faith and to warn them off dangerously false Protestant versions. At the English Redemptorist John Furniss's children's missions, children were rewarded for bringing along any nominally Catholic friends and for informing the clergy of any unbaptized Catholic children.[28] The emphasis was firmly on building up a consciously self-aware Catholic community, bringing its members under the influence and knowledge of their pastors and binding them to the Church through the practice of certain officially approved devotions.

The devotional differences can give the impression of a vast gulf between Catholics and Protestants, and undoubtedly the inculcation of a fully Catholic worldview had the effect of promoting a way of life that was radically different from general working-class culture in Britain.[29] But there was also a shared seriousness about religious matters which seemed to affect the committed members of all denominations. Mary Heimann, the historian of English Catholic devotion, has argued that it was 'the adoption of an excitable approach to sin and grace' which was also expressed in Protestant evangelicalism, rather than the adoption of Italian or Continental forms of devotion (which some earlier historians had seen as being decisive) which 'marked a departure in Victorian Catholic piety from the more gentlemanly tone of the eighteenth century'.[30] This view is endorsed by an account of a London dockland mission in 1855, in which the climax was 'a wild masculine outpouring of emotion as all "burst forth into one long continued wail and lament" for their sins during the closing sermon'.[31] Heimann argues that mission sermons explored all the same themes which Protestants also explored, and were intended to invoke a vivid recognition of sinfulness and inadequacy, and a corresponding desire to renew fervour and earnestness.[32]

In the 1840s, when missions began under the auspices of the Passionists and the Redemptorists, thousands could respond in the space of a week or so. It was reported that at St Mary's, Mulberry Street, Manchester, in January 1847, 30 converts were received, 400 people returned to their religious duties and 1,500 out of the 2,000 parishioners went to Mass.[33] Large numbers attending confession was also a feature of all parish missions, with priests kept busy for hours on end. By the end of the century, the numbers attracted to missions was perceived to be dwindling, with perhaps only 50 per cent of the parish responding in some cases. At Grimsby in 1890 it was claimed that half of the town's Catholics had been left 'totally unimpressed' by the mission and, significantly, were 'deemed to have lapsed altogether'. The remaining 1,000 were earnest enough to wish to attend. In Manchester in 1892 a similarly polar distinction was made between those who attended the mission and those who were 'lost to the Faith'.[34] Missions to children were also changing in character by the early 1870s. The increasing numbers of Catholic schools and parochial organizations changed the way in which the Church related to the young. Father Furniss, who had preached to children in their thousands and had attempted to give them a vivid experience of Catholicism that would remain with them in later life, retired from his work in 1862. When his successors in the 1870s presented children's missions they lasted only a week, and served as a preparation for the adult mission in the same place.[35] By the end of the century the emphasis had shifted even further. In 1893 a priest wrote to a Catholic newspaper complaining that the chief means of bringing boys to the faith was now to urge them to join a club, 'where the principal attractions are a few illustrated papers, some draughts and a box or two of dominoes'.[36] It was a very long way from John Furniss's ghoulishly spellbinding descriptions of the eternal torments in store for those who failed to die in a state of grace.

In the United States of America, Catholic missions were explicitly modelled on the Protestant pattern, and, according to Jay P. Dolan, they were strongly evangelical in tone, emphasizing conversion and the pursuit of personal piety.[37] Although Catholic missions grew in popularity in both America and Europe during the 1850s and 1860s, the American context was, not surprisingly, rather different from the European, although many of the missioners came from Europe. In Europe the purpose of a mission was to restore religion to established congregations, and in countries such as France, Germany and Italy it was often strongly overlaid with political overtones, as Catholics galvanized themselves to withstand the chill winds of secularism. In America the purpose was to establish new congregations, to revive the religion of those who were newly arrived from different nations and to meld them together to create Catholicism in its American form. As there were none of the cultural or political pressures that could be brought to bear on Catholics in Europe, priests conducting missions in America had, like the Protestant preachers, to rely solely on their powers of persuasion. They also knew that as time was short they had to do or say something extraordinary and that there would be little or no likelihood of regular follow-up. Particularly in the earlier part of the period, when Catholic populations were often sparsely scattered, gathering the congregation for Mass on a weekly basis was impossible, and therefore there was little opportunity to instruct Catholics through the usual route of regular teaching. In such circumstances it became even more important that the message preached was very clear and likely to elicit immediate action in the form of repentance. Not surprisingly, mission priests dwelt on the familiar themes of the dangers of dying suddenly and unprepared, and the horrors of hell which awaited those who succumbed to this condition. Indeed it was recorded that one Redemptorist preacher, Henri Giesen, preached so loudly

and vividly on the flames of hell that his booming voice summoned the local
firemen, who arrived at the church to put out the fire that Giesen's oratory
had fabricated![38] Catholics responded just as emotionally as their Protestant neighbours. Weeping, wailing, groaning and other manifestations
that would not have been out of place in early Pentecostalism were often
observed, although mission leaders were usually anxious to prevent matters
getting out of control. Dolan argues that Catholic revivalism should be
included within the history of American evangelicalism, and suggests that
'The Catholic revival was an evangelical summons to conversion'. Furthermore when non-Catholics observed these activities, they too concluded that
it was a revival that was taking place.[39]

Anglo-Catholic revival

At roughly the same time as the second generation of Catholic missioners were beginning to notice that their missions were attracting more of
the already pious and faithful, and fewer of the lapsed and reprobate, and
as evangelicals were beginning to prepare for the visit to Britain of the
celebrated American revivialist duo Dwight L. Moody and Ira D. Sankey,
Anglo-Catholics were planning to preach a mission in London. As a movement within Anglicanism, Anglo-Catholicism sought to bring about the
institutional renewal of the Church. It was in part a reaction against the
Evangelical revival which high-church Anglicans saw as threatening the
Church of England. Calls for conversion and baptism in the Spirit undermined the Anglican doctrine of baptismal regeneration, and prolonged and
over-emotional worship, together with the use of lay preachers, was seen as
inimical to good order and encroaching upon the proper sphere of the clergy.
Yet, as Peter Nockles has shown, the proponents of Anglo-Catholicism
did not shrink from using the language of revival to describe their new
movement. A striking number of the early histories of the Oxford Movement explicit referred to it as the 'Catholic revival', 'the revival of primitive
doctrine', or, in the case of H.P. Denison, writing in 1912, 'one of the most
wonderful revivals in church history'.[40] The major difference, however, is
that the Catholic model of revival included a much greater emphasis on the
corporate life and idea of the Church.

Essentially Anglo-Catholic revivalists saw themselves as restoring and
reviving the old ways of the Church, associated both with the early Church
and with the high-church Caroline divines of the seventeenth century. [41]
At the same time, they wanted to move the Church in a direction which
brought it much closer to contemporary Roman Catholicism. In Chapter
1 we traced the development of the Catholic revival within the Church
of England in its theological, cultural and aesthetic manifestations, and

concluded that by the first decade of the twentieth century, Anglo-Catholics had succeeded in making their own parishes seem much more like Catholic churches. To the casual observer, their services looked not dissimilar to those of the Roman Catholics, with the adoption of the eastward position for the celebration of the Eucharist, greater use of lighted candles and a greater variety of vestments. Anglo-Catholicism, or Ritualism as it was also known, appeared to be taking over the soul of the Church of England, and Evangelicalism appeared to have been beaten into a retreat. Early twentieth-century Church of England clergy were more likely to be seen walking (or cycling) around their parishes in cassocks, and were keener on being called 'Father'. One way in which they had tried to prepare their parishioners for their metamorphosis from English gentlemen to Catholic priests had been through the conduct of parish missions from the late 1860s.

The first large-scale revival campaign in Britain's capital city was led not by James Caughey, or anyone else of his ilk, but by the Church of England. It was known as the Twelve Days Mission, and involved about 112 London parishes in November 1869. There was a follow-up mission of similar proportions in 1874, shortly before Moody and Sankey visited London. Indeed it has been suggested that one reason why Moody met with so much evangelical support was that he was seen as providing a Protestant counterblast to the 'aggressive sacramentalism' of the Anglo-Catholic missions.[42] Both missions drew very consciously on Roman Catholic models, not least in the adoption of its terminology of 'mission' in preference to the term 'revival'. They were led by (among other) members of the Society of the Holy Cross and of the Society of St John the Evangelist, religious orders for men which had been recently founded with the explicit intention of supplying the established Church with mission priests. The catalyst was the desire to reach the 'careless and the ungodly' among the urban poor, who had been identified as the chief neglecters of religion since the publication of the religious census of 1851. The focus was, as might be expected, sacramental. The missioners wanted the parishioners to attend the daily Eucharist services which they provided, and the climax of the mission in some parishes was a service for the renewal of baptismal vows. This again was a direct borrowing from Roman Catholic missions and was the most convenient and the least controversial to reproduce in an Anglican setting. The element which proved most controversial in Anglican churches was something that was taken for granted in Catholic ones, and that was the attempt to persuade those attending the mission to take up the practice of regular confession. The successful introduction of confession mattered to the missioners because it was seen as vital in the creation of an authentically Catholic parish, and it has been argued that one of the principal aims of the

Twelve Days Mission was to popularize the idea of detailed confession to a priest. Nineteenth-century Anglo-Catholic clergy frequently complained that they could not know their parishioners unless they could persuade them into the confessional. For a whole variety of reasons, it was a practice which largely failed to win the support of the Anglican laity.[43]

At its halfway stage, *The Times* reported that the Twelve Days Mission was attracting attendances of about 35,000 people a day. As has already been noted, the mission was parish-based, so activities varied from parish to parish. At St Paul's, Knightsbridge, one of the most fashionable Anglo-Catholic churches in London (where the missioner was chided for preaching against such 'Belgravian' sins as the London season), the daily programme was intense but typical of what was going on in other similar parishes. The day began with Holy Communion at 7 a.m., 8.30 a.m. and 9.15 a.m. Mattins was at 8 a.m.; a litany of penitence and the catechizing of children was at 11 a.m. Various priests were available to hear confessions between noon and eight. Evensong was at 5 p.m., together with an instruction class for women. The mission service proper was at 8 p.m, together with an instruction class for men.[44] It is not clear how many parishioners subjected themselves to the full regime and how many dropped in for just a few of the mission sermons. One Broad Church observer, the journalist and cleric C.M. Davies, attended a mission service at St Albans, Holborn, and found the service 'doleful', as the preacher struggled to popularize the sacrament of penance. He was struck by the hybrid nature of what he saw. 'In fact, the whole affair is a wonderful congeries of the Roman and Ranter elements grafted on the stock of the Church of England as by law established.'[45] The evangelical newspaper *The Record* made a similar point but in a predictably more hostile way. 'The attempt seems to be one which grafts the earnestness of revival preaching on the sacerdotal errors of Romanism, and associates the call to repentance with the deadly poison of the Confessional.'[46] When the second London mission took place, in February 1874, the bishops were anxious to ensure that it included every kind of Anglican, in the hope of smothering a second wave of sacramental revivalism. Their success in this was limited, and once more London witnessed a mission in which the claims of Anglo-Catholicism were forcefully put forth.

Catholic Anglicanism overseas

The Anglican Church in the colonies proved to be fruitful soil for Tractarians, ecclesiologists and ritualists. Indeed, the challenge of working (in some locations at least) with a largely blank canvas could prove more rewarding than trying to grapple with parishioners whose views had become set hard over generations. Furthermore it became an important point of principle to demonstrate to residents of the New World that there was an alternative to evangelical emotionalism and Roman authoritarianism. In 1850 Canterbury colony was set up at Christchurch, New Zealand, by a group of Anglicans who had been influenced by the Oxford Movement. They hoped that a purified Church of England would emerge there, far from the crises of home. John Medley, who had been a close associate of Keble and Pusey, was consecrated as bishop of Fredericton in New Brunswick, Canada, in 1845, and is sometimes given the soubriquet of the first Tractarian bishop.[47] While in England, he had written about the importance of open pews[48] and had been closely associated with the Cambridge Camden Society. Once in Canada he became an enthusiastic builder of 100 Gothic revival churches, including his own cathedral at Fredericton. In many ways he was the model Tractarian bishop, expounding a sacramental theology, composing church music and translating the early Fathers. By the time he left his diocese in 1892 it was quite different from the one to which he had come 47 years earlier. Whilst much change could have been expected over an episcopate of this length, the tendency for episcopates in the colonies to be much longer than those in the English Church, together with the lack of other vested interests, allowed for pioneering, entrepreneurial bishops like Medley to make a huge and lasting impact.[49]

High-church bishops appointed to dioceses overseas varied in the extent to which they sought to avoid exporting the churchmanship conflicts which were such a strong feature of the Victorian Church into their new colonial contexts. Despite his impeccable credentials as an Anglo-Catholic revivalist, Medley was certainly more tolerant of the Evangelicals who composed the majority of the New Brunswick clergy at the time of his arrival than he would probably have been had he been translated to a bishopric in England or Wales. He did not seek to censure a clergyman who denied the doctrine of baptismal regeneration, nor did he withhold licences from those who espoused strongly Evangelical views. Bishop Gray of Cape Town, on the other hand, was much less tolerant of what he saw as Evangelical challenges to his authority, and this resulted in his becoming embroiled in a lengthy and damaging conflict with one of his clergy, William Long, over Long's refusal to attend the diocesan synod. It seems inconceivable that Gray would have taken such draconian action over the non-attendance of one of the clergy had the drama been played out, for example, in the diocese of London.[50] The apogee of the single-minded Anglo-Catholic colonial bishop was reached with Frank Weston (1871–1924) of Zanzibar, who was deeply critical of any missionary cooperation with the Free Churches. In 1923, in his last major public appearance in Britain, he presided over the Second Anglo-Catholic Congress.

Missionary agencies, as well as individual bishops, were also highly influential in spreading more Catholic forms of worship abroad. Certain Anglican missionary agencies, such as the Universities' Mission to Central Africa, worked explicitly to promote more Catholic forms of Anglicanism abroad. As we have seen, the UMCA was founded in 1857 after David Livingstone's appeal, and it was immediately perceived by the much longer-established Society for the Propagation of the Gospel as an undesirable rival. Whereas the traditional high-church SPG had always seen itself as operating ecclesially with due deference to both church and state, the UMCA seemed more intent on fulfilling a Tractarian dream of model dioceses led by missionary bishops beyond the 'blighting influence' of the establishment. Such dioceses could provide a haven for disaffected Tractarians, and also the ideal soil for the nurturing of Anglican religious orders. Following the initiative of Pusey, religious orders were founded from 1845, first for women and then for men. Some religious orders established overseas branches quite independently. Others worked in collaboration with support from the SPG. These included the Society of St John the Evangelist, the Society of the Sacred Mission, the Community of the Resurrection, the Order of the Holy Paraclete, and the Community of St Mary the Virgin. Others were set up by SPG missionaries or by individual bishops as indigenous communities or missionary sisterhoods or brotherhoods.[51] Wherever such religious communities developed, they contributed markedly to what has usually been a lasting Catholic tone to the Anglican Church overseas.

The significance of revival and renewal

In this chapter, we have seen how revival and renewal emerged as important international movements within most of the Christian traditions in the nineteenth century, and how these themes reveal much about both the similarities and the differences between the Churches. We have seen that for at least the first three-quarters of the century, there was an emphasis on large-scale religious gatherings designed to evoke excitement and individual response. Evangelicals, Roman Catholics and Anglo-Catholics emphasized the importance of appealing to the individual soul. They all saw the large group setting as the most effective means of achieving this in the first instance, but they hoped to follow up the mass meeting by offering individual guidance of varying sorts. All considered that they had the solution for dealing with their hearers' sense of sinfulness, whether instantly or more gradually, and all saw their work as having enormous cosmic significance. They believed that they were literally saving souls from hell and eternal damnation, and some of the evangelicals believed that their revivals were hastening the return of Christ and the end of the world. In the immediate term, as well as saved souls, they hoped to win converts, or freshly committed Catholics, who could be fully integrated either into the evangelical subculture or into world of the Roman or Anglo-Catholic parish.

Revival and renewal also brought about lasting changes to the Churches which could not have been anticipated at the beginning of the process. Christians coming out of the Methodist tradition saw the creation of a large new denomination, Primitive Methodism, and then a significant redefinition of Wesley's holiness doctrine, which under Finney, Caughey and Palmer became transformed into a belief in entire sanctification as an essential second stage in Christian life. This in turn spawned new denominations which emphasized holiness as a central tenet, and holiness provided one of the pillars on which rested the foundations of Pentecostalism at the end of the period. For Christians coming out of the Calvinist traditions, the effects of revival contributed to a softening of traditional views of a limited atonement, and for practical purposes blurred some of the theological distinctiveness between themselves and the Arminians. For Roman Catholics, missions helped to develop a sense of catholicity, binding together people of often widely different social and ethnic background, and producing a devotionally well-informed laity, with what Mary Heimann describes as 'a recognisable blend of earnestness with simplicity, notable for its open-mindedness in the face of the marvellous and the supernatural'.[52] For Anglo-Catholics, the wider process of renewal (as opposed to the specific and limited effects of the London missions) assisted in the gradual redefinition of the Anglican ethos, so that by the twentieth century 'central' churchmanship became equated with a form of liberal Catholicism. The missions themselves may have helped in rooting a permanent Catholic subculture in some of the London parishes. Up until at least the middle of the twentieth century, Anglo-Catholics were able to colonize deeper and deeper into the heart of Anglicanism almost wherever it existed in the world.

We have noted the similarities in technique between evangelical revivals and Roman Catholic missions, and also the comments that were made about the hybrid nature of Anglo-Catholic missions, as they fused together elements of the Catholic and the evangelical. Paradoxically, missions and revivals were also crucial in reinforcing the essential separation between Catholics and Protestants and in defining and pointing up the dangers of the 'other'. A major theme running through all of John Furniss's children's missions was the importance of avoiding the 'badness' of all manifestations of Protestantism. Extreme danger lurked in reading Protestant books and tracts, Protestant schools should be avoided at all costs, as should Protestants as prospective marriage partners or employers, although some flexibility might be required in relation to the latter, but not if the demands of work entailed having to miss Sunday Mass.[53] For Anglo-Catholics the 'other' was understood to be the revivalist preacher, who in the 1870s was epitomized by Dwight L. Moody, who was about to evangelize in the very same territory. It is noticeable that Moody and the Anglo-Catholics went head-to-head in radically different interpretations of central Christian doctrines. Sacramental theology, and a particular focus on the significance of baptism and the renewal of baptismal vows, was, as we have seen, at the heart of London missions. Moody's teaching on baptism was that it was something in which one should not put one's trust for salvation. Confession generated even greater controversies and an even deeper sense of the otherness of the other. But controversy always has its place in the history of religious movements. Writing about the hostilities that existed between early Pentecostalists and radical evangelicals in America, Grant Wacker has noted that 'an unresisted movement soon becomes an unknown one. Since Pentecostals, like all successful sects, instinctively appreciated the value of opposition, it was almost inevitable that they would come up with some non-negotiable doctrine or some difficult ritual, or both, that clearly distinguished them from their religious kin.'[54] We may apply Wacker's point more widely to the many different forms of revivalism, mission and renewal that occurred in the nineteenth-century Church.

CHAPTER 7

Dislocation and Decline

Secular pressures

It was suggested in the Introduction that theories about secularization, which have abounded since the middle of the nineteenth century, offer the opposite paradigm to the revival narratives which were explored in the previous chapter. Secularization, like revival, has become something of a blanket term, which encompasses all aspects of the process by which religion and its claims are seen as being detached from their earlier position at the centre of society and relegated to the margins. This results in the decision whether or not to practise a religion being seen as a personal choice in the private lives of citizens, which should have no impact on society at large. The processes which have contributed to secularization are very varied, and include: the shift from rural to urban living, with the attendant collapse of intimate, small-scale societies, and the decline in churchgoing which has often (but by no means always) been seen to accompany it; the increasing belief that scientific theories, rather than religious accounts, provide authentic explanations for the origins and development of humans, and for the existence of the world; the related sense of doubt about the reliability of Scripture; changes in church–state relationships in which the state distanced itself from, and limited the powers of, its established Church; changes in social attitudes in which people became more concerned with making individual choices which suited them, without reference to, or interest in, religious teachings. All these factors, and others, have played an important part in shaping the cultural landscape of European and New World societies over the last century and a half, resulting in, at the very least, a significant shift (and many would argue an actual decline) in the perceived importance of religion. Secularization theories have been developed and utilized by a wide range of sociologists, political thinkers, historians and indeed theologians, to explore these shifts in greater depth and to provide explanations for social, cultural and religious change.

In the tangled skein of circumstances which produced what many would now think of as the largely secularized panorama of Western Europe, some threads were already becoming clearly visible in the nineteenth century, whilst others (such as the widespread abandonment of marriage and the attendant loss of the stigma of illegitimacy) would not become apparent until the final quarter of the twentieth century. In the twenty-first century, however, there has been a heightened awareness of the extent to which the West is failing to develop as the fully secularized society that had long been predicted. Not only does there continue to be much general interest in religion and spiritual experience, but specific factors such as the renewed interest in Christianity in formerly communist Eastern Europe, the continued growth of revivalist and Pentecostal forms of Christianity all over the world and the deep challenges to Western society posed by highly unsecularized forms of Islam have taken many of the proponents of secularization theories by surprise. The early twenty-first century is looking a lot less secular than the late twentieth century did, and secularization is rarely now seen as part of an inevitable process. This is casting a new light even on those aspects of secularization which had their origins long ago. In this chapter, we shall consider some of those parts of the process which were becoming manifest during the nineteenth century.

Politics and secular movements

The roots of the secular mentality may be traced to the intellectual climate of the Enlightenment, which provided men of education with the tools and opportunities to raise questions and to push boundaries which had hitherto been largely untouched. Over the following decades, the consequences were played out in the political process, most dramatically in France, but also in those countries which avoided bloody revolution, such as Britain. Across late eighteenth-century Europe, it had been taken for granted that each state favoured one particular Christian denomination; even if it extended toleration to members of other denominations, it operated elaborate systems of censorship and control which ensured that the odds were always stacked in favour of the officially approved Church. Particular privileges in relation to education, places of worship, preaching, poor relief and the registration of births, marriages and deaths were usually part of this package. Across Europe, the parish was the basic political as well as ecclesiastical unit. It followed that the clergy of the state-favoured denomination were also important for the good ordering of society as well as for the provision of spiritual and pastoral welfare.[1]

During the nineteenth century, changes occurred in respect of the relationship of each state to its established Church. The speed and extent of the changes varied very much from state to state and were determined by the very different political circumstances in each, but by the final quarter of the nineteenth century it was clear that everywhere, real power rested with the politicians, not with clerics. The politicians were increasingly motivated by the need to meet the aspirations of their expanding male electorates, for it was understood that late nineteenth-century men were very much less sympathetic to religion than were the women of the period.[2] The influence of established Churches had been steadily reduced, and in places where there were significant religious minorities, the rights of members of non-established Christian bodies, and of Jews, had been increased, usually to the point of equality for all (male) citizens. Indeed the arrival in Western Europe of large Jewish communities fleeing persecution in Eastern Europe, and increasingly also of members of other faiths, particularly Islam, began very gradually to introduce people to the future possibility of a multifaith society. The role of the clergyman of the established Church contracted as a new professional class of teachers, lawyers, accountants and registrars (among others) arrived in the parish and took over tasks which had previously been assumed by him. In the way in which this process worked out, France and Britain reflect the opposite ends of the spectrum, with France developing a prominent anti-Church secular constituency which had no real parallel in Britain.

The French Revolution, Europe's most violent late eighteenth-century event, in which roughly 2 per cent of France's priests lost their lives, and the vast majority went into precarious exile, set the tone for what followed in that country. There were nine different changes of regime between 1799 and 1870, which brought continuing religious upheaval. In one decade there might be the public embrace of atheism, in the next some attempt at rapprochement, and in the following an extreme assertion of Catholic hegemony, as when Charles X (1824–30) introduced mutilation followed by execution for anyone caught profaning the Eucharist. This triggered a further fierce anti-Catholic reaction. France was a religiously monochrome country in which there were few religious alternatives to Catholicism, and so a struggle developed between those who embraced the *idée laïque*, an untranslatable term which expressed the idea of the desirability of creating a secular state in a secular society, and those who saw themselves as *catholiques avant tout*, 'Catholics before all else'. The two sides engaged in a lengthy *guerre des deux Frances*, or 'war of the two Frances', which at its height, in the period between 1879 and 1905, assumed something of the character of a French version of the *Kulturkampf*.[3] The see-sawing of political regimes meant that France did not experience the full onslaught of secularization until 1879, when the French republicans, who already controlled the Chamber of Deputies, won control of the Senate. A raft of secularizing measures known as the 'laic laws' were passed in the years which followed, which culminated in the disestablishment of the French Church in 1905. They included the repeal of laws designed to promote Sunday rest, the legalization of divorce, a ban on the saying of prayers at meetings of public bodies, the exclusion of priests and nuns from teaching in state schools, the abolition of religion from the syllabus in state schools and the removal of religious symbols, such as crucifixes, from schools and law courts.[4] In some places, a fiercely anti-clerical republican ethos developed, which expressed itself in events such as the holding of public banquets on Good Friday, the day when Catholics fasted in remembrance of the crucifixion of Jesus.

Schools became the most heavily contested territory in the war of the two Frances. For Ultramontane Catholics, the teachers in the secular schools were seen as the most dangerous elements in French society, simultaneously corrupting the young with their religion-free education, whilst challenging the well-established tradition that schooling should be provided by nuns and brothers. Priests sometimes retaliated by making it difficult for pupils in secular schools to be admitted to their first communion, often on the basis that they were ignorant of the catechism; there were also reports of clerical discrimination against the families that used secular schools, verbal abuse and even physical violence.[5] From 1879 onwards the education system and the French Church operated in opposition to each other. The *instituteurs* (schoolmasters) and their female equivalents, the *institutrices*, became the bearers of secular republican values, although in fact one-third considered themselves to be Catholics. It has been argued that it was only during the First World War, when committed Catholics and secular schoolmasters found themselves fighting shoulder to shoulder, that some of the breach between them was healed and an uneasy armistice broke out between Catholic and secular France.[6]

Britain avoided revolution; when Socialist-inspired uprisings rocked Europe in 1848, all that happened in London was that a group of Chartists (campaigners for a variety of political reforms intended to benefit the working man) met for a rally on Kennington Common, after which they went home.[7] The British government extended the franchise and managed the process of giving equality to the country's large number of non-Anglicans through the gradual and orderly implementation of changes to the statutes. This addressed the grievances of Nonconformists and Roman Catholics whilst permitting the Church of England to retain its established status, and arguably to emerge from the age of reform in a strengthened rather than a weakened position. There was an organized secular movement in nineteenth-century Britain, but it lacked the size, influence and venomous hostility towards religion of its French counterpart. Among early nine-teenth-century secular freethinkers, it was really only Richard Carlile who utilized strongly offensive language, for example by describing the clergy as 'black slugs'.

More typical was William Cobbett, who, critical though he was of the Church, sometimes actually attended Anglican services, as long as they did not cut unduly into his writing time. The British secular movement expressed itself mainly through the blasphemous and seditious press which had been in existence since the century's second decade and which had resulted in the prosecution and imprisonment of a number of publishers and booksellers. The staple fare in many such publications was parodies of Prayer Book liturgy, shocking revelations about the supposedly vast wealth of the clergy and cartoons depicting the most morally dubious events in the Old Testament, such as God stoning the Amorites (Joshua 10.11).[8] There was also a systematic programme of re-publication of the works of French Enlightenment thinkers, and of the eighteenth-century English radical Thomas Paine. However, the relatively low levels of literacy in Britain in the first half of the nineteenth century limited the impact of the secular press on the working classes; as late as 1841, 33 per cent of men and 49 per cent of women who married in registry offices were unable to sign their own names.[9] Whereas a person with limited reading skills might attend the meetings of secularist 'preachers', and enjoy cartoons depicting, for exam-ple, the exploits of David with Bathsheba, (II Samuel 11) he (less often she) needed a reasonable level of literacy in order to become fully conversant with the secularists' agenda.

Secularism in Britain seemed to be parasitic upon the Christianity it strove to undermine, and to some extent the fortunes of the two movements waxed and waned together. The National Secular Society, for example, was founded in 1866 and was at its height in 1885, when it had over 100 branches, the date when levels of churchgoing were also reaching an all-time high. But its membership was never much more than 6,000 – insignificant in comparison with the membership of the Churches, and tiny in comparison with the parallel movement in France. After the mid-1880s its membership fell away dramatically, much faster than the almost parallel drop in late nineteenth- and early twentieth-century church attendance. For much of the period of secularist growth, there had been a distinct reticence about declaring an explicitly God-denying (as opposed to a Church-denouncing) position, a reticence even shared by the leading proponent of mid-nineteenth-century secularism in Britain, George Holyoake. As Edward Royle observed, in Britain the word 'atheist' or 'infidel' was not necessarily applied to a person who denied the existence of God, but to 'one who had the temerity to convey to the lower orders the heresies of the respectable'.[10] Holyoake's successor as the leader of the movement, Charles Bradlaugh, had no hesitation in describing himself as an atheist in the God-denying sense, but the continuing influence of the earlier position may be seen in the fact that the most controversial moment for the late nineteenth-century secular movement came when Bradlaugh, together with Annie Besant, the estranged wife of an Anglican clergyman who had become Bradlaugh's devoted disciple, re-published a pamphlet not about God but about family planning. Among middle-class free thinkers in particular, there was stern opposition to any attempt to increase levels of knowledge about contraception. This was for two main reasons: first, it was believed that those who could afford big families should be encouraged to have them, as children brought up in relative affluence would thrive and make a bigger contribution to society than the children of the poor. It was also believed that the poor should be encouraged to avoid having children that they could not afford, by postponing marriage for as long as possible. Secondly, it was considered that telling people how to avoid pregnancy would undermine the moral structures of society, particularly if such knowledge spread to unmarried women. Charles Darwin, a father of ten, was a particularly high-profile opponent of Bradlaugh and Besant.[11] When Bradlaugh and Besant were convicted of obscenity at the Old Bailey in 1877, many moderate secularists concluded that justice had been done, and breathed a sigh of relief that their wives and daughters would not now be at risk of reading scandalous birth-control publications.

Britain lacked the climate of anti-clericalism which existed in parts of Catholic Europe. Very few Englishmen ever seriously contemplated killing a priest, although under extreme provocation a priest might kill them.[12] Less dramatically, although the Anglican clergy were unambiguously linked to the somewhat repressive machinery of government in the first few decades of the nineteenth century, and although they appeared to be storing up increasing amounts of treasure not in heaven but in substantial properties in the English countryside, it is clear that when they inspired negative emotions these were of annoyance and jealousy rather than deep hatred. There is certainly evidence that on occasions English workingmen could find the clergy extremely irritating, but the number of violent flare-ups, which were usually directed towards property rather than priests, was very few. After the mid-1830s a combination of parliamentary reform, tithe reform, a reduction in the number of clerical magistrates and an improvement in labourers' living standards caused some of the tensions to disappear. Later in the century, anti-clericalism emerged in a very different form, with attacks focused on certain clergy as catholicized churchmen who had sold out their Protestant identity. This had nothing to do with them being tithe owners or magistrates, which by this point they would have long ceased to be. Mid-nineteenth-century anti-clericalism was exemplified by the anti-Ritualist riots which affected a number of mainly London churches in the late 1850s and 1860s.[13]

Mary Heimann observes that as the nineteenth century progressed, across Western Europe religion as a whole became more politicized. Conservative politics began to be associated with those who worshipped in state-protected Churches, and liberalism or radicalism with those who were excluded, or chose to exclude themselves, from the establishment.[14] Hugh McLeod argues that the effect of secularizing legislation meant that during the course of 1848 the majority of the Protestant clergy in Germany and of the Catholic clergy in France moved more clearly to the right of the political spectrum.[15] This did not occur in England, where if anything, the Anglican clergy moved steadily towards the left from the middle of the nineteenth and into the twentieth century. They began to reveal an increasing tendency to speak out against social exploitation and to show a desire to support, rather than to control, the poor.

Science and biblical authority

One of the clearest outcomes of the European Enlightenment was the central emphasis which began to be given to scientific endeavours of various types. This included both the ongoing exploration of natural science (which began to be known just as 'science') and the developments in the historical sciences which produced 'scientific' approaches to analysing texts, and the biblical text in particular. In Britain, as in America, science and religion had seemed in harmonious coexistence for decades. In the age before science developed into a number of properly organized professions, which became the preserve of highly trained specialists, scientific investigations were most frequently pursued in the home by those clergy who liked to spend their off-duty hours gathering fossils or subjecting flora and fauna to microscopic examination. Such investigations were usually approached in a reverential spirit which led the investigators to marvel at and give thanks for the beauty, intricate design and endless variation in the natural world. The clergymen-scientists had usually been heavily influenced by the eighteenth-century Anglican theologian William Paley, whose famous work, *Natural Theology; or Evidence of the Existence and Attributes of the Deity, collected from the Appearances of Nature*, had first appeared in 1802. It was to remain a key text on the syllabus for all Anglican ordinands for the next 100 years. As the title of his book indicated, Paley believed that evidence for the existence of God could be found by studying the intricacies of nature. For many

English-speaking Christians, it seemed that Paley had offered a formal and attractive proof for the existence of God and a modern version of the classical argument for God's existence from design. Furthermore it was one in which science seemed to become the handmaid of theology.

In the 1820s William Buckland, an Oxford University geologist and a clergyman, found himself arguing that the scientific evidence from fossils could be made to support the Old Testament accounts of creation and Noah's flood. However, as further investigations began to reveal the bones of dinosaurs (who seemed conspicuously absent from the biblical record) and as people began to wonder if the timescale for the existence of the world was significantly longer than the 6,000 years posited by Archbishop Ussher, the ground began to shift. By the second half of the nineteenth century there was a parting of the ways which led to 'science' being cast out of the family fold of Christianity and sent into exile; it began to be seen as an arrogant black sheep that failed to acknowledge divine supremacy and threatened the souls of the faithful with its new, deity-free versions of how life on earth began and how it evolved over millennia. For some scientists, particularly those who believed that Christianity and the pursuit of truth must be ultimately reconcilable, this was a deeply distressing experience; for others, who relished the prospect of creating an alternative intellectual universe for the modern rational man that was cut free of all theological moorings and clerical interventions, it was distinctly liberating.

In 1859 Charles Darwin published his work *On the Origin of Species by Means of Natural Selection*, which effectively demolished Paley's natural theology by offering a religiously agnostic account of the development of species which was predicated upon the theory that over an extremely long time span the stronger species survived and gradually adapted to suit their environment, while the weaker varieties became extinct. His second major work, *The Descent of Man* (1871), specifically included mankind in his evolutionary scheme, thus raising a host of doubts for Christians about the existence of the soul, humanity's special relationship with God, and its ultimate destiny.[16]

The episode involving the discussion of Darwin's work at the meeting of the British Association for the Advancement of Science in 1860, culminating in an exchange between Darwin's agnostic disciple Thomas Huxley, and the Bishop of Oxford, Samuel Wilberforce, provides the iconic moment in the history of the nineteenth-century 'struggle' between science and religion. It is a secular counterweight to the nineteenth-century Church's other iconic moment, that of Henry Morton Stanley's heroic 'discovery' of the exhausted David Livingstone in deepest East Africa. Indeed, for the millions of children who were educated in the secular schools of twentieth-century Britain, the only two 'facts' that they learned about the nineteenth-century Church were that Darwin had disproved the Bible, and that Bishop Wilberforce had made a fool of himself by asking the scientist Huxley if he was descended from an ape on his mother's or his father's side. In fact none of those who were present at the meeting of the British Association were able to recall the precise words of this celebrated dialogue, although an exchange between Huxley and Wilberforce on the scientific validity of Darwin's theories, rather than their theological implications, certainly did take place. As Mary Heimann reminds us, in retrospect Darwin's work 'seems less significant for its thesis, than for the symbolic importance which was attributed to it in what gradually came to be seen as an antithesis between something loosely called "religion" and something equally loosely called "science"'.[17] Although Darwin's work was not original, and drew heavily on the theories of others, a fact that he was always ready to admit, 'his recombination of familiar elements led to a theory which was at once as evocative as Paley's while at the same time being more economical, since it could account for apparently useless variations and solve the moral problem of suffering in the world without having recourse to divine agency'.[18] As for the issue of the 'struggle' between the religious and scientific world-views, this was an idea promoted by Huxley, who was anxious to dramatize and capitalize upon the gulf between 'backward' religious perspectives and 'modern' scientific ones.

The significance of Darwin went far beyond the shores of Britain. As noted earlier, *The Origin of Species* was translated into French in 1862, and it was an instant hit with the French intelligentsia, who saw it as perfectly in harmony with the writings of Auguste Comte. Comte's positivism, which was widely adopted in France in the 1850s and 1860s, was a very successful attempt to devise a systematic alternative to supernaturalist forms of faith. He classified theology as a primitive, although necessary, stage in under-standing the world, which had now been replaced by the age of science, which provided a persuasive way of explaining, and indeed explaining away, religion. Comte was hailed by secularists as the greatest French thinker of the nineteenth century, and his works were made compulsory in the state schools. Meanwhile Darwin was seen as providing the Third Republic with the justification which it needed to ban clerical influence in universities, and to re-focus the syllabus on 'scientific' and 'modern' subjects. In Germany Darwin was taken up as part of an intellectual package that included homage to Marx, as well as to a number of other anti-religious thinkers. Although their interests appeared to be very different, once fused together, the ideas of Marx and Darwin provided a framework out of which subse-quent generations could argue that religion was a social construct within a materialist universe. In 1868 Ernst Haeckel published *History of Creation*, which was the first book in German to use Darwinism as the basis for a whole worldview. He developed his ideas more fully in his *Riddle of the Universe* (1899) which became an international bestseller. [19] Haeckel dwelt on the potential for Darwin's theories to be given a racist interpretation, giving them the dreadful twist which was to be fully exploited in the twentieth century.

In America Darwin's theories burst into a Protestant world which thought that it had been founded upon, and had indeed actually achieved, a harmonious relationship between faith and science. Less temperamentally conservative than their European counterparts, the vast majority of Americans saw themselves as the beneficiaries of various types of scientific advances and as the heirs of the liberating intellectual amalgam that was the American Enlightenment. The American Enlightenment was a distinctive synthesis of European components, and emphasized the ideals of order and religious compromise derived from Newton and Locke, the scepticism associated with Voltaire and Hume, the utopianism which grew out of Rousseau, and the 'common sense' philosophy embodied in eighteenth-century Scotland. Of these four stands, the first and the fourth had the biggest influence, and the ideas of the Scottish Enlightenment dominated American intellectual life for the first six or seven decades of the nineteenth century. [20] Indeed they had a more significant 'afterlife' in America than they did in Scotland. Even among those with impeccably orthodox credentials, George Marsden argues that there was a tendency to adopt a Deist perspective, which saw the universe as a machine run according to natural laws and set in motion by a somewhat distant creator. This produced a mindset, also noted in Britain, which placed religion in a scientific context whilst using science apologetically to emphasize the harmony and excellence of the design in nature.

By the 1830s the Baptist author Francis Wayland was using what became a popular college text book, *Elements of Moral Science* (1835), to argue that ethics was as much a branch of science as physics and that Scripture and rational moral science operated independently but completely harmoniously. In a later volume, *The Elements of Political Economy* (1837), he pushed the argument further to suggest that political economy, as a 'pure science', had nothing to do with ethical questions. As both George Marsden and Martin Marty have noted, this type of approach contributed to the subtle secularization of American life. With the minimum of fuss and without apparent thought to the larger consequences, avowedly religious thinkers were neatly re-classifying the major components of life and the world into either secular-scientific or religious categories. [21] Although the impact of

Darwin was also important, arguably it was these activities which did as much, if not more, to fray the fabric which had woven religion deep into American culture.

Because Christianity and science had been closely intertwined in the first half of the nineteenth century, and indeed earlier, American Christians, like British Christians, reacted to Darwin in complex ways. Initially at least there was no straightforward split between conservatives and liberals, with the former being hostile and the latter cautiously welcoming, although this did undoubtedly come later. In the short term, whilst some theological conservatives would make no concessions to new interpretations of the Bible, others sought to find ways to reconcile Darwinism with traditional Christianity. In particular it was maintained that some revisions might be needed to the literal understanding of Genesis, so that the six 'days' of creation could be reinterpreted as long periods of time. Perhaps too, God had created man as a distinct species at a late point in the evolutionary process, thus ensuring that his moral nature was intact from the beginning and not itself subject to evolutionary change. By these and other means, conservative Christians tried to make sense of the rapidly changing intellectual climate.[22] In the period between 1876 and 1906, almost every major Protestant denomination experienced at least one heresy trial, usually involving a seminary professor who was seen to have taken his interpretation of the Bible beyond the limits accepted by his Church.[23] In the final quarter of the century, fundamentalism, the most significant legacy of the anti-Darwinian reaction in America, began to emerge in tandem with a number of other conservative religious movements, including Pentecostalism, the holiness movement and Dispensationalism (a pessimistic theology which divided biblical and post-biblical time into seven 'dispensations' or eras, in each of which humanity failed God's test). All these groups attempted to read Scripture in order to discern its literal meaning, and an increasingly wide chasm developed between them and the numerous 'modernists' who attempted various forms of contextual interpretation.

The high point of fundamentalism was not achieved until the early years of the twentieth century, and the tide turned against it in the period after the Scopes trial (1925), in which fundamentalists were heavily lampooned in the press as naive country simpletons. In the post-Scopes era, from 1927 to 1930, legislators in 19 states rejected anti-evolution bills, the new discipline of genetics began to get underway, and the astronomer Edwin Hubble proved conclusively that the universe was indeed very old and expanding, thus providing the first formal scientific evidence for Darwin's theory about the vast length of time over which evolution had occurred.[24] It was only at this date, therefore, that Darwin's arguments of 70 years earlier seemed finally to be unassailable. Creationists did not, however, take this as the signal to give up. They continued to promote their account of human and planetary origins based on a literal reading of Scripture, although their unambiguously fundamentalist worldview made them seem more marginal in the eyes of the liberal majority.

Undoubtedly, then, debates about science and biblical authority contributed significantly, if subtly, to the development of a more secular outlook in America. But most American Christians seem to have swallowed the change that Darwinism brought about without really tasting the difference. Marsden notes that in the 1850s the vast majority of American colleges had had as their presidents evangelical clergymen who ensured a distinctly moral and evangelical flavour to the courses, with science professors confidently proclaiming scientific confirmation of the Bible. By the end of the century all this had changed. The best colleges were now 'universities', or were trying to become so. In undertaking this transition, they modelled themselves on the German scientific university, now seen as leading the field in existing disciplines, as well as in rapidly developing new ones. New syllabuses paid attention to cutting-edge approaches and professionally demanded standards. Increasingly few people really any longer believed that science supported the argument from design, and many were turning to liberal or modernist versions of Christianity in order to salvage what could be 'rescued' from Christian orthodoxy. The cumulative effect was that within hardly a generation, vast areas of American thought and academic life had been removed from all reference to Protestantism or the Bible.[25] It would be an exaggeration to suggest that America had become secular, but it had certainly adopted a strongly compartmentalized approach which separated religious and secular matters.

American Christians faced another very significant challenge to biblical authority, this time one that was not replicated in Europe. As we saw in Chapter 4, the Bible did not provide clear and unambiguous answers on the slavery question, and slavery became the issue which preoccupied America most during the middle decades of the nineteenth century. This meant that in the eyes of many, the authority of the Bible was undermined; no common meaning could be found in the sacred text which almost everyone in the United States professed to honour and which was also the most widely read text of any kind in the whole country.[26] In the decades which preceded the Civil War, and during the conflict itself, religious leaders of all persuasions devoted hundreds of thousands of words to discussing the Bible and slavery. As Mark Noll puts it, many were eager to raise a trumpet for the Lord, but collectively the trumpets blown so forthrightly produced a cacophony.[27] Some abolitionists concluded that if a clear case against slavery could not be made from the Bible, then the Bible would have to be jettisoned; some anti-abolitionists concluded that the abolitionists were scoffing at Scripture. Pro-abolitionists argued violently amongst themselves about how the Bible should be interpreted. The result was a theological crisis of major proportions. As Noll has argued, at the heart of the problem was that whereas pro-slavery texts could be lifted out of the Bible by those adopting a 'common sense' reading of Scripture, the anti-slavery case required a much more nuanced approach, based on a reflective reading of the entirety of Scripture and a detailed knowledge of the historical circumstances and operation of the Roman and Ancient Near Eastern slave systems. But this latter approach, open only to those of the educated elite, contradicted the democratic and republican instincts of the United States, in which evangelical Bible believers were not prepared to defer to their intellectual betters. 'The supreme crisis over the Bible was that there existed no apparent biblical resolution to the crisis.'[28] Shockingly, what finally resolved the question of how to interpret the Bible was recourse to several years of civil war.

The decline of hell

We noted at the beginning of this chapter that one of the processes which contributed to secularization was people's growing willingness to make personal choices without reference to, or interest in, religious teachings. Quite how this somewhat amorphous phenomenon occurred among individuals is not something about which generalizations can easily be made, but it is apparent that during the final quarter of the nineteenth century new attitudes began to develop to some matters about which there had been little noticeable change for decades. One issue which is often cited is changing views on death and the afterlife, as terrifying fears about torment in an eternity of hell began quite rapidly to fade away. Another is people's increasing willingness to attribute circumstances to readily explainable practical rather than theological factors. As John Kent memorably put it, 'Did a baby throw his bread and butter to the floor because of his federal alliance with Adam, or because of a surfeit of plum cake?'[29] Late nineteenth-century Christians were more likely to come to the latter conclusion, and had often developed an emollient, even sentimentalized approach to infants and childhood which meant that they could no longer tolerate traditional views about the fate of naughty children and the unbaptized. In the 1870s, a decade after the retirement of the celebrated Catholic children's missioner, John Furniss, his hell-fire methods began to come under sustained attack. It was disgraceful, Furniss's critics maintained, that he should have sought the religious commitment of children through fear, and should have penned blood-curdling publications with titles such as the *Sight of Hell*. If the idea of eternal punishment was becoming increasingly abhorrent, the thought of preaching it to children was becoming even more so.[30]

The attitude of missionaries to the eternal fate of those whom they sought to evangelize also began to alter, although Brian Stanley notes that it would be simplistic to imply that British Protestantism moved conclusively from an unquestioned belief that all the 'heathen' were destined for hell to a more optimistic or agnostic view. Later in the century, as attacks on the traditional doctrine of eternal punishment gathered strength, Congregationalists and those Anglicans who had been influenced by F.D. Maurice (who had been dismissed from his professorship at King's College London for denying the eternal punishment of the wicked) began to reflect scepticism about the eternal suffering of the lost. Citing the work of G.A. Oddie, Stanley notes that a comparison of doctrinal papers submitted by candidates of the LMS between 1845 and 1858 and between 1876 and 1888 reveals that in the later period, 'candidates were not only less inclined to state a belief in the doctrine of everlasting punishment, but in a number of cases questioned its validity'.[31] Stanley concludes that probably the majority of Congregational ministers and missionaries had abandoned the traditional eschatology by the 1880s, and among the Methodists and Baptists, the process had begun but was less advanced. In contrast, however, a renewed formal adherence to the traditional doctrine began to be seen as an important issue by the more conservative missionary organizations, and when James Hudson Taylor devised a new doctrinal formulary for the China Inland Mission in 1884, he inserted a clause requiring assent to the doctrine of the everlasting punishment of the lost. He had declared when he founded the mission in 1865 that saving the 'million a month' in China whom he claimed were destined for hell was one of his primary purposes, and in the 1880s he still evidently believed that watering down his eschatology would weaken the effectiveness of the mission.[32]

Attitudes to the related issues of death and salvation were also changing. Traditionally the question at the core of Protestant Christianity had always been, 'what must I do to be saved?' Quite what it meant, even in the earlier part of the century, involved different things for different types of Protestant. For the Swiss participants in the *reveil*, 'being saved' was likely to mean a question about conversion; [33] for members of the Church of England, it was more likely to be a question about preparation for a holy death, a shorthand for 'being saved from hell and eternal damnation'. [34] For those whose piety was forged in the liturgical tradition of the Book of Common Prayer, the starkness of the question was to some extent mitigated by the generally comforting tone of the liturgy. The frequent use of the first person plural reinforced the sense of a community of believers, an example of the corporate still being emphasized ahead of the individual. The liturgy itself was penitential, but not exactly unworldly, intimate, without being over-familiar. God desired not the death of a sinner, but that he may turn from his wickedness and live. The purpose of hearing the word in the liturgy was to plant it firmly in the mind and heart of the believer, in part at least so that it could be accessed at the time of death.

Protestants viewed mental confusion, or loss of the power of speech at the time of death as a serious risk. This was because it would be necessary to make a sign that one accepted Christ at the point of death, and it was widely believed that at this moment the destiny of the individual soul was fixed for ever. Protestantism knew no gentle purgatorial dipping of the soul in the lake of penal waters, the image made famous by the Catholic John Henry Newman's poem *The Dream of Gerontius* (1865).[35] The Protestant death had become, and remained, a strictly individual affair, a personal trauma in which family, clergy and friends could offer only limited assistance. Anglicans began to write prayers for use at the death bed, but they stopped short of implying that anything they said or did could alter the soul's post-mortem state. Protestants had only one chance to die well, and so it was important that however frail they became, they had fully internalized the appropriate responses long before hand. This explains the enormous popularity of nineteenth-century death-bed literature, both the many fictionalized and supposedly factual accounts that were published in the cheap evangelical prints, and the more sophisticated versions penned by poets and novelists. People did not read about other people's deaths for entirely lurid reasons. They read about them in order to know what they should do and say themselves.[36] David Hempton has argued that Methodist death-bed scenes, melodramatic, ritualistic and paradigmatic as they were, were intended to show that the faith of Methodists worked unto death itself. 'If Methodists of all people could not die well, then what had been the point of it all? For all those who had invested in, and sacrificed for, the Methodist message, a holy and peaceful death not only was an authentication of the way they spent their lives but also a powerful and final evangelistic gesture.'[37]

By the end of the nineteenth century, some Christians were adopting a universalist position in which all were destined for heaven and others were moving towards a sense of frank agnosticism about the post-mortem state. On moral grounds Christians of many (although not all) theological complexions were finding it increasingly difficult to believe that a loving God could consign large parts of his creation to eternal damnation. Indeed it was the ethical objections to the content of some traditional Christian teachings, and to eternal damnation in particular, which caused a number of former Christians to restyle themselves as freethinkers or honest doubters.[38]

Moreover, as improvements in living conditions and medical science steadily reduced what had previously been the very real risks of sudden or early demise, extensive and constant preparation for a holy death began to seem less important. People began to focus rather more on the quality of their life than on the likely quality of their death.

Meanwhile, in France and Britain especially, from the 1850s there developed an increasingly widespread interest in Spiritualism (known as 'Spiritism' in France) which remained strong until after the First World War. Mary Heimann suggests that it was partly doubts about traditional Christian faith and ethics raised by Darwin's *Descent of Man* that caused the popularity of Spiritualism to take off from the 1870s, as people became overwhelmed with the need to find empirical evidence for the existence of the soul.[39] The possibility of being able to make contact with the spirits of one's dead relatives was something which could appeal to many of all religious persuasions and none, and an added attraction for secularists was that it provided an emotionally absorbing, 'spiritual' activity in which the Church had no involvement or control. The Catholic Church voiced strong disapproval, and in France such activities became strongly overlaid with anti-clericalism.[40] According to Hugh McLeod, 'perhaps the most attractive aspect of Spiritualism was that it purported to prove the fact of immortality, while rejecting hell'.[41] Spiritualism was also particularly attractive to those who had become disillusioned, either with orthodox Christianity, or with scientific materialism, and who were intent on personal exploration and experimentation. Devotees frequently became involved in a wider nexus of interests, which sometimes included vegetarianism, Eastern religions, free love or, conversely, celibacy. Spiritualist mediums sometimes developed a distinctively pastoral function, and offered what would today be described as a range of alternative therapies, from counselling to herbal medicine. By the mid-1860s, British scientists and academics were becoming increasingly interested in psychic phenomena, and in 1882 the subject gained a new respectability when the Society of Psychic Research was founded to conduct scientific investigations.

The rise of leisure

Whilst it might seem over-simplistic to chart the rise of leisure against the decline of hell, there is possibly a subtle linkage which is worthy of exploration. Just as religious revivals tended to occur with greatest intensity during periods of epidemic, so declining churchgoing (where it occurred) tended to take place as the likelihood of illness resulting in sudden death receded. Furthermore a whole variety of later nineteenth-century developments opened up greater leisure opportunities, thus making possible the transformation of Sunday, which for many was still the only completely work-free day in the week, from a day of worship and rest to a day of leisure activity. People who lost the habit of regular Sunday churchgoing often found that it was a difficult habit to regain. Former churchgoers who had found churchgoing tedious but had continued to attend because they feared incurring divine wrath if they were absent were likely to decide to make their absence permanent when no bolt from the heavens had been visited on them after several weeks. Increasingly late nineteenth-century urban dwellers, in particular, could avoid church without incurring scandal, or indeed perhaps even notice.

The period from about 1870 to 1914 witnessed what Hugh McLeod has termed a 'leisure revolution', as a hitherto unimagined range of leisure activities became available for those of all social classes.[42] Holiday resorts developed to suit all tastes and pockets. In Britain they were often by the seaside, and made readily accessible by rail links and the rapid expansion of hotels and guesthouses. In Europe fashionable and exclusive resorts such as Biarritz and Monte Carlo took off, providing a magnet for wealthy Europeans of all nationalities. Sport developed everywhere as a national obsession, with the formation of local, regional and national sports teams which increasingly became the bearers of regional pride and identity. The provision of municipally provided sports pitches, tennis courts and gyms allowed the participation of boys and men, fuelling their aspirations to become like their heroes. Whether as participants or as spectators, sport began to take up a large amount of emotional space in the male psyche. It became fused with a range of other opportunities: soccer became a key bonding mechanism for working-class males; cricket and rowing established one's status in school and university; golf was the essential form of relaxation for business and professional men. Men who professed no interest in sport were increasingly likely to be seen as unmanly 'oddities'. Public dances and other forms of musical and theatrical entertainment also expanded rapidly. For the first time they were aimed at the mass market rather than simply catering for the tastes of the upper classes. They created an expectation in people who had hitherto made their own entertainment that they now needed to 'be entertained' – by professional actors, musicians and music hall artistes. Meeting the expectation laid the foundations for the modern entertainment industry, and for the twentieth-century development of cinema, the gramophone, radio and television. Meanwhile William Booth borrowed explicitly from the repertoire of the new entertainment culture when he created Salvation Army bands and 'citadels', which were meant to look more like music halls than churches.

The mass production of the bicycle was the most important leisure-related invention of the period, allowing people the freedom to travel considerable distances at the time and to the place of their choosing. For suburban and city dwellers, the bicycle gave unique opportunities to escape into the countryside or to the coast and to engage in courtship and social activities at a much greater distance from home; a fit man would think nothing of cycling the sorts of distances that today would only be contemplated by car owners. In 1890s Britain Sunday became the great day for cycling, a development which had occurred somewhat earlier in the more secular climate of France and Germany. McLeod notes that the bicycle became 'the supreme symbol of a new kind of Sunday, unpuritan without necessarily being irreligious, best described by a contributor to a newspaper correspondence on Sunday observance in 1905, who praised the man who "takes his bicycle, entailing no Sunday labour on others, and goes forth to worship God in His bright sunshine, amid His wonderful lakes and fells"'. [43] In Britain the introduction of bank holidays from the 1870s, the new tendency of employers to give a half holiday on Saturday afternoon, and for factories to close for several weeks in the summer, all significantly increased the amount of time that men in particular could devote to leisure. Women never really featured as equal participants in the leisure revolution, although some women obtained bicycles and some participated in certain sports, such as tennis and croquet. Theatre-based entertainment, and day trips or holidays, were open to both sexes, although women often lacked the economic or social independence to undertake them without male assistance.

Since the middle of the nineteenth century, and particularly in its final quarter, many British clergy had realized that they needed to provide some form of leisure facilities in their churches. This enabled them to give their church members the opportunity to socialize in a wholesome atmosphere that was free from alcohol (and in the case of Catholics, free from Protestants), and also to offer convenient and inexpensive recreational facilities to the whole community, sometimes where no secular alternatives as yet existed. Thus many London boxing clubs developed out of churches, as did some football teams. In Birmingham in 1880, 83 out of 344 football clubs had a religious affiliation;[44] the most famous example was to become Aston Villa. Clergy, who had often been influenced by the sporting ethos at school and university, were frequently keen to introduce sport into the parish and to use it as an evangelistic mechanism for maintaining the interest of boys and men. But as McLeod notes, using church-based leisure facilities to attract unchurched sports fanatics was seldom hugely successful, as they might be happy to use the gym but reluctant to appear regularly at worship. Church boxing clubs also became problematic if gambling started, and church dances were sometimes seen as needing preventative clerical intervention if the styles of dancing became excessively intimate.[45] In France and Germany the links between Catholic churches and sports clubs were if anything stronger than in Britain, providing an important element in the development of an all-encompassing Catholic culture which was an alternative to the secular world. In France in 1905, when the Catholic soccer champions played the champions of the secular league, their 2-1 victory was hailed in the Catholic press as an event of both political and spiritual significance.[46]

Back in Britain the clergy were more successful at maintaining the interest of women, after their attempts with sportsmen began to fade. They had long realized that there was a particular need to offer social facilities to women, who had always been excluded from the nineteenth-century's great male social facility, the public house. Certainly Mothers' Unions and Women's Institutes continued on church premises long after equivalent male social organizations had bitten the dust. Many clergy tried hard to adapt to the changing times. Specialist publications designed for worshippers on the move, like the *Tourist's Church Guide* (from 1874), were designed to help Anglo-Catholics seek out suitable places of worship. Meanwhile some of the incumbents of churches in scenic locations began to advertise themselves as being particularly welcoming to passing cyclists. But while the Churches continued to work hard to extol the virtues of Christian sportsmen (of whom there were many celebrated examples), or of an invigorating cycle ride after one had been to church, the truth was that in late nineteenth-century Britain people were becoming more interested in sport for its own sake and in pursing their varied leisure interests without the impediment of building church attendance into Sunday's activities.

The significance of secularization

By the end of the nineteenth century, educated Americans had increasingly divided their world into neat compartments of the secular and the religious, and most of them knew that the status of the Bible would never be the same as it had been in the pre-Civil War and pre-Darwin era. Meanwhile European secular thinkers had colonized more and more intellectual territory and had evolved a number of multi-layered perspectives on the world, differing versions of which could be embraced equally enthusiastically by working men in Berlin or Parisian professionals. Socialism, popular science, progress, a belief in the ever-increasing intellectual power and wisdom of humanity, a cultural aesthetic expressed in opera, painting and literature and sometimes an interest in psychoanalysis, which helped people to understand why they were the way they were, or spiritualism, which opened up the possibility of gaining controlled access to dead relatives: all these things provided people with the raw materials to create absorbing and compelling accounts of what it meant to be human. Meanwhile the civic authorities in late nineteenth-century European cities – as well as individual entrepreneurs – were increasingly seeing it as their duty to provide ambitious leisure facilities for their citizens: theatres, music halls, sports stadiums, pleasure gardens, fun fairs – all became part of the fabric of late nineteenth-century life. Other facilities, such as public libraries, museums, art galleries and swimming baths were intended to provide educational and health benefits. In Britain people were expressing their desire for freedom and to enjoy their lives and their leisure without an oppressive sense of Victorian puritan restraint. Everywhere people yearned for entertainment, and they expected to be able to travel, whether by train, tram or bicycle. There was a greater expectation of individual freedom of choice than had hitherto ever been seen.

The balance had begun to shift between people who were primarily motivated by religious considerations, and people who were not. The priest saying Mass in his little country church, the women and girls wondering if there might be another Marian apparition, the revivalist preacher wondering if anyone would come and hear his message, the biblical fundamentalist wondering about the effect of the whale's digestive system on Jonah; from a secularist perspective, all these people began to look hopelessly simple, credulous, naive even; individuals in thrall to a providentially driven view of the universe, who had somehow missed the point of the intellectual and cultural revolution which had occurred in the second half of the nineteenth century.

CHAPTER 8

Conclusion: The Uniqueness of the Church in the Nineteenth Century

In this concluding chapter we shall attempt to draw together some of the threads from earlier chapters by briefly considering three further themes which seem to highlight in a particular way the uniqueness of the nineteenth-century Church. In doing so we shall also return to a theme which was outlined in the Introduction, namely that of the gulf between Roman Catholicism and Protestantism. The three final topics – piety, femininity and sobriety – have been selected because they seem to highlight the differences between the two great rival versions of Christianity, whilst at the same time pointing up some of the similarities.

Piety

Even the choice of the word 'piety' reveals a Protestant bias. Whereas Protestants cultivated their piety, Catholics preferred the term 'devotion'. But for both it meant paying attention to those aspects of religious life which went beyond the bare minimum of fulfilling the obligation of Sunday church attendance. It meant cultivating the extra elements which helped to shape a distinctive Catholic or Protestant outlook, although other factors, particularly the influence of home and the immediately surrounding environment, were probably just as important in the formation of a strong denominational identity. Common to both Catholics and Protestants at this period was a strong emphasis on personal religion, which, as we have seen, was forged in reaction against both what people perceived as the cold rationalism of the eighteenth century and the atheistic lawlessness of the revolutionary period. Nineteenth-century Christians of all types, whether consciously or not, often found solace in the ideas associated with the Romantic movement; they wanted to place feeling above logic and to give attention to maintaining a personal, individual relationship with God. Personal, experiential religion was not of course unique to the nineteenth century. It had had powerful antecedents in earlier Moravianism and Methodism, and would have a huge impact in later Pentecostalism. But, as we shall see, personal piety was also transposed into a distinctively nineteenth-century key.

Some of the distinctiveness of Protestant piety came from its reaction against Rome. At the heart of the Reformation break with Rome had been an objection to the pious practices of late medieval Christians: indulgences, pilgrimages, shrines, miracles, Masses for the dead and for special intentions; all were seen as corruptions which needed to be swept away in the Protestant world. From their earliest generations, Protestants had emphasized instead word over sacrament, and personal commitment over corporate belonging. Reading and hearing the Bible and listening to sermons replaced attendance at Mass, and extra-liturgical devotions were seen as dangerous distractions from the essential duty of responding to the word. Jesus's mother disappeared from the religious landscape. Theological study itself could become a ritualized activity, and with the spread of literacy in the nineteenth century everyone could become their own interpreter of Scripture. Indeed this was exactly what William Miller became, when he decided that he would put away the biblical commentaries in the library at Poultney, Vermont, and read only the Bible itself. The result of most people's Scripture study was of course less eccentric than that of Miller, who, as we saw in Chapter 4, concluded by prophesying the end of the world in 1843, and again in 1844. But the emphasis on every Protestant becoming their own theologian, assisted by the publication of large amounts of easily available religious material, a devotion to sermons, and a culture where the discussion of theological issues was seen as a normal part of ordinary life, was a unique feature of the nineteenth-century Church. In South Wales the Rhymney baptismal fair of 1844 is a good example, as Nonconformists with different theologies of baptism engaged each other in debate for hours on end from stages set up on wagons.[1]

Nineteenth-century evangelicals, as we saw in Chapter 6, placed a great emphasis upon conversion. It was an essential part of the revival process. But once converted, what were they supposed to do? Regular attendance at Sunday worship, keeping the Sabbath day holy, diligent Bible study and regular prayer in the home had long been seen as the obvious Protestant requirements. This produced a routine for seven days of the week, but it lacked the longer-term, cyclical approach to Christian time, with the emphasis on the feasts and fasts of the liturgical year, that was a feature of Catholic countries. Several centuries earlier, the Protestant nations had severely curtailed the observance of saints' and holy days, although they had not always been successful at eliminating them entirely. The Annunciation of the Blessed Virgin Mary on 25 March, known as Lady Day, was in nineteenth-century Britain still an important day when rents fell due, and in Britain today, Old Lady Day (6 April) still starts the fiscal year for tax purposes – although this seems rather far removed from its original meaning as a religious festival! For Protestants traditional cyclical patterns of religious observance had become linear, and with it the notion of progress in the spiritual life had come to the fore. Spiritual progress was not of course an idea that was alien to Catholicism, but the emphasis on ordinary individuals (as opposed to those destined for sainthood) progressing to states of holiness and sanctification was less pronounced. One of the most enduringly popular Protestant devotional books of all time, translated into many languages and still widely read in the nineteenth century, was John Bunyan's *The Pilgrim's Progress*, which was first published in 1678. *The Pilgrim's Progress* encapsulates the centrality of this idea in its title, and works it out as the central character, Christian, makes his progress from the City of Destruction to the Heavenly City.

Another key feature of Protestant piety was the use of the regular meeting for the committed, an idea that began within Methodism and was taken up more widely, to permit the godly to meet with the like minded for mutual support, encouragement, and, if necessary, reproof. Meetings, usually held on week nights, separated out those who merely attended worship on Sunday from those who were actively engaged in seeking their salvation, 'fleeing from the wrath to come', as the early Methodists had put it. Class meetings were for people who wanted to cultivate godly language, temperance, honesty, plainness, seriousness, frugality, diligence, charity and economic loyalty within the Methodist connection. Band meetings were smaller and segregated by gender and marital status. They were seen as places of confession for committed Christians who were intent upon pursuing sanctification. Originally Methodist classes had had about 12 members in one geographical area meeting with one identified leader, but in time they grew larger, to around 25 to 35 people. Women predominated on a ratio of about three to two. David Hempton has argued that class meetings were the most important building blocks of religion in America.[2] The issuing of quarterly membership tickets created a strong sense of loyalty and the importance of maintaining high spiritual standards, as tickets were withheld from those who were seen to be backsliders. Thus Methodism created a series of short-term contracts with its membership, in contrast to the permanency which was a stronger feature in those denominations which emphasized baptism as the sacrament through which one obtained membership of the Church.

Evangelicals who were committed to remaining within state Churches usually borrowed from Dissent by organizing their own separate meetings for the devout. In England evangelical Anglican clergy often arranged cottage meetings in conscious imitation of the Methodists. These consisted of Bible readings, a short address and extempore prayer. The idea was that they should be much less formal than Sunday worship, and that the rigid social hierarchy that was usually reinforced should, in theory at least, be temporarily suspended. But they differed crucially from Methodism in not being lay-led.[3] In Vaud, Switzerland, Félix Neff was influenced by the Moravians when he insisted that there should be separate associations within the established Church that were composed specifically of devout believers. He believed that although the converted and the unconverted should mix together in church, the leaven should permeate the lump whilst remaining hidden itself.[4] In the very different environment of nineteenth-century America, Sydney Ahlstrom argued that Puritan piety helped to create a nation of individualists who were also fervent moral athletes.[5] Arguably this was among the strongest features of nineteenth-century Protestant piety wherever it occurred.

As indicated earlier, Catholics also drew on the inspiration of the Romantic movement, and, like their Protestant neighbours, they were on the look out for a deeper form of religious experience. As Mary Heimann puts it 'much of the argument which surrounded [Catholic] devotional change in England during the second half of the nineteenth century turned precisely on the question of how much importance ought to be attributed to feeling, and the degree to which specific devotions ought to be seen as the measure of, or the means of inculcating, a more fervent love of God'.[6] We saw in Chapter 6 that there was often a striking similarity between the form (but not of course the content) of Protestant revivals and Catholic missions, and the same is true of Protestant piety and Catholic devotion. Ultimately developments in Catholic devotion may have been more a matter of changing taste than anything that was either theologically determined or clerically controlled. Heimann notes that there was a general shift away from the more gentlemanly piety of the eighteenth century, which began to be seen as cold and rationalistic. Quite why so many new forms of devotion, such as to the rosary, to the Sacred Heart of Jesus, to the stations of the Cross, and to services such as Benediction, should have become so suddenly popular does not yet seem to have been fully explained, although mass manufacture of religious objects and easier travel to holy sites may have had something to do with it. It does not, however, seem adequate to attribute it (as many Protestants did) to ever greater levels of Vatican control. Whilst the impact of Ultramontanism may have had some influence in some places, the reality was that no papal pronouncements could have had the degree of influence that would have been required to bring about a sea-change in the enormously complex global entity that was the nineteenth-century Catholic Church. As Heimann reminds us, 'However compelling arguments for an "Ultramontane" triumph over "Liberal Catholicism" or "Gallicanism" in the nineteenth century might at first appear, their very functionalism ought to put us on our guard: real life is seldom so tidy as to consist merely of the straightforward imposition of "power" by one group over another.'[7] Ecclesiastical authorities may have taught the use of the rosary as an aid to prayer and as a means to promote devotion to the Virgin Mary, but they could do little to stop the way in which ordinary people would choose to use the beads, whether it was rural Irish peasants placing rosaries on the corpses of dead girls, or villagers in West Africa hanging them on the walls of their homes like charms to ward off evil.[8] The further away the Church moved from its European heartland, the more it had to turn a blind eye to unconventional or unorthodox expressions of Catholicism, as we saw in Chapter 5.

For Catholics, membership of exclusively Catholic societies, known as guilds, confraternities or sodalities, took the place of the Protestant class, band or cottage meeting, and participation in processions, missions and pilgrimages took the place of camp meetings or other revivalist gatherings. The validity of direct religious experience among Catholics began to be emphasized with as much fervour as it was among Protestant evangelicals, and the same tensions were present between those who were cautious about the emotional element in religious experience and those who wished to embrace it with ever more fervour. Certainly the Vatican seems to have struggled to keep up with the explosion of different devotional forms that were appearing all over the world.

Femininity

Mary Heimann argues that the fashion for 'vulgar piety' which emerged in the nineteenth century made piety more feminine (and proletarian) than what had gone before. She suggests that this veneration of feminine piety was perfectly encapsulated in the most famous of the nineteenth-century Marian visionaries, Bernadette Soubirous (St Bernadette), who herself became something of an icon of feminine spirituality in the Catholic world.[9] As noted in Chapter 3, when the Virgin Mary appeared in Lourdes she declared that she was 'the Immaculate Conception', but it is worth reflecting a little further here on how the enormous cult of Mary contributed to the feminization of faith. Mary herself was honoured as virgin and mother, thereby enhancing the status of both of these conditions, and a very large proportion of those who claimed to have witnessed her were girls or young women. Whereas

Marian visions had had a long history, female visionaries were a distinctively nineteenth-century development. Most young, female visionaries came from impoverished backgrounds, and had had damaged relationships with their own parents.[10] Soubirous herself, a social outcast from the Pyrenean town of Lourdes who had 18 separate visions of the Virgin Mary in the period from 1858, was in many ways the archetype. Such girls offered an unexpected challenge to the established male authority of the Church.

The Virgin Mary herself became a truly transnational figure in the nineteenth-century Catholic world. Marian apparitions were reported in numerous locations in France and Italy, in Spain and Portugal, in Knock in Ireland, and in Marpingen and Kevelaer in Germany; some of these were authenticated by the ecclesiastical authorities and gave rise to enormous pilgrimage centres, but many were not. Although non-European apparitions seem to be less well documented, they occurred nevertheless, particularly in Latin America. There were even two Marian pilgrimage sites that developed in Vietnam, following apparitions at Tra Kieu and La Vang.[11] Although both sexes flocked to Marian pilgrimage sites, it was always women that outnumbered men. There was, however, more to the Marianization of nineteenth-century Catholicism than apparitions, as David Blackbourn has shown. Her influence could be seen in the articulation of new doctrine (the Immaculate Conception), the naming of new congregations and in Marian hymnals and new popular devotions.[12] In part, Mary was seen as Catholicism's answer to the growth of secularism. She started making frequent appearances just at the point when Darwin's ideas were beginning to spread, and the miraculous nature of her appearances provided its own challenge to the cult of scientific rationalism, a triumphant reassertion of supernatural power. It was perhaps not surprising that sceptics tried to dismiss Marian visionaries as gullible, attention-seeking peasants, in rather the same way that American liberals tried to dismiss fundamentalists as naive country bumpkins who would shed their silliness if they were exposed to the sophistication of city life. But the fact remained that Mary became a central figure in the lives of many hundreds of thousands of Catholics, female and male, urban and rural, educated and uneducated, all over the world. She offered comfort and solace to those who were suffering the effects of poverty, sickness, marginalization or political persecution of the type embodied in the *Kulturkampf*. To those who were more fortunate, she offered a perfect exemplar of purity, faithfulness and love; she combined the paradox of virginity and motherhood with extraordinary power. To a remarkable degree, the nineteenth century was Mary's century.

The nineteenth century was also the age of the nun. Susan O'Brien has estimated that in the 100 years from the end of the Napoleonic Wars to the start of the First World War, as many as 400,000 women became nuns or religious sisters within the Catholic Church, and about 10,000 women spent some time in an Anglican sisterhood in Britain, of whom perhaps 5,000 stayed for life.[13] Over 90 per cent of these women joined active rather than contemplative orders, and a very high proportion were involved either in teaching or nursing. Indeed it would not have been possible for the Church to achieve its highly prized goal of separate schooling had it not been for all the teaching sisters who were available to staff schools, with huge commitment and without the desire for personal financial reward. The vast majority of the orders that these women joined were either new or re-founded, and many of them originated in French-speaking Belgium or in France, where the desire of Catholics to atone for the sacrilege of the revolutionary period was very strong. The revitalization of the religious life was seen as one way of achieving this. From francophone Europe these orders spread to the rest of the world and played a large role in Catholic missionary efforts. The Daughters of Jesus and Mary was typical. It had been founded by Marie-Claudine Thévenet, who had endured the horror of watching her brothers being executed during the revolutionary period. Her order began life as a teaching congregation in the archdiocese of Lyons, with its focus on running schools and orphanages. In 1841 it started work in northern India, and from then on turned itself into an international missionary congregation, with further houses in Spain, Canada and England, and later expansion into Mexico, the United States and Ireland.[14]

As the century progressed, in some countries the number of nuns began to outstrip the combined number of priests, monks, friars and brothers. This had occurred in Ireland by 1900, at which date women comprised 64 per cent of the Church's personnel, and also in Australia, where women massively outnumbered men. This profound change in the religious life was in its way as significant as the great monastic reform movements of the Middle Ages. It certainly contributed to the feminization of the Church, as well as to the development of its particular international perspective, as increasingly large numbers of women found themselves in active ministry abroad, especially in the aftermath of expulsions from Germany following the *Kulturkampf* in the 1870s, and the separation of church and state in France in 1904. For large numbers of women, life as a nun was an attractive proposition, and not the refuge of the desperate, as many Protestants believed. It offered opportunities for activity, usefulness, travel, some degree of authority and freedom from the trials of reproduction in its gruesome nineteenth-century form. Nuns were thus able to override the tightly constructed gender identity that was enforced on other women. They changed their names and their appearance, and they exchanged family life for community life. Foundresses of religious houses and reverend mothers were able to exercise leadership without attracting censure for being unwomanly. By the end of the century, not only did women comprise a very large proportion of Catholicism's active personnel, but they also formed an increasingly large number of active churchgoers. In Europe at least it was becoming a common pattern for men to leave religion to their wives and daughters. As Blackbourn puts it, as religion increasingly became a woman's sphere, the Church seemed to offer women a 'respite from powerlessness'.[15] The fact that women lacked formal power in the Catholic Church seemed less extraordinary in a world where women lacked formal power in most other institutions also.

Protestantism too was becoming a feminine space. Indeed one of the criticisms which has been made of older versions of the secularization thesis is that they were gender-blind. When contemporary observers, or indeed some twentieth-century scholars, commented that they saw fewer churchgoers in the late nineteenth-century Church, what they usually meant was that they saw fewer male churchgoers. Women often continued to go as before, or even more frequently, but seem to have remained invisible to many male observers.[16] Churchgoing and participation in church-related activities continued to be important for women of all classes, particularly as so many of the secular alternatives were largely or wholly aimed at men, as we saw in the last chapter. Meanwhile much has been written about the transformation of British middle-class women from the commercially or agriculturally active people that they so often were in the eighteenth century to the passive, sofa-bound creatures that they became in the nineteenth. As women's work no longer began to be seen as respectable, Victorian men came under increasing pressure to bring home an income large enough to support the entire family, and Victorian women came under pressure to behave like domestic angels with clipped wings. As the English Congregationalist John Angell James put it in 1852, 'There are few words in the language around which cluster so many blissful associations as that delight of every English heart, the word HOME ... One of the most hallowed, and lovely, and beautiful sights in our world is, woman at home.'[17]

Amongst the middle classes, it was believed that women's greater religiosity was fuelled by their greater leisure for contemplation, and by their being shielded from the knowledge and temptations of the world. Contemporary views of feminine faith, gentleness and passivity became subtly interlinked to make women appear more 'naturally' religious. Meanwhile a husband toiling endlessly in his grubby city office might well be tempted to invest his wife with the virtues which he felt that he sacrificed in the business world – purity, faith, charity and hope. It was hardly surprising that in a society that remained so clearly obsessed with religion, men wanted their wives to be religious.[18] It was sometimes argued (admittedly by Christian commentators) that even an atheist or an infidel would want his wife to be religious, in order to ensure a happy home.[19] On the whole women seem to have been willing to be regarded as more 'naturally' spiritual than men, with a greater capacity for making sense of religion. Jeffrey Cox has argued that among the working classes, it was women who made the decisions about their family's religious observance.[20]

There was a tension between the Protestant desire to sanctify the home, and to place women on a pillar of piety, and the traditional evangelical requirement for activism. Evangelicals believed that all Christians needed to be actively promoting the salvation of others and also that they had a special duty towards those less fortunate than themselves. A survey of women's work in Britain carried out in 1893 by Louisa Hubbard and Angela Burdett-Coutts estimated that a staggering 500,000 women laboured 'continuously and semi-professionally in philanthropy' and another 20,000 supported themselves as the paid officials in charitable societies.[21] For the vast majority who worked on a voluntary basis the absence of payment was beside the point. First and foremost, they were fulfilling their religious duty of relieving the sufferings of others, and, they hoped, pointing to the path that led to salvation through faith in Jesus Christ.[22]

Philanthropy was unique in being the only form of church work that was open to women of all denominations. Other activities were likely to be circumscribed as much by the religious ethos of the denomination as by the limitations imposed by being a nineteenth-century female. No Primitive Methodist would consider becoming a nun, any more than a Roman Catholic woman would consider engaging in an itinerant preaching ministry. Female preaching and leadership in worship were associated with Nonconformist revivalism. Rachel Stearns, the Massachusetts Methodist whom we met in Chapter 6, commented that after the staid environment of Congregationalism, she enjoyed being able to participate in Methodist services by leading prayers and by shouting. There were many women like Rachel Stearns, but they were able to express themselves more vocally at the beginning of the century than at the end. Deborah Valenze has shown that within English Methodism, female preaching was a feature of the eighteenth and the very early nineteenth centuries, but that it was stamped out as the Methodist denominations became institutionalized and governed by male-led bureaucracies.[23] The same was generally true elsewhere in the Protestant world, with the exception of organizations such as the Salvation Army.

On the other hand, and somewhat paradoxically, by the second half of the century a few women had emerged as well-known religious leaders.

Phoebe Palmer, Ellen White, Catherine Booth and Mary Baker Eddy are all still revered today as originators of new, distinctive and continuing Christian movements. In the late eighteenth and early nineteenth centuries, it was usually only extremely emotionally distressed women who tried to become religious leaders, and they were normally dismissed as mad. Examples include Joanna Southcott, who claimed that she was giving birth to a messianic child in 1814, and Ann Lee, who had to escape Britain for America in order to put her religious ideas into practice by founding the Shakers, as we saw in Chapter 4.

Sobriety

In the second half of the nineteenth century, Christians of all types became increasingly engaged in social campaigns, and the development of Christian social thought and action was to become one of the central features of the Churches in the twentieth century. It was, however, the campaign against drink that had a uniquely late nineteenth- and early twentieth-century flavour, dying out in many places after the First World War almost as rapidly as it had arisen in the 1850s. Because, almost uniquely at this period, it received widespread support from all Christian groups and also from secularists, and was seen as carrying the hopes of a better world by both theological liberals and theological conservatives, the worldwide temperance campaign makes a fitting topic with which to conclude a book on the Church in the nineteenth century.

Protestants tended to be critical of Catholics for engaging in (or being suspected of engaging in) recreational activities of which they disapproved, such as drinking, gambling and dancing, but in fact the leadership of the Catholic Church at this period was strong in its advocacy of teetotalism. In England the Roman Catholic Church founded 11 societies specifically devoted to temperance or to total abstinence in the 15 years between 1860 and 1875,[24] and Cardinal Manning was a notable supporter. In Ireland, increasingly stiff penalties were invoked against parishioners who promised to renounce alcohol but failed to keep the pledge. Father Theobald Mathew started a temperance crusade in the south west of Ireland in 1838, and signed up many thousands to a promise of teetotalism. He became Catholicism's best-known anti-drink campaigner. His campaign had, however, peaked by the late 1840s, rather earlier than in America or Britain. Mathew himself, worn out by his preaching tours, had come under suspicion from the bishops, who saw him as a Roman Catholic version of the evangelical pulpit orators they so much despised.[25] Sheridan Gilley has suggested that the inability to overcome the drunkenness prevalent in Irish rural life before 1850 explains why many emigrants to the New World failed to make the transition to the Tridentine norm of Sunday Mass-going, and rapidly lost touch with their religion. In order to sustain the new Irish Church of the diaspora, it was necessary to create a respectable and well-behaved body of worshippers who could cope with the complexities of urban life; the temperance campaign was therefore necessary to ease the Church's transition into the New World.[26] In a similar vein, S.J. Connolly has argued that in rural Ireland, temperance developed as a revivalist movement with strong millenarian overtones. 'Among urban artisans, on the other hand, it became a vehicle for the culture of self-improvement, highly organised, emphasising values of thrift, self-discipline and literacy, and closely linked to political self-assertion.'[27]

In America the Catholic temperance movement achieved its first peak during a visit from Father Mathew in 1849. Thousands of Catholics took the pledge from Father Mathew, and the number of total abstinence societies markedly increased. Temperance became a preoccupation of all religious orders involved in parish missions. As Jay P. Dolan puts it, temperance 'did not originate with the emergence of revivalism, but the mission reinforced the crusade for temperance and enveloped the pledge in an aura of a life or death decision. The drunken sinner was a nightly visitor to the revival meeting. He appeared in just about every sermon as a classic example of the sinner, and his vice was always singled out as one of the most destructive plagues to have befallen mankind.'[28] The Paulist missioner Walter Elliott even refused to give absolution to saloon keepers unless they abandoned the trade. As we saw in Chapter 4, in America there were considerable tensions between Catholics of different national origins, and this extended to differing approaches to the temperance question. The Germans were notably more reticent about recommending the pledge, except as a last resort for habitual drunkards. They made a distinction between beer (particularly beer), wine and cider, which they saw as natural products which could be imbibed in moderation, and liquor which was the product of distilling, which they believed should only be taken as medicine, and then in the smallest possible quantities.[29]

Temperance was an equally important issue in the Protestant world, where it also loomed large in the minds of the reform-minded. It somewhat predated the Catholic campaign, with the first American Society for the Promotion of Temperance being formed in 1826, although in reality this organization was limited in its activities to Massachusetts. From America, the movement spread to Canada, Britain and Ireland. Like the Catholics, Protestants became equally divided about which alcoholic drinks could be consumed in moderation and which should be abstained from completely. There was also concern that taking the pledge could be seen as a secular substitute for evangelical conversion, and this resulted in the majority of British evangelicals deciding to delay their support for teetotalism until the 1860s.[30] Indeed, the London Baptist Association only abandoned wine at its dinners in 1880.[31]

By the 1870s temperance had become associated with a number of other progressive causes, particularly women's rights. Mark Noll argues that America's temperance and prohibition movements were the direct successors of antebellum movements like the fight against slavery. Just as some had laboured to win freedom for the slaves, after the Civil War many made great efforts to free the nation from 'slavery' to alcohol. The American Protestant temperance campaign was headed by a Methodist woman, Frances Willard, who was an associate of the leading revivalist preacher Dwight L. Moody. Willard organized activities in conjunction with Moody's urban revivals. She was a persistent advocate of women's right to preach, although her denomination, the Methodist Episcopal Church, did not ordain women.[32] Willard's Women's Christian Temperance Union (WCTU), founded in American in 1874, rapidly spread to Canada, Europe and the Antipodes. In Australia and New Zealand temperance campaigners believed that giving women the vote would lead to strong anti-drink legislation, and thus the issue became linked to women's suffrage, resulting in the WCTU obtaining votes for women in New Zealand in 1893.[33] In America the WCTU was largely responsible for raising the age of consent in some states to 16. Temperance campaigners throughout the world were united by the belief that the abuse of women and children could only be lessened when men became sober, and thus sobriety was the starting point for orderly family life.

By the end of the First World War temperance as a global movement had become completely divided. On the one hand, the United States passed the Eighteenth Amendment to the constitution, which imposed prohibition on the whole of the country until its repeal in 1933. A similar course of action was contemplated in Scotland, as we saw in Chapter 2. Elsewhere the movement was in retreat, as legislatures around the world generally declined to pass anti-drink legislation. In England Anglican clergy of the 1920s, whose fathers would have regarded total abstinence as a defining element in clerical culture, were beginning to enjoy the occasional half pint with a clear conscience. The clergy became much more likely to make a clear distinction between the moderate use of alcohol in the form of non-addictive social drinking, sometimes sanctified as the 'enjoyment of God's good gifts', and the classical late nineteenth-century scenario, which maintained that total abstinence was the only way to keep off the slippery slope that led to alcoholism and destitution.[34]

By the same token, Roman Catholics and Protestants were finally moving towards the point where those who allowed themselves that half-pint glass would be able to propose a toast – not to the conversion of the world to Christianity, which had been their great nineteenth-century dream, but to an ecumenical future in which Christians of very different beliefs and practices would be able to reach out to each other in friendship rather than hostility. As Europe tried to rebuild itself after the deep emotional, political and theological shocks of the Great War, the antagonisms that had existed for centuries between Christians of different Churches were seen to have increasingly less power. In the twentieth-century world, personal choice would continue to be as important a factor in determining individual religious allegiance as it had been in mid-nineteenth century Nottingham on the day of the religious census. But no Anglican vicar would look upon all the non-Anglican Christians in the town with feelings of anxiety and dread, as Joshua Brooks had done. Instead he would be thankful that there were others at hand who shared most, if not all, of his values.

The purpose of this book has been to describe and explain something of the extraordinary global expansion of the Church in the nineteenth century, how it fared in its European heartlands and in the New World, and how the powerful twin forces of revival and renewal, and dislocation and decline worked upon it. I have argued that the narratives of both revival and renewal, and dislocation and decline, provide the structures for the interpretative frameworks which are currently favoured by historians. Ultimately it is for the reader to decide which of these forces was the most powerful, which of the narratives is the most satisfying, and whether the Church in the nineteenth century was more strongly shaped by revival, renewal and global expansion than by secularization and decline, or whether in fact both were present and at work simultaneously.

Notes

Introduction: Interpreting the Church in the Nineteenth Century

1. See in particular Callum G. Brown, *The Death of Christian Britain: Understanding Secularisation 1800–2000* (London, 2001).
2. See Hugh McLeod, *Secularisation in Western Europe, 1848–1914* (New York, 2000), pp 1–30, for an excellent introduction to the secularization thesis as it is being currently applied to the study of nineteenth-century Christianity.
3. Jeffrey Cox, 'Master Narratives of Long-Term Religious Change', in Hugh McLeod and Werner Ustorf (eds), *The Decline of Christendom in Western Europe, 1750–2000* (Cambridge, 2001), p 208.
4. Dag Thorkildsen, 'Scandinavia, Lutheranism and National Identity', in Sheridan Gilley and Brian Stanley (eds), *The Cambridge History of Christianity: World Christianities c.1815–1914* (Cambridge, 2006), p 349.
5. Thomas Kselman, 'The Varieties of Religious Experience in Urban France', in Hugh McLeod (ed), *European Religion in the Age of Great Cities 1830–1930* (London, 1995), pp 167–8.
6. Others who have come to a similar (although by no means identical) position on pluralism are Kselman, 'Varieties of Religious Experience', pp 165–90, and Hugh McLeod, *Secularisation in Western Europe*, p 28.
7. I am grateful to the Canadian scholars Hannah Lane, Michael Gauvreau and Nancy Christie who have all made this point to me. See also Frances Knight, *The Nineteenth-Century Church and English Society* (Cambridge, 1995), pp 24–36.
8. McLeod, *Secularisation in Western Europe*, p 14.
9. Terence J. Fay, *A History of Canadian Catholics: Gallicanism, Romanism and Canadianism* (Montreal and Kingston, 2002), p xii.
10. David W. Bebbington, *The Dominance of Evangelicalism: The Age of Spurgeon and Moody* (Leicester, 2005), p 20. See also David W. Bebbington, *Evangelicalism in Modern Britain: A History from the 1730s to the 1980s* (London, 1989), pp 2–17.
11. Edwin Scott Gaustad and Philip L. Barlow, *New Historical Atlas of Religion in America* (Oxford and New York, 2001), figure C.17.

Chapter 1. England and Wales

1. This reconstruction of Joshua Brooks's reaction to the 1851 religious census is mainly based on his letter to George Graham, 1 April 1851. The letter is published in Michael Watts, *Religion in Victorian Nottinghamshire: The Religious Census of 1851*, vol. 2 (Nottingham, 1988), p 183. Additional information has been derived from Michael Watts's work on the 1851 census, correspondence relating to St Mary's Nottingham and Joshua Brooks held at the Lincolnshire Archives Office (LAO CorB5/8/18, CorB5/8/19 and CorB5/8/20), *Nottingham Review*, 13 January 1843, and David M. Thompson, 'The 1851 Religious Census: Problems and Possibilities', *Victorian Studies* xi/1 (1967), pp 87–97.

2. Richard Dennis, *English Industrial Cities in the Nineteenth Century: A Social Geography* (Cambridge, 1984), pp 30–1.

3. Watts, *Religion in Victorian Nottinghamshire*, vol. 2, pp 176–94.

4. Anonymous pamphlet allegedly circulated by Irish Protestant clergy resident in Nottingham, entitled *Interesting to Protestants and Roman Catholics*, n.d. but *c.*1844. It accused Catholics of ignoring the Second Commandment, Exodus 20.4–6, which prohibits making and worshipping idols. A copy survives in LAO CorB5/8/31/1/169.

5. Hugh McLeod, *Religion and Society in England, 1850–1914* (Basingstoke, 1996), pp 29, 33; K.D.M. Snell and Paul S. Ell, *Rival Jerusalems: The Geography of Victorian Religion* (Cambridge, 2000).

6. Snell and Ell, *Rival Jerusalems*, p 71.

7. *Ibid.*, pp 124–6.

8. *Ibid.*, p 137.

9. McLeod, *Religion and Society in England*, p 28.

10. *Ibid.*, p 38.

11. Horace Mann, who was responsible for organizing the census and presenting the data, attempted to compensate for the number of multiple attendances by the operation of a very crude formula which involved counting all who attended morning services, half of those who attended in the afternoon, and one-third of those who attended in the evening. Mann reasoned that those who attended after lunch were more likely to have also attended in the morning. In fact, this formula had the effect of deflating the numbers of Nonconformist and working-class worshippers, who typically attended services later in the day.

12. McLeod, *Religion and Society in England*, p 12.

13. Editions of the census for the whole of Wales have been published in Ieuan Gwynedd Jones and David Williams (eds), *The Religious Census of 1851: A Calendar of the Returns Relating to Wales, vol. 1: South Wales* (Cardiff, 1976), and Ieuan Gwynedd Jones (ed), *The Religious Census of 1851: A Calendar of the Returns Relating to Wales, vol. 2: North Wales* (Cardiff, 1981).

14. Ieuan Gwynedd Jones, *Mid-Victorian Wales: The Observers and the Observed* (Cardiff, 1992), p 131.

15. Ieuan Gwynedd Jones, 'Denominationalism in Caernarvonshire in the Mid-Nineteenth Century as Shown in the Religious Census of 1851', *Transactions of the Caernarvonshire Historical Society* 31 (1970), pp 82–3.

16. John Wolffe, *God and Greater Britain: Religion and National Life in Britain and Ireland 1843–1945* (London, 1994), p 66.

17. Jones, 'Denominationalism in Caernarvonshire', pp 88–9. See also John Davies, *A History of Wales* (London, 1993), pp 424–6, which provides a very helpful set of maps indicating all the places of worship recorded in the 1851 census for Anglicans, Congregationalists, Baptists, Calvinistic Methodists, Wesleyan Methodists, Catholics, Unitarians and Mormons.

18. Snell and Ell, *Rival Jerusalems*, pp 55–8.

19. Michael Watts, *The Dissenters: From the Reformation to the French Revolution* (Oxford, 1978), pp 1–2. See also Clyde Binfield, *So Down to Prayers: Studies in English Nonconformity 1780–1920* (London, 1977), for a detailed discussion of the meanings of 'Dissent', 'Nonconformity' and 'Free Churchmanship'.

20. Glanmor Williams, William Jacob, Nigel Yates and Frances Knight, *The Welsh Church from Reformation to Disestablishment 1603–1920* (Cardiff, 2007), p 211, citing the curate of Amlwch, Anglesey, in 1801. National Library of Wales B/QA/14.

21. David M. Thompson, *Nonconformity in the Nineteenth Century* (London, 1972), pp 13–15.

22. James Munson, *The Nonconformists: In Search of a Lost Culture* (London, 1991), pp 6–34.

23. Williams, Jacob, Yates and Knight, *The Welsh Church*, p 221.

24. Bebbington, *Evangelicalism in Modern Britain*, pp 106–7.

25. These were the Repeal of the Test and Corporation Acts (1828), Catholic Emancipation (1829) and the Reform Act (1832). The Corporation Act of 1661 required all members of municipal corporations to receive Holy Communion in the year preceding their election to office. The Test Act required the same of all who held office under the Crown. In fact, since 1727, in most years an annual Indemnity Act had been passed, which had effectively allowed Protestant Nonconformists to serve anyway, thus making the Repeal of the Test and Corporation Acts of greater symbolic than actual significance. Catholic emancipation was of more genuine significance to Roman Catholics, particularly as their exclusion from the parliamentary process had been more acutely felt since the Act of Union with Ireland in 1800. The Bill met with violent opposition in much of mainland Britain. The Reform Act extended the franchise a little and altered some constituency boundaries in a manner that paid greater attention to where people actually lived.

26. John Keble, *Sermons Academical and Occasional* (1848), p 127.

27. The Thirty-Nine Articles did not achieve their final form until 1571, some 15 years after Cranmer's death. He did, however, have significant input into most of the texts on which they were based, namely the Ten Articles (1536), the Bishops' Book (1537), the Six Articles (1539), the King's Book (1543) and

the Forty-Two Articles (1553).

28. Owen Chadwick, *The Victorian Church*, Part 1, 3rd ed. (1971), pp 181–9.

29. Nigel Yates, *Anglican Ritualism in Victorian Britain 1830–1910* (Oxford, 1999), pp 48–63.

30. *Ibid.*, p 3.

31. These were the Cambridge Camden Society and the Oxford Society for Promoting the Study of Gothic Architecture.

32. Clive Dewey, *The Passing of Barchester* (London 1991), p 86.

33. Frances Knight, 'The Influence of the Oxford Movement in the Parishes *c*.1833–1860: A Reassessment', in Paul Vaiss (ed), *From Oxford to the People: Reconsidering Newman and the Oxford Movement* (Leominster, 1996), pp 136–7.

34. Howard Colvin, *Biographical Dictionary of British Architects 1600–1840* (London, 1978). See under L.N. Cottingham.

35. Lincolnshire Archives Office (LAO CorB5/8A/3). C. Neville to J. Kaye, 9 May, no year.

36. LAO CorB5/8A/3. C. Neville to J. Kaye, 17 September, no year.

37. Pusey House Mss HAM/2/1/1, 30 September 1856. I am grateful to Colin Cunningham for discussions on Cottingham and Teulon.

38. This was what had previously happened at Beeston, Nottinghamshire, but by 1843 the incumbent felt that this was no longer right and began to store the bread and wine in an 'ancient but broken niche for holy water within the rails'. LAO CorB5/8A/2. J. Wolley to J. Kaye, 3 January 1843.

39. In 1853 W.J. Conybeare estimated the number of Tractarian clergy to be 1,000 out of a total clerical body of 18,000. See W.J. Conybeare, 'Church Parties', ed Arthur Burns, in Stephen Taylor (ed), *From Cranmer to Davidson: A Miscellany*, Church of England Record Society 7 (1999), p 357. One hundred and thirty years later, George Herring estimated the number active between 1840 and 1870 at 958, and that included those who converted to Rome. George Herring, 'Tractarianism to Ritualism: A study of some aspects of Tractarianism outside Oxford, from the time of Newman's conversion in 1845 until the first Ritual Commission in 1867' (University of Oxford, DPhil thesis, 1984). See also George Herring, *What Was the Oxford Movement?* (London, 2002), p 76.

40. Alexandra Walsham, *Church Papists: Catholicism, Conformity and Confessional Polemic in Early Modern England* (Woodbridge, 1993), p 17.

41. John Bossy, 'English Catholics after 1688', in O.P. Grell, J.I. Israel and N. Tyacke (eds), *From Persecution to Toleration: The Glorious Revolution and Religion in England* (Oxford, 1991), p 374.

42. Gerald Parsons, 'Victorian Roman Catholicism: Emancipation, Expansion and Achievement', in G. Parsons (ed), *Religion in Victorian Britain. Volume 1: Traditions* (Manchester, 1988), p 150.

43. See Mary Heimann, *Catholic Devotion in Victorian England* (Oxford, 1995), pp 1–37, for the best analysis of both contemporary and current understandings

of the sociological make-up of Catholicism in nineteenth-century England, and its religious implications. See also Gerald Parsons, 'Victorian Roman Catholicism'.

44. Edward Norman, *The English Catholic Church in the Nineteenth Century* (Oxford, 1984), p 1; Jennifer Supple, 'The Catholic Clergy of Yorkshire 1850–1900: A Profile', *Northern History* 21 (1985), pp 212–35; G.P. Connolly, '"With more than ordinary devotion to God": The secular missioner of the North in the Evangelical age of the English mission', *North West Catholic History* 10 (1983), pp 8–31; all noted by Parsons, 'Victorian Roman Catholicism', p 181.

45. The best recent account of the resolution of these grievances has been supplied by Timothy Larsen, *Friends of Religious Equality: Nonconformist Politics in Mid-Victorian England* (Woodbridge, 1999), pp 39–75.

46. Larsen, *Friends of Religious Equality*, pp 57–9. The issue was not resolved until 1856, when the place of notification was shifted to the registrar's office.

47. *Ibid.*, pp 70, 45.

48. Michael Watts, *The Dissenters. Volume II: The Expansion of Evangelical Nonconformity* (Oxford, 1995), p 483.

49. Kenneth O. Morgan, *Wales in British Politics 1868–1922* (Cardiff, 1980), pp 181–98. The two 'renegade' counties were Brecknockshire and Radnorshire.

50. A.G. Edwards, bishop of St Asaph, attempted to act as a mediatorial figure, although his fellow bishops were less conciliatory on this occasion.

51. For a more detailed account of the Church of England, see Knight, *The Nineteenth-Century Church and English Society*.

52. Frances Knight, 'The Cultural Aspirations of the Welsh Clergy', in David Bebbington and Timothy Larsen (eds), *Modern Christianity and Cultural Aspirations* (London, 2003); Frances Knight, 'The Pastoral Ministry in the Anglican Church in England and Wales *c*.1840–1950', in *The Pastor Bonus: The Dutch Review of Church History* 83 (Leiden, 2004); Frances Knight, Part IV, *The Welsh Church from Reformation to Disestablishment 1603–1920* (Cardiff, 2007).

53. Frances Knight, '"A Church without Discipline is no Church at All": Discipline and Diversity in Nineteenth- and Twentieth-Century Anglicanism', in Kate Cooper and Jeremy Gregory (eds), *Discipline and Diversity: Studies in Church History* 43 (Woodbridge, 2007).

54. Yates, *Anglican Ritualism*, pp 278–9.

55. Gerard Connolly has argued on the basis of a case-study of Manchester and Salford that Catholicism in those towns in the years between 1770 and 1850 was in the process of being absorbed into English life as another variety of Nonconformity. G.P. Connolly, 'The Transubstantiation of Myth: Towards a New Popular History of Nineteenth-Century Catholicism in England', *Journal of Ecclesiastical History* 35 (1984), pp 78–104. Mary Heimann has argued on the basis of a detailed study of devotional practice that what was taking place within Catholicism, in England and elsewhere, is more accurately seen as 'evangelical' in tone and 'revivalist' in spirit, rather than

as Ultramontane (orchestrated from Rome). Heimann, *Catholic Devotion in Victorian England*, p 35.
56. Clyde Binfield, *So Down to Prayers*, pp 145–61.

Chapter 2. Protestant Europe

1. Urs Altermatt and Franziska Metzger, 'Switzerland. Religion, Politics and the Nation: Competing and Overlapping Identities', in Gilley and Stanley (eds), *World Christianities*, p 326.
2. Urs Altermatt, 'Conservatism in Switzerland: A Study in Anti-Modernism', in 'A Century of Conservatism, Part 2', *Journal of Contemporary History* 14 (1979), pp 581–610.
3. Altermatt and Metzger, 'Switzerland', in Gilley and Stanley (eds), *World Christianities*, pp 324–5.
4. Michael Wintle, 'The Netherlands', in Gilley and Stanley (eds), *World Christianities*, p 335.
5. Hugh McLeod, *Religion and the People of Western Europe 1789–1989*, 2nd ed. (Oxford, 1997), p 18.
6. Wintle, 'The Netherlands', in Gilley and Stanley (eds), *World Christianities*, pp 333–4.
7. Mary Heimann, 'Christianity in Western Europe from the Enlightenment', in Adrian Hastings (ed), *A World History of Christianity* (London, 1999), p 459.
8. Callum G. Brown, *Religion and Society in Scotland since 1707* (Edinburgh, 1997), p 32.
9. Thorkildsen, 'Scandinavia', in Gilley and Stanley (eds), *World Christianities*, pp 350–1.
10. There were also Presbyterians in Ireland, but many of these were of Scottish ancestry.
11. Callum Brown has argued that when independence for Scotland was being much discussed during the 1990s, politicians began to turn to Scotland's religious history, and particularly to the Disruption of 1843, in order to develop arguments which linked Scotland's modern national identity with its previous religious identity. Brown concluded that these arguments were entirely spurious. See Brown, 'Religion and National Identity: Scotland since the Union of 1707', in Ingmar Brohed (ed), *Church and People in Britain and Scandinavia* (Lund, 1996), pp 283–99. In the same year, David Hempton also suggested that 'while Presbyterianism in Scotland has played a major role in defining Scottishness it has played almost no part in fostering Scottish nationalism'. David Hempton, *Religion and Political Culture in Britain and Ireland* (Cambridge, 1996), p 63.
12. Brown, *Religion and Society in Scotland*, p 17.
13. *Ibid.*, p 20.
14. *Ibid.*, p 21.
15. Brown, 'Religion and National Identity', in Brohed (ed), *Church and People*,

p 287.

16. John Wolffe, 'Anglicanism, Presbyterianism and the Religious Identities of the United Kingdom', in Gilley and Stanley (eds), *World Christianities*, p 317.

17. S.J. Brown, *Thomas Chalmers and the Godly Commonwealth in Scotland* (Oxford, 1982).

18. Hempton, *Religion and Political Culture*, pp 63–4.

19. *Ibid.*, p 66.

20. *Ibid.*, p 68.

21. Brown, *Religion and Society in Scotland*, p 68.

22. The major difference between tithes in England and teinds in Scotland was that tithes were calculated as a proportion of produce, whereas teinds were calculated as a proportion of the rateable value of agricultural land set against current prices of produce. This made Scottish ministers in general more vulnerable to loss of income than the English clergy, particularly after poor harvests. See Callum G. Brown, 'Rotavating the Kailyard: Re-imagining the Scottish "meenister" in discourse and the parish state since 1707', in Nigel Aston and Matthew Cragoe (eds), *Anticlericalism in Britain c.1500–1914* (Stroud, 2001), p 140.

23. Brown, *Religion and Society in Scotland*, p 69.

24. *Ibid.*, p 70.

25. *Ibid.*, p 99.

26. *Ibid.*, p 142.

27. *Ibid.*, p 146.

28. *Ibid.*, p 2.

29. Hempton, *Religion and Political Culture*, p 90.

30. Brown, *Religion and Society in Scotland*, p 60.

31. *Ibid.*, pp 44–55.

32. For more on the sudden loss of support experienced around 1890, see *ibid.*, Chapter 6.

33. Mary Fulbrook, *A Concise History of Germany* (Cambridge, 1990), pp 101–2.

34. Nicholas Hope, *German and Scandinavian Protestantism 1700–1918* (Oxford, 1995), p 232.

35. Anthony J. Steinhoff, 'Christianity and the Creation of Germany', in Gilley and Stanley (eds), *World Christianities*, p 282.

36. David Blackbourn, *The Fontana History of Germany 1780–1918: The Long Nineteenth Century* (London, 1997), p 293.

37. Steinhoff, 'Christianity and the Creation of Germany', p 285.

38. Hope, *German and Scandinavian Protestantism*, pp 238–55.

39. Eda Sagarra, *A Social History of Germany 1648–1914* (London, 1977), pp 208–10.

40. *Ibid.*, pp 204–5.

41. Fulbrook, *A Concise History of Germany*, pp 92–3.

42. Thorkildsen, 'Scandinavia', in Gilley and Stanley (eds), *World Christianities*,

pp 343–4.

43. Lars Österlin, *Churches of Northern Europe in Profile: A Thousand Years of Anglo-Nordic Relations* (Norwich, 1995), p 189.

44. *Ibid.*, p 193.

45. Dag Thorkildsen, 'Church and Nation in the 19th Century: The Case of Norway', in Brohed, *Church and People*, pp 249–66.

46. Österlin, *Churches of Northern Europe*, pp 159–60.

47. Hope, *German and Scandinavian Protestantism*, pp 359–62.

48. Österlin, *Churches of Northern Europe*, p 177.

49. *Ibid.*, p 178.

50. Thorkildsen, 'Scandinavia', in Gilley and Stanley (eds), *World Christianities*, pp 346–9.

Chapter 3. Catholic Europe

1. Nicholas Atkin and Frank Tallett, *Priests, Prelates and People: A History of European Catholicism since 1750* (London, 2003), pp 69–70.

2. Eamon Duffy, *Saints and Sinners: A History of the Popes* (New Haven, 1997), p 202.

3. Atkin and Tallet, *Priests, Prelates and People*, p 71.

4. *Ibid.*, pp 72–4.

5. Owen Chadwick, *The Popes and the European Revolution* (Oxford, 1981), p 520.

6. Duffy, *Saints and Sinners*, p 214.

7. *Ibid.*, p 194.

8. Sheridan Gilley, 'The Papacy', in Gilley and Stanley (eds), *World Christianities*, p 14.

9. Duffy, *Saints and Sinners*, p 216.

10. *Ibid.*, p 222.

11. Frank Coppa, 'Italy: The church and the *Risorgimento*', in Gilley and Stanley (eds), *World Christianities*, p 239.

12. Gilley, 'The Papacy', in Gilley and Stanley (eds), *World Christianities*, p 18.

13. *Ibid.*

14. Atkin and Tallet, *Priests, Prelates and People*, p 131.

15. *Ibid.*, p 138.

16. Duffy, *Saints and Sinners*, pp 230–2.

17. Atkin and Tallet, *Priests, Prelates and People*, pp 145–6; Steinhoff, 'Christianity and the Creation of Germany', in Gilley and Stanley (eds), *World Christianities*, p 295.

18. For an excellent account of events at Marpingen, and of the phenomenon of nineteenth-century Marian apparitions more generally, see David Blackbourn, *Marpingen: Apparitions of the Virgin Mary in Bismarckian Germany* (Oxford, 1993).

19. James F. McMillan, 'Catholic Christianity in France, 1815–1905', in Gilley and Stanley (eds), *World Christianities*, pp 218, 224.

20. *Ibid.*, p 227.

21. Patrick Corish, *The Irish Catholic Experience: A Historical Survey* (Dublin, 1985), p 133.

22. See S.J. Connolly, *Priests and People in Pre-Famine Ireland, 1780–1845* (Dublin, 2001), pp 21–3, 102–12, for a discussion of the state of opinion on this matter. Following David Miller, Connolly argued that it was around 40 per cent in 1834. Some scholars have put it higher, others lower. The most recent work on this question has been done by Nigel Yates, who analysed the diocese of Raphoe, on the basis that the proportions of Catholics, Anglicans and Presbyterians who lived there most closely replicated the national religious divide. He placed the Roman Catholic figure (35.7 per cent) in the context of an Anglican church attendance of 20.8 per cent and a Presbyterian attendance of 32.0 per cent. See Nigel Yates, *The Religious Condition of Ireland 1770–1850* (Oxford, 2006) pp 153–7.

23. Sheridan Gilley, 'Catholicism, Ireland and the Irish diaspora', in Gilley and Stanley (eds), *World Christianities*, p 250; Corish, *The Irish Catholic Experience*, p 215.

24. Hastings, *A World History of Christianity*, p 4.

25. Yates, *The Religious Condition of Ireland*, pp 301–4.

26. S.J. Connolly, *Religion and Society in Nineteenth-Century Ireland* (Dundalk, 1985), p 3.

27. Corish, *The Irish Catholic Experience*, p 149.

28. *Ibid.*, p 156.

29. Gerald Parsons, 'Irish Disestablishment', in Gerald Parsons (ed), *Religion in Victorian Britain. Volume II. Controversies* (Manchester, 1988), p 138.

30. Gilley, 'Catholicism, Ireland and the Irish diaspora', in Gilley and Stanley (eds), *World Christianities*, p 250.

31. Yates, *The Religious Condition of Ireland*, pp 99–116.

32. *Ibid.*, p 116.

33. Duffy, *Saints and Sinners*, p 235.

34. Atkin and Tallet, *Priests, Prelates and People*, p 176.

35. *Ibid.*, p 161.

36. Duffy, *Saints and Sinners*, p 242.

37. *Ibid.*

38. Atkin and Tallet, *Priests, Prelates and People*, p 163.

Chapter 4. The United States and Canada

1. For example, Quakers and Baptists had been persecuted by Congregationalists in the 1650s.

2. Sydney E. Ahlstrom, *A Religious History of the American People* (New Haven and London, 2004), pp 370–3.

3. Massachusetts continued to give special privileges to the old Congregational parishes until 1833, but this was exceptional.

4. Ahlstrom, *Religious History*, p 380.

5. Alexis de Tocqueville, *Democracy in America* (1835), 2 vols., ed Phillips Bradley (New York, 1966), vol. I, p 308.

6. *Ibid.*, pp 308–14.

7. Dietrich Bonhoeffer, *No Rusty Swords: Letters, Lectures and Notes, 1928–1936, from the Collected Works of Dietrich Bonhoeffer*, vol. 1, ed Edwin Robinson (New York, 1965), cited in Ahlstrom, *Religious History*, p 5.

8. Edwin Scott Gaustad and Philip L. Barlow, *A New Historical Atlas of Religion in America* (Oxford and New York, 2001), p 6, fig. 1.6.

9. *Ibid.*, p 61, fig. 2.3.

10. Mark A. Noll, *The Old Religion in a New World: The History of North American Christianity* (Grand Rapids, 2002), pp 121–2.

11. De Tocqueville, *Democracy in America*, vol. II, pp 29–30.

12. Thomas O'Loughlin, 'The Demand and Supply of Priests to the United States from All Hallows College, Ireland, between 1842 and 1860', *Records of the American Catholic Records Society* 95 (1984), pp 39–60.

13. Ahlstrom, *Religious History*, pp 555–68.

14. This occurred in the case of Bishop Michael Egan, the first bishop of Philadelphia, who was publicly ridiculed by an Irish priest named William Hogan in the early 1820s. Ahlstrom, *Religious History*, p 537.

15. Mark A. Noll, *A History of Christianity in the United States and Canada* (Grand Rapids, 1992), p 227.

16. *Ibid.*, pp 229–30.

17. *Ibid.*, pp 238–9.

18. Ahlstrom, *Religious History*, p 475.

19. Cited in *ibid.*, p 479.

20. David T. Arthur, 'Joshua V. Himes and the Cause of Adventism', in Ronald L. Numbers and Jonathan M. Butler (eds), *The Disappointed: Millerism and Millenarianism in the Nineteenth Century* (Knoxville, 1993), p 50.

21. David L. Rowe, 'Millerites: A Shadow Portrait', in Numbers and Butler (eds), *The Disappointed*, p 15.

22. Wayne R. Judd, 'William Miller: Disappointed Prophet', in Numbers and Butler (eds), *The Disappointed*, p 33.

23. Gaustad and Barlow, *New Historical Atlas*, p 165.

24. Lawrence Foster, 'Had Prophecy Failed? Contrasting Perspectives of the Millerites and the Shakers', in Numbers and Butler (eds), *The Disappointed*, p 183.

25. Gaustad and Barlow, *New Historical Atlas*, p 238.

26. Leonard J. Arrington and Davis Bitton, *The Mormon Experience: A History of the Latter-Day Saints* (London, 1979), p 198.

27. Charles Joyner, '"Believer I Know": The Emergence of African-American Christianity', in Paul E. Johnson (ed), *African-American Christianity: Essays in History* (Berkeley and Los Angeles, 1994), pp 19–20.

28. *Ibid.*, p 24.

29. Paul's comments on the equality brought about through baptism are found

at Gal. 3.28, I Cor. 12.13 and Col. 3.11. In Col. 3.24 and 4.1 he urges slaves to obey their earthly masters, and slave owners to treat their slaves justly and fairly.

30. William E. Montgomery, *Under Their Own Vine and Fig Tree: The African-American Church in the South 1865–1900* (Baton Rouge, 1993), p 6.

31. David W. Kling, 'The New Divinity and the Origins of the American Board of Commissioners for Foreign Missions', *Church History* 72.4 (2003), pp 791–819.

32. David Hempton, *Methodism: Empire of the Spirit* (New Haven and London, 2005), p 42.

33. *Ibid.*, pp 105–8.

34. A rather different view is provided in Jewel L. Spangler, 'Becoming Baptists: Conversion in Colonial and Early National Virginia', *Journal of Southern History* LXVII, 2 (2001), pp 243–86. She argues that in at least some well-documented Virginia Baptist churches, the positive approach towards justice for slaves has been overestimated on the basis of fragmentary pieces of evidence. She sees the churches as basically conservative institutions, with a strong emphasis on order and self-discipline. Church leaders were careful not to go too far in advocating any departures from the status quo, or to threaten the ascendancy of free white men within the congregations.

35. Albert J. Raboteau, 'African-Americans, Exodus, and the American Israel', in Johnson (ed), *African-American Christianity*, p 6.

36. Montgomery, *Vine and Fig Tree*, pp 19–24.

37. Joyner, '"Believer I Know"', pp 18–37.

38. 'Shouting' was not yelling aloud. Rather, it denoted bodily movements accompanied by handclapping, foot-stomping and singing. Joyner, '"Believer I Know"', p 30.

39. William G. Kephart to L. Tappen, 9 May 1864, American Missionary Association Archives, Decatur, Alabama, reel 2. Cited by Raboteau, 'African-Americans', p 13.

40. Noll, *History of Christianity in the USA and Canada*, pp 201–3.

41. *Ibid.*, p 320.

42. *Ibid.*, p 323.

43. Montgomery, *Vine and Fig Tree*, pp 52–5.

44. *Ibid.*, p 334.

45. Noll, *History of Christianity in the USA and Canada*, p 342.

46. Montgomery, *Vine and Fig Tree*, pp 343–4.

47. Gaustad and Barlow, *New Historical Atlas*, p 68.

48. Mark A. Noll, '"Christian America" and "Christian Canada"', in Gilley and Stanley (eds), *World Christianities*, p 376.

49. George A. Rawlyk, '"A Total Revolution in Religious and Civil Government": The Maritimes, New England, and the Evolving Evangelical Ethos 1776–1812', in Mark A. Noll, David W. Bebbington and George A. Rawlyk (eds), *Evangelicalism: Comparative Studies of Popular Protestantism in North America,*

the British Isles and Beyond, 1700–1990 (New York and Oxford, 1994), pp 137–55.

50. Marguerite Van Die, '"The Double Vision": Evangelical Piety as Derivative and Indigenous in Victorian English Canada', in Noll, Bebbington and Rawlyk (eds), *Evangelicalism*, pp 256–9.

51. Noll, *History of Christianity in the USA and Canada*, p 284.

52. Fay, *A History of Canadian Catholics*, pp 5–28.

53. *Ibid.*, pp 33–4.

54. Noll, *History of Christianity in the USA and Canada*, pp 260–1.

55. Alan L. Hayes, *Anglicans in Canada: Controversies and Identity in Historical Perspective* (Urbana and Chicago, 2004), pp 13–6.

56. *Ibid.*, pp 67–8.

57. For a discussion of the Clergy Reserves and the other ways in which the Anglican Church in Canada was funded, see *ibid.*, pp 59–61.

58. The influence of Ireland was particularly strong. Of 91 Anglican clergy in Upper Canada in 1841, 31 were born in Ireland and 19 had been educated at Trinity College Dublin. *Ibid.*, p 6.

Chapter 5. Outcomes of World Mission

1. Daniel H. Bays (ed), *Christianity in China from the Eighteenth Century to the Present* (Stanford, 1996), pp 266–7. See also Brian Stanley, 'Christian Missions, Anti-Slavery and the Claims of Humanity, *c.*1813–1873', in Gilley and Stanley (eds), *World Christianities*, pp 454–7.

2. Andrew F. Walls, *The Cross-Cultural Process in Christian History* (New York and Edinburgh, 2002), pp 39–41.

3. *Ibid.*, p 34.

4. Stanley, 'Christian Missions', p 443.

5. Duffy, *Saints and Sinners*, p 221.

6. *Evangelical Christendom* (London, January 1850), pp 8–28, cited in Bebbington, *The Dominance of Evangelicalism*, p 102.

7. W.M. Jacob, *The Making of the Anglican Church Worldwide* (London 1997), p 87.

8. Heleen Murre-Van Den Berg, 'The Middle East; Western Missions and the Eastern Churches, Islam and Judaism', in Gilley and Stanley (eds), *World Christianities*, p 468.

9. R.E. Frykenberg, 'India', in Hastings (ed), *A World History of Christianity*, pp 173–4.

10. Daniel O'Connor, *Three Centuries of Mission: The United Society for the Propagation of the Gospel 1701–2000* (London and New York, 2000), p 25.

11. Frykenberg, 'India', p 190.

12. Frykenberg, 'Christians and Religious Traditions in the Indian Empire', in Gilley and Stanley (eds), *World Christianities*, p 492.

13. Joint pastoral letter of the Catholic bishops in New South Wales (July 1879) quoted in David Hilliard, 'Australasia and the Pacific', in Hastings (ed), *A*

World History of Christianity, p 525.

14. Hilliard, 'Australasia and the Pacific', p 525.
15. Walls, *Cross-Cultural Process*, p 102.
16. Frykenberg, 'India', p 183.
17. See Brian Stanley, *The Bible and the Flag: Protestant Missions and British Imperialism in the Nineteenth and Twentieth Centuries* (Leicester, 1990), p 11, for the best discussion of the relationship between missions and colonialism. The very negative interpretation of missionaries' motivations dates from the 1960s. The reference to the 'Bible in one hand and a gun in another' occurred at a World Council of Churches meeting in Nairobi in 1975.
18. Kevin Ward, 'Africa', in Hastings (ed), *World History of Christianity*, pp 216–17.
19. Stanley, *The Bible and the Flag*, p 56.
20. *Ibid.*, p 61. This was partly due to the loss of financial support from the British government, which meant that it had to rely, like the other missionary societies, on donations from its supporters.
21. David W. Kling, 'The New Divinity and the Origins of the American Board of Commissioners for Foreign Missions', *Church History* 72.4 (December 2003), p 804.
22. Andrew Fuller wrote *The Gospel Worthy of all Acceptation* in 1785. See Stanley, *The Bible and the Flag*, pp 59–60.
23. Kling, 'The New Divinity', p 807.
24. Walls, *Cross-Cultural Process*, p 28. See also A.F. Walls, 'A Christian Experiment: The Sierra Leone Colony', in G.J. Cuming (ed), *The Mission of the Church and the Propagation of the Faith*, Studies in Church History 6 (Cambridge, 1970), pp 107–29.
25. Walls, 'The Sierra Leone Colony', p 107.
26. Walls, *Cross-Cultural Process*, pp 168–9.
27. This account is largely drawn from Walls, *Cross-Cultural Process*, pp 155–64.
28. See Jacob, *Anglican Church Worldwide*, pp 199–200, for more on the Niger expedition.
29. Walls, *Cross-Cultural Process*, p 159.
30. See, for example, *Sunday at Home: A Family Magazine for Sabbath Reading*, 5, 12, 19 December 1861.
31. Jacob, *Anglican Church Worldwide*, p 207.
32. *Ibid.*, pp 207–11.
33. Ogbu U. Kalu, 'Ethiopianism and the Roots of Modern African Christianity', in Gilley and Stanley (eds), *World Christianities*, pp 576–92.
34. Ward, 'Africa', pp 209–10.
35. *Ibid.*, p 210.
36. *Ibid.*, p 212. It was also true that many of the first generation of nationalist leaders in Africa more generally had been the product of mission schools. See Stanley, *The Bible and the Flag*, pp 16–17.
37. Ward, 'Africa', p 213.

38. For more on African missionaries as medical men, see Paul S. Landau, 'Explaining Surgical Evangelism in Colonial Southern Africa: Teeth, Pain and Faith', *Journal of African History* 37 (1996), pp 261–81.

39. Ward, 'Africa', p 214.

40. Adrian Hastings, *African Catholicism: Essays in Discovery* (London, 1989), pp 9, 12, 71.

41. Frykenberg, 'India', pp 176–8.

42. Stanley, *The Bible and the Flag*, pp 98–100.

43. Frykenberg, 'India', p 181; Stanley, *The Bible and the Flag*, pp 99–101.

44. Frykenberg, 'India', p 181; Frykenberg, 'Christians and Religious Traditions in the Indian Empire', p 475.

45. Stanley, *The Bible and the Flag*, p 101.

46. Frykenberg, 'India', pp 184–5.

47. *Ibid.*, p 187.

48. Robert E. Entenmann, 'Catholics and Society in Eighteenth-Century Sichuan', in Bays (ed), *Christianity in China*, pp 8–23.

49. Entenmann, 'Catholics and Society'; Entenmann, 'Christian Virgins in Eighteenth-Century Sichuan' Sichuan', in Bays (ed), *Christianity in China*, pp 180–93.

50. Entenmann, 'Christian Virgins', p 183.

51. For the catechists, see Alan Richard Sweeten, 'Catholic Converts in Jiangxi Province: Conflict and Accommodation, 1860–1900', in Bays (ed), *Christianity in China*, p 27.

52. R.G. Tiedemann, 'China and its Neighbours', in Hastings (ed), *A World History of Christianity*, p 391.

53. Entenmann, 'Christian Virgins', p 192.

54. Daniel H. Bays and James H. Grayson, 'Christianity in East Asia: China, Korea and Japan', in Gilley and Stanley (eds), *World Christianities*, p 496.

55. For more on Gützlaff, see Jessie G. Lutz and R. Ray Lutz, 'Karl Gützlaff's Approach to Indigenization: The Chinese Union', in Bays (ed), *Christianity in China*, pp 269–91.

56. Tiedemann, 'China', p 392.

57. Stanley, *The Bible and the Flag*, p 105.

58. *Ibid.*, pp 106–9.

59. Lutz and Lutz, 'Karl Gützlaff', pp 271, 279.

60. Stanley, 'Christian Missions', p 445.

61. Andrew Porter, 'Missions and Empire *c.*1873–1914', in Gilley and Stanley (eds), *World Christianities*, pp 561–3.

62. Porter, 'Missions and Empire', p 562. The CMS remained the largest British missionary organization.

63. Andrew F. Walls, 'The Multiple Conversions of Timothy Richard', in *Cross-Cultural Process*, pp 236–58. The quotation is on p 250.

64. China Inland Mission, *Days of Blessing*, p 52, cited in Roger R. Thompson, 'Twilight of the Gods in the Chinese Countryside: Christians, Confucians

and the Modernising State, 1861–1911', in Bays (ed), *Christianity in China*, p 61.

65. Stanley, *The Bible and the Flag*, p 139.
66. Hilliard, 'Australasia and the Pacific', p 509.
67. Stuart Piggin and Allan Davidson, 'Christianity in Australasia and the Pacific', in Gilley and Stanley (eds), *World Christianities*, p 542.
68. *Ibid.*, pp 556–7.
69. Hilliard, 'Australasia and the Pacific', p 511.
70. *Ibid.*, p 512.
71. *Ibid.*, p 513.
72. Walls, *Cross-Cultural Process*, pp 53–64.

Chapter 6. Revival and Renewal

1. The account of Rachel Stearns is taken from Candy Gunther, 'The Spiritual Pilgrimage of Rachel Stearns, 1834–1837: Reinterpreting Women's Religious and Social Experiences in the Methodist Revivals of Nineteenth-Century America', *Church History* 65 (1996), pp 577–95.
2. The first Great Awakening is conventionally dated as being from *c.*1726 to the 1740s, and the second from about 1795 to the early decades of the nineteenth century. A further revival period, from *c.*1875 to 1914, is sometimes termed the third Great Awakening. Some scholars, for example, James D. Bratt, 'The Reorientation of American Protestantism, 1835–1845', *Church History* 67:1 (March 1998), pp 52–82, have argued that the whole century from 1740 to 1840 is better termed as a period of 'Awakening', while others, for example Jon Butler, 'Enthusiasm Described and Decried: The Great Awakening as Interpretive Fiction', *Journal of American History* 69 (September 1982), pp 305–25, have questioned the usefulness of the term at all.
3. Noll, *A History of Christianity in the USA and Canada*, p 166.
4. Noll, *The Old Religion in a New World*, p 84.
5. I am grateful to David Bebbington for providing clarification on this matter. The use of the term 'altar call' was seen as uncontroversial in American revivalist circles, but caused some consternation when American evangelists used it in Britain, where the word 'altar' was seen as having alarming Catholic overtones.
6. Richard Carwardine, *Trans-Atlantic Revivalism: Popular Evangelicalism in Britain and America 1790–1865* (Westport, Connecticut, 1978), pp 45–9.
7. Stuart Piggin and Allan Davidson, 'Christianity in Australia and the Pacific', in Gilley and Stanley (eds), *World Christianities*, p 543.
8. Stuart Piggin, 'The American and British Contributions to Evangelicalism in Australia', in Noll, Bebbington and Rawlyk (eds), *Evangelicalism*, pp 290–309.
9. Noll, *A History of Christianity in the USA and Canada*, pp 263–4.
10. Walls, *Cross-Cultural Process*, pp 20–1.
11. Like many similar groups in America, the Catholic Apostolic Church,

a British denomination founded by Edward Irving in the 1830s, believed that the second coming of Christ would occur shortly. In preparation, they re-established the primitive offices of the Church: Apostles, prophets, evangelists, pastors and teachers, to which 'angels' (bishops) and deacons were added later. From their headquarters in London's Gordon Square, they sought to evangelize mainland Europe and America. In doctrine and worship, their outlook was Catholic, and they used vestments and incense, which was regarded as extraordinary in millenarian and revivalist circles. They had expected that at least one of their Apostles would survive until the second advent, but when the last one died, in 1901, the movement went into terminal decline.

12. Timothy C.F. Stunt, *From Awakening to Succession: Radical Evangelicals in Switzerland and Britain 1815–35* (Edinburgh, 2000).

13. A classic study is John Kent, *Holding the Fort: Studies in Victorian Revivalism* (London, 1978).

14. Carwardine, *Trans-Atlantic Revivalism*, p 35.

15. Kent, *Holding the Fort*, pp 57–9.

16. Carwardine, *Trans-Atlantic Revivalism*, pp 104–7.

17. Hempton, *Methodism: Empire of the Spirit*, p 57.

18. Bebbington, *The Dominance of Evangelicalism*, pp 188–9.

19. Carwardine, *Trans-Atlantic Revivalism*, pp 107–33.

20. *Ibid.*, pp 85–94, 173–4.

21. Bebbington, *The Dominance of Evangelicalism*, p 101. John Kent, on the other hand, disputed the link between the events in America and the Ulster revival, claiming that the only discernible link between them was that both occurred in communities that felt threatened by resurgent Catholicism. *Holding the Fort*, p 72.

22. Carwardine, *Trans-Atlantic Revivalism*, pp 159–97. Carwardine's graphs on pp 161, 194–5 illustrate the patterns of growth and decline experienced by the American Episcopal Church and the British Nonconformist denominations in the period around 1860.

23. Joe Creech, 'Visions of Glory: The Place of the Azusa Street Revival in Pentecostal History', *Church History* 65.1 (1996), pp 405–24.

24. *Ibid.*, p 406.

25. For a perceptive study of the very strained early relations between Pentecostalists and radical evangelicals, see Grant Wacker, 'Travail of a Broken Family: Evangelical Responses to Pentecostalism in America, 1906–1916', *Journal of Ecclesiastical History* 47, 3 (1996), pp 505–28.

26. Conrad Charles, 'The Origins of Parish Mission in England and the Early Passionist Apostolate, 1840–1850', *Journal of Ecclesiastical History* 15 (1964), p 66.

27. Sheridan Gilley, 'Catholic Faith of the Irish Slums: London, 1840–70', in H.J. Dyos and Michael Wolff (eds), *The Victorian City: Images and Realities*, vol. 2 (London, 1973), p 839.

28. John Sharp, 'Juvenile Holiness: Catholic Revivalism among Children in Victorian Britain', *Journal of Ecclesiastical History* 35, 2 (1984), pp 225, 227.
29. *Ibid.*, p 232.
30. Heimann, *Catholic Devotion in Victorian England*, p 146.
31. Gilley, 'Catholic Faith', p 839, citing *Tablet*, 3 February 1855; 11 April 1857.
32. Heimann, *Catholic Devotion in Victorian England*, p 148.
33. Charles, 'Origins of Parish Mission', p 69.
34. Heimann, *Catholic Devotion in Victorian England*, p 172, citing John Sharp, *Reapers of the Harvest: The Redemptorists in Great Britain and Ireland 1843–1898* (Dublin, 1989), p 224.
35. Sharp, 'Juvenile Holiness', p 235.
36. Heimann, *Catholic Devotion in Victorian England*, p 171, citing G.E. Anstruther, 'What Shall We Do with Our Boys in their Teens', *Ransomer* I (1893), p 150.
37. Jay P. Dolan, *Catholic Revivalism: The American Experience 1830–1900* (Notre Dame, Indiana, 1978).
38. *Ibid.*, pp 94–5.
39. *Ibid.*, pp 19, 91.
40. Peter B. Nockles, 'The Oxford Movement as a Religious Revival and Resurgence'. Paper read at the Ecclesiastical History Society conference, Cardiff, July 2006. I am very grateful to Peter Nockles for allowing me a copy of his paper, in which he argues that although 'revival' is a word that had tended to become synonymous with evangelicalism, it needs to be recovered to accommodate both contemporary and modern usages, so that it can be extended to include Catholic movements.
41. Peter B. Nockles, *The Oxford Movement in Context: Anglican High Churchmanship 1760–1857* (Cambridge, 1994); Yates, *Anglican Ritualism in Victorian Britain 1830–1910*, pp 10–39.
42. Kent, *Holding the Fort*, p 236.
43. *Ibid.*, pp 271–89.
44. *Ibid.*, p 259.
45. C.M. Davies, *Orthodox London*, 2nd ed. (1876), pp 151–2, cited in Kent, *Holding the Fort*, p 261.
46. *The Record*, 22 November 1869; Kent, *Holding the Fort*, p 266.
47. Eugene R. Fairweather, 'A Tractarian Patriarch: John Medley of Fredericton', *Canadian Journal of Theology* VI (1962), pp 208–11. For the most recent reassessment of Medley's Tractarianism in the light of modern scholarship, see Barry Craig, 'Bishop John Medley: Missionary and Reformer' (University of Wales, Lampeter, PhD thesis, 2001), pp 268–76.
48. John Medley, *The Advantages of Open Seats* (Oxford, 1843).
49. Barry Craig has argued that the influence of Medley is still very strongly felt in the diocese of Fredericton. Craig, 'Bishop John Medley', pp 1–2.
50. For a full discussion of the significance of the conflict between Gray and Long, see Knight, 'A Church without Discipline is no Church at All': Discipline

and Diversity in Nineteenth- and Twentieth-Century Anglicanism', *Studies in Church History* 43 (Woodbridge, 2007). I am grateful to Bill Jacob for making various observations about Gray.

51. Daniel O'Connor, *Three Centuries of Mission: The United Society for the Propagation of the Gospel 1701–2000* (London and New York, 2000), pp 62–3.

52. Heimann, *Catholic Devotion in Victorian England*, p 172.

53. Sharp, 'Juvenile Holiness', p 233.

54. Wacker, 'Travail of a Broken Family', pp 525–6.

Chapter 7. Dislocation and Decline

1. McLeod, *Secularisation in Western Europe*, p 52. This chapter is much indebted to this particularly useful book.

2. It has been argued that one of the reasons why France did not extend the vote to women during the interwar period of the twentieth century was because it was believed that women voters would be susceptible to manipulation from the clergy in favour of voting for pro-Church candidates. James F. McMillan, '"Priest Hits Girl": On the Front Line in the "War of the Two Frances"', in Christopher Clark and Wolfram Kaiser (eds), *Culture Wars: Secular-Catholic Conflict in Nineteenth-Century Europe* (Cambridge, 2003), p 100.

3. McMillan, '"Priest Hits Girl"', pp 77–101.

4. McLeod, *Secularisation in Western Europe*, p 60.

5. McMillan, '"Priest Hits Girl"', pp 77–101.

6. Joseph F. Byrnes, *Catholic and French Forever: Religious and National Identity in Modern France* (Pennsylvania, 2005), p 156.

7. Chartism was not so peaceful in Wales, however, where there was a large number of fatalities in the Newport Rising of 1839.

8. A cartoon depicting this Old Testament scene dating from an early issue of *The Freethinker* in 1882 is republished in James R. Moore (ed), *Religion in Victorian Britain. Volume III: Sources* (Manchester, 1988), p 359. God is depicted with human limbs but with a devil's face, raining down stones from the clouds.

9. Edward Royle, *Radical Politics 1790–1900: Religion and Unbelief* (London, 1971), p 12.

10. *Ibid.*, p 18.

11. James R. Moore, 'Freethought, Secularism and Agnosticism: The Case of Charles Darwin', in Parsons (ed), *Religion in Victorian Britain. Volume I: Traditions*, pp 305–7.

12. This occurred in Littleport in Cambridgeshire in 1816, when the Revd Sir Henry Bate-Dudley, a prebendary of Ely Cathedral and a local magistrate, shot dead a rioter while trying to quell a disturbance.

13. Frances Knight, 'Did Anticlericalism Exist in the English Countryside in the Early Nineteenth Century?', in *Anticlericalism in Britain c.1500–1914* (Stroud, 2000), pp 159–78.

14. Mary Heimann, 'Christianity in Western Europe from the Enlightenment', in Hastings (ed), *A World History of Christianity*, p 485.
15. McLeod, *Secularisation in Western Europe*, p 36.
16. Heimann, 'Christianity in Western Europe', pp 490–7.
17. *Ibid.*, p 492.
18. *Ibid.*, p 493.
19. McLeod, *Secularisation in Western Europe*, pp 154–5.
20. George M. Marsden, *Understanding Fundamentalism and Evangelicalism* (Grand Rapids, 1991), pp 126–9. Marsden is following the work of Henry F. May, *The Enlightenment in America* (New York, 1976).
21. Marsden, *Understanding Fundamentalism*, p 133; Martin Marty, *The Modern Schism: Three Paths to the Secular* (New York, 1969), p 98.
22. Marsden, *Understanding Fundamentalism*, pp 135–8.
23. *Ibid.*, p 38.
24. Keith A. Francis, *Charles Darwin and The Origin of Species* (Westport, Connecticut, 2007), pp 77–81.
25. Marsden, *Understanding Fundamentalism*, p 15.
26. Mark A. Noll, *The Civil War as a Theological Crisis* (Chapel Hill, 2006), p 4.
27. *Ibid.*, p 1.
28. *Ibid.*, pp 49–50.
29. Kent, *Holding the Fort*, p 34.
30. Sharp, 'Juvenile Holiness', pp 236–8.
31. G.A. Oddie, 'India and Missionary Motives 1850–1900', *Journal of Ecclesiastical History* 25 (1974), p 69, cited in Stanley, *The Bible and the Flag*, p 66.
32. Stanley, *The Bible and the Flag*, p 67. By 1903 Taylor was expressing regret about the 1884 clause, and was far less certain about the fate of the unevangelized.
33. Stunt, *From Awakening to Succession*, p 61.
34. Knight, *The Nineteenth-Century Church*, p 211.
35. The poem became better known when Edward Elgar set it as an oratorio in 1900. The stanza, which the Angel speaks, comes towards the end of poem as Gerontius's soul is 'consumed, yet quickened by the glance of God'. It reads 'Softly and gently, dearly-ransomed soul,/In my most loving arms I now enfold thee,/And, o'er the penal waters as they roll,/I poise thee, and I lower thee and hold thee.' The poem concludes by indicating that the welfare of the Catholic soul in purgatory will be ensured by 'Masses on the earth, and prayers in heaven'. It was a completely different concept from the Protestant one.
36. See Knight, *The Nineteenth-Century Church*, pp 49–53, for a more detailed account of the Anglican approach to death during this period.
37. Hempton, *Methodism: Empire of the Spirit*, pp 67–8.
38. Michael Bartholomew, 'The Moral Critique of Christian Orthodoxy', and Gerald Parsons, '"Honest Doubt" and the Ethics of Belief', both in Parsons (ed), *Religion in Victorian Britain. Volume II: Controversies*, pp 166–219.
39. Heimann, 'Christianity in Western Europe', p 492.

40. Thomas Kselman, 'The Varieties of Religious Experience in Urban France', in McLeod (ed), *European Religion in the Age of Great Cities*, pp 176–9.
41. McLeod, *Secularisation in Western Europe*, p 160.
42. For a discussion of the 'leisure revolution' in England, see McLeod, *Religion and Society in England*, pp 196–201.
43. *Ibid.*, p 199, citing the *Daily Telegraph*, 6 October 1905.
44. McLeod, *Secularisation in Western Europe*, p 272.
45. McLeod, *Religion and Society in England*, p 90.
46. McLeod, *Secularisation in Western Europe*, p 69.

Chapter 8. Conclusion: The Uniqueness of the Church in the Nineteenth Century

1. E.T. Davies, *Religion in the Industrial Revolution in South Wales* (Cardiff, 1965), pp 51–2.
2. Hempton, *Methodism: Empire of the Spirit*, p 78.
3. Knight, *The Nineteenth-Century Church*, pp 40–2.
4. Stunt, *From Awakening to Succession*, pp 65–72.
5. Ahlstrom, *A Religious History of the American People*, p 348.
6. Heimann, *Catholic Devotion in Victorian England*, p 30.
7. Mary Heimann, 'Catholic Revivalism in Worship and Devotion', in Gilley and Stanley (eds), *World Christianities*, p 75.
8. *Ibid.*, pp 80–1.
9. *Ibid.*, p 82.
10. Blackbourn, *Marpingen*, p 18.
11. Peter C. Phan, 'Christianity in Indochina', in Gilley and Stanley (eds), *World Christianities*, pp 521–2.
12. Blackbourn, *Marpingen*, p 396.
13. Susan O'Brien, 'New Religious Orders for Women', in Gilley and Stanley (eds), *World Christianities*, pp 94–5.
14. *Ibid.*, p 94.
15. Blackbourn, *Marpingen*, p 46.
16. Frances Knight, '"Male and Female He Created Them": Men, Women and the Question of Gender', in John Wolffe (ed), *Religion in Victorian Britain. V: Culture and Empire* (Manchester, 1997), p 25.
17. John Angell James, *Female Piety or the Young Woman's Friend and Guide through Life to Immortality* (London, 1852)
18. Knight, '"Male and Female"', pp 27–8.
19. Dale A. Johnson, *Women in English Religion 1700–1925* (New York and Toronto, 1983), pp 39, 106.
20. Jeffrey Cox, *The English Churches in a Secular Society: Lambeth 1870–1930* (Oxford, 1982), pp 34–5.
21. Frank Prochaska, *Women and Philanthropy in Nineteenth-Century England* (Oxford, 1980), pp 222–5.
22. Knight, '"Male and Female"', p 49.

23. Deborah Valenze, *Prophetic Sons and Daughters: Female Preaching and Popular Religion in Industrial England* (Princeton, New Jersey, 1985).

24. Heimann, *Catholic Devotion in Victorian England*, pp 196–8.

25. Yates, *The Religious Condition of Ireland 1770–1850*, pp 176–7.

26. Sheridan Gilley, 'Catholicism, Ireland and the Irish Diaspora', in Gilley and Stanley (eds), *World Christianities*, p 253.

27. Connolly, *Priests and People in Pre-Famine Ireland 1780–1845*, p 25.

28. Dolan, *Catholic Revivalism*, p 148.

29. *Ibid.*, pp 148–9; Ahlstrom, *Religious History*, p 830.

30. John Wolffe, *The Expansion of Evangelicalism: The Age of Wilberforce, More, Chalmers and Finney* (Leicester, 2006), pp 171–3.

31. Bebbington, *The Dominance of Evangelicalism*, p 228.

32. Noll, *The Old Religion in a New World*, pp 134–5.

33. Piggin and Davidson, 'Christianity in Australia and the Pacific', in Gilley and Stanley (eds), *World Christianities*, pp 547–8, 559.

34. Frances Knight, 'The Pastoral Ministry in the Anglican Church in England and Wales, c.1840–1950', in *The Dutch Review of Church History* 83 (2003), p 418.

Select Bibliography

This is only a select list of some of the books that are most likely to be of interest to readers. Most of the titles have been published in the last 20 years.

Works with global or multinational coverage

Bebbington, D.W., *The Dominance of Evangelicalism: The Age of Spurgeon and Moody* (Leicester, 2005)

Gilley, S. and Stanley, B. (eds), *The Cambridge History of Christianity. Volume VIII: World Christianities c.1815–c.1914* (Cambridge, 2006)

Hastings, A. (ed), *A World History of Christianity* (London 1999)

Hempton, D., *Methodism: Empire of the Spirit* (New Haven and London, 2005)

Jacob, W.M., *The Making of the Anglican Church Worldwide* (London, 1997)

McLeod, H., *Piety and Poverty: Working-Class Religion in Berlin, London and New York 1870–1914* (New York and London, 1996)

McManners, J. (ed), *The Oxford Illustrated History of Christianity* (Oxford, 1992)

Noll, M.A., Bebbington, D.W. and Rawlyk, G.A. (eds), *Evangelicalism: Comparative Studies of Popular Protestantism in North America, the British Isles, and Beyond, 1700–1990* (New York and Oxford, 1994)

Norman, E., *Christianity in the Southern Hemisphere: The Churches in Latin America and South Africa* (Oxford, 1981)

Tallet, F and Atkin, N. (eds), *Catholicism in Britain and France since 1789* (London, 1996)

Wolffe, J., *The Expansion of Evangelicalism: The Age of Wilberforce, More, Chalmers and Finney* (Leicester, 2006)

The British Isles

Brown, C.G., *Religion and Society in Scotland since 1707* (Edinburgh, 1997)

——, *The Death of Christian Britain: Understanding Secularisation 1800–2000* (London, 2001)

Brown, S.J., *Thomas Chalmers and the Godly Commonwealth in Scotland* (Oxford, 1982)

——, *The National Churches of England, Ireland and Scotland 1801–46* (Oxford, 2001)

Burns, A., *The Diocesan Revival in the Church of England c.1800–1870* (Oxford,

1999)

Connolly, S.J., *Religion and Society in Nineteenth-Century Ireland* (Dundalk, 1985)

——, *Priests and People in Pre-Famine Ireland, 1780–1845* (Dublin, 2001)

Green, S.J.D., *Religion in the Age of Decline: Organisation and Experience in Industrial Yorkshire 1870–1920* (Cambridge, 1996)

Heimann, M., *Catholic Devotion in Victorian England* (Oxford, 1995)

Hempton, D., *Religion and Political Culture in Britain and Ireland* (Cambridge, 1996)

——, *The Religion of the People: Methodism and Popular Religion c.1750–1900* (London and New York, 1996)

Holmes, J., *Religious Revivals in Britain and Ireland, 1859–1905* (Dublin, 2000)

Knight, F., *The Nineteenth-Century Church and English Society* (Cambridge, 1995)

Larsen, T., *Friends of Religious Equality: Nonconformist Politics in Mid-Victorian England* (Woodbridge, 1999)

McLeod, H., *Religion and Society in England 1850–1914* (Basingstoke, 1996)

Magray, M.P., *The Transforming Power of the Nuns: Women, Religion and Cultural Change in Ireland, 1750–1900* (New York and Oxford, 1998)

Mumm, S., *Stolen Daughters, Virgin Mothers: Anglican Sisterhoods in Victorian Britain* (London and New York, 1999)

Munson, J., *The Nonconformists: In Search of a Lost Culture* (London, 1991)

Parsons, G. (ed), *Religion in Victorian Britain. Volume I: Traditions* (Manchester, 1988)

——, *Religion in Victorian Britain. Volume II: Controversies* (Manchester, 1988)

Smith, M., *Religion in Industrial Society: Oldham and Saddleworth, 1740–1865* (Oxford, 1994)

Snell, K.D.M. and Ell, Paul S., *Rival Jerusalems: The Geography of Victorian Religion* (Cambridge, 2000)

Strong, R., *Episcopalianism in Nineteenth-Century Scotland* (Oxford, 2002)

Walker, P., *Pulling the Devil's Kingdom Down: The Salvation Army in Victorian Britain* (Berkeley, 2001)

Walsh, B., *Roman Catholic Nuns in England and Wales 1800–1937: A Social History* (Dublin, 2002)

Watts, M., *The Dissenters. Volume II: The Expansion of Evangelical Nonconformity* (Oxford, 1995)

Williams, G., Jacob, W., Yates, N. and Knight, F., *The Welsh Church from Reformation to Disestablishment* (Cardiff, 2007)

Wolffe, J., *God and Greater Britain: Religion and National Life in Britain and Ireland 1843–1945* (London and New York, 1994)

——(ed), *Religion in Victorian Britain. Volume V: Culture and Empire* (Manchester, 1997)

Yates, N., *Anglican Ritualism in Victorian Britain 1830–1910* (Oxford, 1999)

——, *The Religious Condition of Ireland 1770–1850* (Oxford, 2006)

Europe

Aston, N., *Christianity and Revolutionary Europe, c.1750–1830* (Cambridge, 2002)

Atkin, N and Tallett, F., *Priests, Prelates and People: A History of European Catholicism since 1750* (London, 2003)

Blackbourn, D., *Marpingen: Apparitions of the Virgin Mary in Bismarckian Germany* (Oxford, 1993)

Byrnes, J.F., *Catholic and French Forever: Religious and National Identity in Modern France* (Pennsylvania, 2005)

Callahan, W., *Church, Politics and Society in Spain, 1750–1874* (Cambridge, Massachusetts, 1984)

——, *The Catholic Church in Spain, 1874–1998* (Washington, 2000)

Chadwick, O., *A History of the Popes 1830–1914* (Oxford, 1998)

Clark, C. and Kaiser, W. (eds), *Culture Wars: Secular-Catholic Conflict in Nineteenth-Century Europe* (Cambridge, 2003)

Coppa, F., *The Modern Papacy since 1789* (London and New York, 1998)

Gibson, R., *A Social History of French Catholicism* (London and New York, 1989)

Harris, R., *Lourdes: Body and Spirit in the Secular Age* (London, 1999)

Hope, N., *German and Scandinavian Protestantism 1700–1918* (Oxford, 1995)

Kselman, T., *Miracles and Prophecies in Nineteenth-Century France* (New Brunswick, 1983)

Lannon, F., *Privilege, Persecution and Prophecy: The Catholic Church in Spain, 1875–1975* (Oxford, 1987)

Lausten, M.F., *A Church History of Denmark* (Aldershot, 2002)

McLeod, H. (ed), *European Religion in the Age of Great Cities* (London, 1995)

——, *Religion and the People of Western Europe 1789–1989* (Oxford, 1997)

——, *Secularisation in Western Europe, 1848–1914* (New York, 2000)

Molland, E., *Church Life in Norway, 1800–1950* (Minneapolis, 1947)

Sperber, J., *Popular Catholicism in Nineteenth-Century Germany* (Princeton, 1984)

Stunt, T.C.F., *From Awakening to Succession: Radical Evangelicals in Switzerland and Britain, 1815–35* (Edinburgh, 2000)

Wintle, M., *Pillars of Piety: Religion in the Netherlands in the Nineteenth Century* (Hull, 1987)

The United States and Canada

Ahlstrom, S.E., *A Religious History of the American People*, 2nd ed. (New Haven and London, 2004)

Brekus, C.A., *Strangers and Pilgrims: Female Preaching in America, 1740–1845* (Chapel Hill and London, 1998)

Brown, C.G., *The Word in the World: Evangelical Writing, Publishing, and Reading in America 1789–1880* (Chapel Hill, 2004)

Campbell, J.T., *Songs of Zion: The African Methodist Episcopal Church in the United States and South Africa* (New York, 1995)

Carwardine, R., *Evangelicals and Politics in Antebellum America* (New Haven 1993)

Dolan, J.P., *The Immigrant Church: New York's Irish and German Catholics, 1815–1865* (Baltimore and London, 1975)

Fay, T.J., *A History of Canadian Catholics* (Montreal and Kingston, 2002)

Gaustad, E.S. and Barlow, P.L., *New Historical Atlas of Religion in America* (Oxford and New York, 2001)

Gauvreau, M. *The Evangelical Century: College and Creed in English Canada from the Great Revival to the Great Depression* (Montreal and Kingston, 1991)

Handy, R.T., *A History of the Churches in the United States and Canada* (New York, 1976)

Hatch, N.O., *The Democratisation of American Christianity* (New Haven, 1989)

Hayes, A.L., *Anglicans in Canada* (Urbana and Chicago, 2004)

Hennesey, J., *American Catholics: A History of the Roman Catholic Community in the United States* (Oxford, 1981)

Montgomery, W.E., *Under Their Own Vine and Fig Tree: The African-American Church in the South, 1865–1900* (Baton Rouge, 1993)

Noll, M.A., *A History of Christianity in the United States and Canada* (Grand Rapids, 1992)

——, *The Old Religion in a New World* (Grand Rapids, 2002)

——, *The Civil War as a Theological Crisis* (Chapel Hill, 2006)

Raboteau, A.J., *Slave Religion: The 'Invisible Institution' in the Antebellum South* (New York, 1978)

Rawlyk, G.A., *Aspects of the Canadian Evangelical Experience* (Montreal and Kingston, 1997)

Taves, A., *The Household of Faith: Roman Catholic Devotions in Mid-Nineteenth Century America* (Notre Dame, 1986)

Missions

Harris, P., *Nothing but Christ: Rufus Anderson and the Ideology of Protestant Foreign Missions* (New York, 1999)

Hutchison, W., *Errand to the World: American Protestant Thought and Foreign Missions* (Chicago and London, 1987)

Jacobs, S.M., *Black Americans and the Missionary Movement in Africa* (Westport, Connecticut, 1982)

Porter, A.N., *Missions versus Empire* (Manchester, 2004)

Stanley, B., *The Bible and the Flag* (Leicester, 1990)

—— (ed), *Christian Missions and the Enlightenment* (Grand Rapids, 2001)

Walls, A.F., *The Cross-Cultural Process in Christian History* (New York and Edinburgh, 2002)

Ward, K. and Stanley, B. (eds), *The Church Mission Society and World Christianity, 1799–1999* (Grand Rapids, Cambridge and Richmond, 2000)

Some other parts of the world

Ballhatchet, K.A., *Caste, Class and Catholicism in India: 1789–1914* (Richmond, Surrey, 1998)

Bayly, S., *Saints, Goddesses and Kings: Muslims and Christians in South Indian Society, 1700–1900* (Cambridge, 1989)

Bays, D.H. (ed), *Christianity in China: From the Eighteenth Century to the Present* (Stanford, 1996)

Bediako, K., *Christianity in Africa: The Renewal of a Non-Western Religion* (Edinburgh, 1995)

Blakely, T., van Beek, W. and Thompson, D.L. (eds), *Religion in Africa* (London, 1994)

Breward, I., *A History of the Australian Churches* (Sydney, 1993)

Cox, J., *Imperial Fault Lines: Christianity and Colonial Power in India, 1818–1940* (Stanford, 2002)

Dunch, R., *Fuzhou Protestants and the Making of Modern China 1857–1927* (New Haven, 2001)

Frykenberg, R.E., *Christians and Missionaries in India: Cross-Cultural Communication since 1500* (Grand Rapids and London, 2003)

Hastings, A., *The Church in Africa 1450–1950* (Oxford, 1994)

Hutchinson, M. and Campion, E. (eds), *Re-visioning Australian Colonial Christianity: New Essays in the Australian Christian Experience, 1788–1900* (Sydney, 1994)

Isichei, E., *A History of Christianity in Africa* (London, 1995)

Kaye, B. (ed), *Anglicanism in Australia* (Carlton South, 2002)

King, M., *God's Farthest Outpost: A History of Catholics in New Zealand* (Auckland, 1997)

O'Farrell, P., *The Irish in Australia* (Kensington, New South Wales, 1987)

Piggin, S., *Evangelical Christianity in Australia: Spirit, Word and World* (Melbourne, 1996)

Sweeten, A.R., *Christianity in Rural China: Conflict and Accommodation in Jiangxi Province 1860–1900* (Ann Arbor, 2001)

Whyte, B., *Unfinished Encounter: China and Christianity* (London, 1988)

Withycombe, R.S.M., *Australian and New Zealand Religious History, 1788–1988* (Canberra, 1988)

Wright, D. and Clancy, E., *The Methodists: A History of Methodism in New South Wales* (Sydney, 1993)

Index